A KIPLING COMPANION

A KIPLING COMPANION

NORMAN PAGE

MACMILLAN PRESS
LONDON

First published 1984 by
THE MACMILLAN PRESS LTD
London and Basingstoke
Companies and representatives
throughout the world

Typeset in Great Britain by
WESSEX TYPESETTERS LTD
Frome, Somerset

Printed in Hong Kong

British Library Cataloguing in Publication Data
Page, Norman
A Kipling companion. – (Macmillan
literary companions)
1. Kipling, Rudyard – Criticism and
interpretation
I. Title
828'.809   PR4807
ISBN 0–333–31538–3

To Alison White
who, like Kipling, is a lover of language, and
children, and England

Contents

List of Plates

Preface

The young Kipling's precocity and popularity have few parallels in literature. As a youth still in his teens or hardly out of them, he published large quantities of prose and verse, including some sketches and stories of remarkable quality: 'The City of Dreadful Night', for instance, shows an extraordinary confidence and skill for an author of nineteen, and Kipling was the same age when he wrote the even more powerful and haunting story 'The Strange Ride of Morrowbie Jukes', with its nightmarish symbolical presentation of the Anglo-Indian predicament. An American critic, Louis L. Cornell, has recently said of another story, 'The Hill of Illusion', 'I doubt whether any Englishman writing in 1888 could have exposed so coldly and neatly the itch of mutual distrust that afflicts a couple on the eve of an adulterous elopement' – and Kipling was twenty-two when he wrote that story. No wonder 'precocity' and even 'genius' were words readily applied to him: when *The Story of the Gadsbys* was issued in London in 1890 *Blackwood's Magazine* described it as 'the most amazing monument of precocity in all literature', and three years earlier Henry James had written to his brother: 'Kipling strikes me personally as the most complete man of genius (as distinct from fine intelligence) that I have ever known'. 'Genius' was a word that even his sworn enemies found themselves using of Kipling: Max Beerbohm, who detested him with unswerving consistency, admitted that 'even *I* can't help *knowing* him to be that'. After reading *The Light that Failed*, William James declared: 'He's more of a Shakespeare than anyone yet in this generation of ours' – praise that seems wildly extravagant, especially in relation to that rather feeble novel, but that provides a glimpse of how Kipling struck a contemporary; and it was Henry James again who found him 'prodigious' and 'shockingly precocious', and described him as 'the infant monster

of a Kipling' – phrases that Kipling may have been recalling at the
end of his life when he spoke in his autobiography of what was
regarded as his 'indecent immaturity' (an immaturity, of course,
of years, not of literary power). When Kipling was only twenty-
five, W. E. Henley referred facetiously to his 'works of youth' and
'those of his riper years'; and G. K. Chesterton later found an
element of 'precocious old age' in his work. There was even
something oddly precocious about his physical appearance:
school photographs show him with a heavy moustache, and
suggest a mature man unsuccessfully disguised as a schoolboy;
and when Edmonia Hill met him in 1887 she wrote that 'Mr
Kipling looks about forty, as he is beginning to be bald, but he is,
in reality, just twenty-two.'

Success came rapidly to Kipling. At twenty-two he was already
famous, receiving the remarkable accolade of a leading article in
The Times; and he had only just turned twenty-five when J. K.
Stephen published in the *Cambridge Review* the excellent satirical
verses 'To R. K.' (Kipling later said that he wished *he* had written
them):

> Will there never come a season
> Which shall rid us from the curse
> Of a prose that knows no reason
> And an unmelodious verse:
> When the world shall cease to wonder
> At the genius of an Ass,
> And a boy's eccentric blunder
> Shall not bring success to pass;
>
> When mankind shall be delivered
> From the clash of magazines,
> And the inkstands shall be shivered
> Into countless smithereens:
> When there stands a muzzled stripling,
> Mute, beside a muzzled bore:
> When the Rudyards cease from Kipling
> And the Haggards Ride no more?

Kipling's main offence in Stephen's eyes seems to have been his
success combined with his youth, and not many boys and
striplings have enjoyed a celebrity capable of provoking such an

outburst (Rider Haggard was nine years older). There were other parodies which, if not the sincerest form of flattery, were certainly a tribute to his meteoric rise to fame. Even earlier than Stephen's poem, Barry Pain had parodied the *Plain Tales* in the *Cornhill* (October 1890), and soon afterwards (1892) E. V. Lucas gave a recipe in the *Privateer* for 'Kipling Chutnee'. Such attacks imply a widely familiar target. Within a few years a flurry of more substantial and more serious publications attested to the widespread interest in Kipling's work: a *Kipling Birthday Book*, for instance, appeared in 1896, and biographies, bibliographies and critical studies from around the turn of the century. The year 1899 alone saw the appearance of (among other titles) *A Kipling Primer*, *The Kipling Guide Book*, *The Religion of Mr Kipling*, *Kipling: A Biographical Sketch*, *Kipling the Artist*, *Kiplingiana*, even 'A Japanese View of Kipling' – all this prompted by the work of a man still in his early thirties. At the same time Kipling began to collect honorary degrees, and in his early forties (and at what must be well below the average age) he became the first English author to receive the Nobel prize for Literature. Earlier, he had become the youngest member of the Savile Club; had been elected to the Athenaeum at thirty-one under Rule Two, which 'provides for admitting distinguished persons without ballot' (Dickens had beaten him, though, by being elected at twenty-six); and according to one report had been mentioned by Tennyson as a possible successor in the Laureateship. The world-wide concern over his serious illness in 1899 is very impressive, the more so since he was not a grand old man of literature but still young.

These tributes, academic and popular, acknowledged a body of work remarkable in its range and vitality as well as its sheer volume (the bibliography of Kipling's early years makes dizzying reading). *Plain Tales from the Hills* (1888) and its immediate successors annexed new fictional territory in the late-Victorian period: no one had written of India, Indians and Anglo-Indians with such authority and power; nowhere since Shakespeare's *Henry V* had the British private soldier been depicted so fully and sympathetically; no English writer of fiction had been so fascinated by the ways in which men and things work, and so well informed on these often arcane subjects. The energy of Kipling's style in prose and verse could lead to stridency and vulgarity, but it was like a gust of fresh air in the close, stale atmosphere of much English writing of the period. There was nothing *fin de siècle* about

Kipling except the dates of his early appearances: as Lionel
Johnson wrote in 1891,

> The reader of contemporary books, driven mad by the distract-
> ing affectations, the contemptible pettiness of so much modern
> work, feels his whole heart go out to a writer with mind and
> muscle in him, not only nerves and sentiment.

And as the author of an obituary article in the *Times Literary
Supplement* was to put it forty-five years later,

> He was definitely the man of the hour, a milestone on the path
> of letters like Byron and Chateaubriand. He appeared at a
> moment when literature in this country was being sicklied o'er,
> not with the pale cast of thought but with the unnatural bloom
> of cosmetics.

Kipling offered something that was genuinely new: no wonder the
magnificent ballad 'Danny Deever' moved the staid Edinburgh
professor David Masson to exclaim to his students in February
1890, 'Here's Literature at last!'

Comparisons with Dickens are irresistible, and ought not to be
resisted. Kipling was not, of course, ultimately in the Dickens
class (who among English novelists is?); but his beginnings were
at least as phenomenal, and there are some suggestive points of
resemblance that quickly struck his contemporaries. Dickens had
died in 1870, the year before Kipling as a small child saw England
for the first time, and his place had not been filled; but with
Kipling's appearance on the literary scene some believed that a
new Dickens had arisen from the east. W. E. Henley wrote that
'Here is such a promise as has not been perceived in English
letters since young Mr Dickens broke in suddenly upon the
precincts of immortality'; an anonymous reviewer (possibly
Theodore Watts-Dunton) suggested in the *Athenaeum* that Kipling
'might conceivably become a second Dickens'; and Sidney Low,
editor of the *St James's Gazette*, even declared portentously at a
dinner-party that 'It may be . . . that a greater than Dickens is
here.' Nearly fifty years later Kipling himself noted wryly in his
autobiography that 'People talked, quite reasonably, of rockets
and sticks' (recalling the famous unfulfilled prediction of a
reviewer in the 1830s that the author of *Pickwick*, having gone up
like a rocket, would come down like the stick).

Both writers began as journalists; both were smallish men of
enormous energy and with a formidable capacity for work; both
had endured periods of intense despair during childhood and
suffered from lifelong insomnia; both were extraordinarily obser-
vant and make telling use of minute and significant detail; both
became, and have remained, cult figures (the Dickens Fellowship
was founded in 1905, the Kipling Society, more promptly, in
1927, and both flourish to this day). When the Public Orator at
Oxford presented Kipling for an honorary degree in 1907, he used
a phrase that might as readily have been applied to Dickens: *auctor
movendarum lacrimarum ac risuum potentissime* (an author supremely
capable of moving men to laughter and tears).

As with Dickens, the reader of Kipling finds himself compelled
to come to terms with, or at least to confront, certain elements that
have been fiercely attacked. Both writers have been charged with
vulgarity, sentimentality, a preoccupation with violence and
sadism, false rhetoric and overstatement, and inadequacy in the
presentation of women – though some of these charges tell us as
much about cultural changes as about the authors in question. In
addition, Kipling has been found irritatingly knowing ('cocky' is
T. S. Eliot's word for this trait) in his early work, and wilfully and
intolerably obscure in some of his later work. His political
attitudes have been found repellent: W. H. Auden said that time
would 'pardon Kipling and his views', but time has not been eager
to do so. The obituary article already cited observed that 'seldom
had a famous national institution been the object of more hostile
criticism'; H. E. Bates, writing in 1941, compared him to Hitler.
R. L. Green has described him as 'the most controversial author
in English literature', and C. S. Lewis has said that 'Kipling is
intensely loved and hated. Hardly any reader likes him a little.'

Under the impact of deep personal sorrows, physical pain and
mental anxiety, Kipling's energies waned somewhat in his later
years, as indeed did those of Dickens; but he went on writing, and
such late stories as 'The Wish House', 'The Gardener', and
'Dayspring Mishandled' are arguably among the best he ever
wrote, and for that matter among the best in the English
language. His critical reputation declined in the last twenty or so
years of his life; but since his career extended from the age of
Oscar Wilde to that of Virginia Woolf, and since he outlived
Conrad and Lawrence, it would have been surprising if it had not.
T. S. Eliot described him as early as 1919 as 'a neglected

celebrity', and added that 'the arrival of a new book of his verse is not likely to stir the slightest ripple on the surface of our conversational intelligentsia'; twenty years later Edmund Wilson wrote of 'the Kipling that nobody read'. But the 'conversational intelligentsia' – presumably including the women who come and go talking of Michelangelo – do not enjoy exclusive admission to the house of literature: the fact is that Kipling has never lacked readers, and his books have never been out of print. Not long after Kipling's death, George Orwell wrote that his name had been 'a byword for fifty years'. Orwell added: 'During five literary generations every enlightened person has despised him, and at the end of that time nine-tenths of those enlightened persons are forgotten and Kipling is in some sense still there.'

Over a long period Kipling has in fact attracted the attention, and often earned the admiration, of many of the most distinguished critics. Bonamy Dobrée wrote discerningly of him as early as 1927, and later Kipling critics include Lionel Trilling, Randall Jarrell, W. L. Renwick, W. W. Robson, Angus Wilson, Kingsley Amis and John Bayley. More than forty years after Orwell's comment, Kipling is 'still there'. C. S. Lewis has described him as 'a very great writer', and J. I. M. Stewart finds him comparable to Maupassant and Chekhov as a master of the short story, 'a position which no other English-born writer has remotely approached'. Perhaps Kipling's absence from lecture-courses and syllabuses is partly accounted for by the failure of English academic criticism to deal at all adequately with the short story as a literary genre. And certainly his political attitudes – or, what is rather a different matter, the political attitudes that have been attributed to him – have prevented many people from seeing him steadily and whole.

Like Dickens (yet again), Kipling has long enjoyed an international celebrity reflected in numerous translations: *The Jungle Book*, for instance, has been reborn as (among other reincarnations) *Le livre de la jungle*, *Junglebogen*, *Kniha džunglí*, *Mowgli*, *o menino lobo*, *Door wolven opgevoed*, *Das dschungelbuch*, *Il libro della jungla*, *Jungelboken*, and *Ksiega puszczy*; not to mention other versions from Braille to Yiddish. More profoundly, his influence has made itself felt in unexpected places: Freud liked to read *The Jungle Book*, Brecht translated *Barrack-Room Ballads* into German, and Borges is among Kipling's admirers.

Again like Dickens, Kipling has enriched the common stock of language: if poetry is 'memorable speech', Kipling is certainly a poet. Orwell praised his 'power to create telling phrases' and nominated him as 'the only English writer of our time who has added phrases to the language'. Today many talk of the white man's burden or lesser breeds without the law or assure us that never the twain shall meet without realizing that they are quoting Kipling, who is represented by over two hundred entries in the latest edition of the *Oxford Dictionary of Quotations*. (One wonders, though, at the omission of 'But that is another story', probably the first Kipling quotation to become widely repeated: Richard Le Gallienne recalled in 1900 that 'In 1890 we were saying to each other, with a sense of freemasonry in a new cult, "But that is another story". Today we are exhorting each other to: "Take up the white man's burden".') 'If' is, for better or worse, one of the most widely familiar poems in the language; 'Recessional' may possibly be the most widely misunderstood; and the wolf cub movement has made Kipling perhaps the most influential of all writers for the young. Even if, nearly fifty years after his death, Kipling is less obviously a 'national institution' than he once was, it is surprising how often he turns up in public and private discourse: scarcely a week goes by, for instance, without a phrase of Kipling's, acknowledged or (more often) unacknowledged, appearing in the press (during the Falklands crisis of 1982, *The Times*, which published so many of Kipling's own topical verses, printed a parody of his 'The Dutch in the Medway').

Like Dickens, then, Kipling belongs to the common reader, and even the non-reader, as well as to critics, scholars and literary and cultural historians. It would be regrettable, though, if the different segments of his readership were to be seen as having dug themselves into different camps. The thousands who still read Kipling for no other motive than delight ensure his continuing vitality as a classic; but they can be served, and their pleasure and understanding can be enhanced, by the labours of the professional. The recent quickening of interest in Kipling's life and career, manifested by the appearance or reappearance of several biographies, makes available a mass of information on a complex and fascinating personality who enjoyed a fame such as comes to few men in their lifetime. Two generations after his death, Kipling shows no sign of being forgotten; and that there is as yet no critical consensus on such questions as the relative merits of his earlier and later stories may be seen as a tribute to his powers. The only

writers who fail to provoke disagreement, partisanship and
argument are those who deserve to be forgotten. A recent critic,
Robert F. Moss, has spoken of 'the maddening sprawl of Kipling's
work'. Certainly Kipling was immensely productive (a shelf-full
of prose works, a massive volume of verse, and more uncollected
pieces than the most pertinacious bibliographer is ever likely to
track down); certainly his ideology is inconsistent, and the best
often lies alongside the worst in his writings. But no less is true of
Dickens – or for that matter of Shakespeare.

There have been many guides to Kipling, not all of them aiming
at comprehensiveness and not many of them now readily
available. I have taken advantage of the discoveries, judgements
and interpretations of recent biographers and critics and have
tried to produce a volume to which the student and the enthusiast
alike can turn with pleasure and profit (sometimes, one hopes,
they will be the same person), whether to check a specific point or
to find a broader area of Kipling's achievement conveniently
summarized. Since I believe Kipling's short stories to represent
his finest contribution to literature – indeed, I consider him to
have no serious rivals among English writers in this genre – I have
devoted more space to them than to anything else; but all the main
aspects of his life and work are covered, however incompletely. I
have been greatly aided by the biographies by Charles Carrington
and Lord Birkenhead, and by the more recent studies by Angus
Wilson and Kingsley Amis. R. E. Harbord's *Reader's Guide*, an
extraordinary labour of love, has been a valuable reference
source, as have Roger Lancelyn Green's *Kipling: The Critical
Heritage* and various bibliographies listed later in this volume,
where fuller details of all these works will be found.

I should add that no attempt has been made to provide more
than a minimum of bibliographical information concerning the
complex publishing history of Kipling's works; considerations
both of space and of the needs of most readers have led me to limit
myself to noting the most important early appearances of each
item. The reader desirous of fuller details is referred to the
standard sources.

If I hereafter refer to Kipling's most important critics without
professorial or other titles, this is intended to imply no disrespect
for them or their work; indeed, it is further evidence (if any is
needed) of Kipling's qualities that he has elicited such a large
body of sensitive, perceptive and enthusiastic commentary from

such scholars as Louis L. Cornell, Elliot L. Gilbert, C. A. Bodelsen, J. I. M. Stewart and J. M. S. Tompkins, and evidence of my great debt to them that I have had occasion to refer to them so often. The Select Bibliography supplies details of their important contributions to Kipling studies. *KJ* refers throughout to the *Kipling Journal*, which for over half a century has published useful small-scale discussions of Kipling's life and work.

N.P.

A Kipling Chronology

1865   (30 December) Joseph Rudyard Kipling born in Bombay, the son of John Lockwood Kipling and Alice Kipling, née Macdonald. (RK never used the name Joseph, which was that of his paternal grandfather; the name Rudyard was from Lake Rudyard in Staffordshire, where his parents met.)

1868   Accompanied by her son, Mrs Kipling travels to England for the birth (11 June) of her second child, Alice (later nicknamed 'Trix'); the family then returns to Bombay.

1870   Death of the Kiplings' newborn second son.

1871   (15 April) The Kipling family sail for England. In December the parents return to India, leaving RK and his sister with foster-parents at Southsea, the Holloways of Lorne Lodge ('The House of Desolation'). RK stays there for more than five years, with occasional holidays at The Grange in Fulham, the home of Mr and Mrs Edward Burne-Jones ('Aunt Georgie' and 'Uncle Ned'). RK attends school in Southsea.

1877   (March) Probably prompted by a letter from 'Aunt Georgie', Alice Kipling arrives in England and removes her son from Lorne Lodge. She and the two children spend the summer on a farm near Loughton on the edge of Epping Forest, and the autumn in lodgings in the Brompton Road.

(c. 1877)   RK writes a poem on the loss of the *Carolina*.

1878   (January) RK goes to the United Services College at

Westward Ho!, north Devon, where the headmaster, Cormell
Price, was acquainted with the Kiplings. RK is nicknamed
'Gig-lamps' ('Giggers') as the only boy in school wearing
spectacles. His friends there include George C. Beresford and
Lionel C. Dunsterville. In the summer of 1878 RK is taken by his
father to Paris (Lockwood Kipling had come home in order to
supervise the Indian exhibit at the Paris Exposition). During his
school years he pays holiday visits to the homes of his Burne-Jones
and Poynter cousins, and also spends holidays at the South
Kensington home of three sisters (Mrs Winnard and the two Miss
Craiks) who were family friends.

1879   (summer) RK contributes to *The Scribbler*, a homemade
magazine in which he collaborated with the Burne-Jones and
Morris children.

1880   RK visits his sister at Southsea and falls in love with
Florence Garrard, another boarder at Lorne Lodge, eventually
becoming unofficially engaged to her. During this year his mother
pays a visit to England.

1881   Unknown to RK, his mother has *Schoolboy Lyrics* privately printed in Lahore. From June 1881 to July 1882 RK edits
the *United Services College Chronicle*.

1882   (March) The *Chronicle* prints RK's poem 'Ave Imperatrix!'. At the end of the summer term he leaves school and (20
September) sails for Bombay, arriving on 18 October; thence he
travels by train to Lahore. He becomes a sub-editor on the staff of
the *Civil & Military Gazette* (Lahore), a daily newspaper edited at
first by Stephen Wheeler and from the summer of 1886 by E. Kay
Robinson. RK lives with his parents and becomes a member of the
Punjab Club. (8 November) His sonnet 'Two Lives' is published
anonymously in the British periodical *The World*.

1883   (summer) RK spends a month at Simla.

1884   (*c.* July) Florence Garrard writes to RK to break off their
engagement. Trix returns to India to rejoin the family group. (26
September) 'The Gate of the Hundred Sorrows', RK's first
published short story, appears in the *Civil & Military Gazette*.

(November) *Echoes* is published (collection of 39 parodies: 32 by RK, the remainder by his sister).

1885 (March) RK goes to Peshawar to cover for his paper the ceremonial reception of the Amir Abdurrahman by the new Viceroy, Lord Dufferin; he ventures briefly into the Khyber Pass, 'his first and last experience of the North-West Frontier' (Carrington). He again spends a season in Simla. (7 March) He conceives the idea of a full-length Anglo-Indian novel, *Mother Maturin*; by 30 July he has written '237 foolscap pages', but it is never completed and is subsequently lost. At the end of the year *Quartette* is published, a collection of prose and verse 'By Four Anglo-Indian Writers' (i.e. RK, his parents and his sister); it contains four stories and five poems by RK, of which only two stories ('The Strange Ride of Morrowbie Jukes' and 'The Phantom Rickshaw') are later reprinted.

1886 The original series of 'Departmental Ditties' appears in the *Gazette* from 5 February to 13 April; later the volume *Departmental Ditties* is published anonymously in Lahore (a second edition, published in Calcutta, has RK's name on the title-page). In October, the book is reviewed by Andrew Lang in *Longman's Magazine*. RK is again in Simla in August. On 2 November, a series of 'Plain Tales from the Hills' begins in the *Gazette*. During this year RK is admitted as a Freemason to the Lodge 'Hope & Perseverance, No. 782 E.C.' (initiated 5 April; passed into Second Degree 3 May; raised to Sublime Degree 6 December).

1887 RK spends the summer in Simla. On his return he is transferred to the offices of the Allahabad *Pioneer* and embarks on what he later called 'a furious spell of work' that lasted until his departure from India eighteen months later. At the *Pioneer* he edits *The Week's News*, writes a story for it weekly, continues to contribute to the *Gazette*, and travels widely in quest of material for travel sketches (for example, in November 1887 he goes to Benares and Calcutta), as well as turning out essays and poems. 'His stories, poems and sketches appeared at an average rate of three a week; nor is it unusual to find weeks wherein the rate of production reaches a piece a day' (Cornell). In August he resigns from the Lahore Lodge and later joins a Lodge in Allahabad.

1888   (January) *Plain Tales from the Hills* is published in Calcutta and London. *Soldiers Three*, *The Story of the Gadsbys*, *In Black and White*, *Under the Deodars*, *The Phantom Rickshaw* and *Wee Willie Winkie* are published in Allahabad. RK returns to Lahore for a time to deputize for Kay Robinson during the latter's leave; in June and July he is in Simla; later he returns to Allahabad.

1889   (February) RK goes to Lahore to say goodbye to his family, and on 9 March sails from Calcutta to England via Rangoon, Singapore, Hong Kong, Yokohama, San Francisco and New York, reaching Liverpool on 5 October. In London he meets Wolcott Balestier and (in 1890) Caroline ('Carrie') Balestier.

1890   From 22 February the *Scots Observer* publishes a number of RK's poems later collected in *Barrack-Room Ballads*. (25 March) *The Times* devotes a leading article to RK's work. *The Light that Failed* is probably completed by August and is published in the USA in November. In September RK suffers a breakdown in health and (October) visits Italy.

1891   (March) *The Light that Failed* is published in England. RK visits the USA briefly; then, in August, he sets off on a trip round the world, visiting South Africa, Australia and New Zealand, and paying his last visit to India. At Lahore news reaches him of the death of Wolcott Balestier from typhoid; on receiving the news RK returns to England. *Life's Handicap* is published in London and New York.

1892   (10 January) RK arrives back in London. (18 January) He marries Carrie Balestier by special licence at All Souls', Langham Place; and (3 February) they set off to travel round the world. From New York they proceed to visit Carrie's family at Brattleboro, Vermont, and then cross the continent to Vancouver and sail to Yokohama. RK finds that he has lost his savings in the failure of the Oriental Banking Company and they are compelled to abandon their trip. They leave Japan on 27 June and arrive in Brattleboro on 26 July. There they live in a cottage on the Balestier family estate, where Josephine Kipling is born on 29 December. *The Naulahka*, written jointly with Wolcott Balestier, is serialized (November 1891–July 1892). *Barrack-Room Ballads* published.

1893   (spring) The Kiplings begin to build a house (Naulakha) on the estate, and move in at the end of the summer. *Many Inventions* published.

1894   *The Jungle Book* published. The Kiplings visit Bermuda and England.

1895   *The Second Jungle Book* published. The Kiplings visit England.

1896   (2 February) Elsie Kipling born. After a quarrel with his brother-in-law that leads to court proceedings (August), RK takes his wife and children back to England. They live near Torquay. *The Seven Seas* published.

1897   (2 April) RK elected to the Athenaeum. (June) The Kiplings move to Rottingdean, Sussex. (17 July) 'Recessional' published in *The Times*. (17 August) John Kipling born. *Captains Courageous* published.

1898   (8 January) The Kiplings sail to Cape Town and remain in South Africa until April (the first of many winters spent there). *The Day's Work* published.

1899   (January) The Kiplings sail to New York. (February) RK falls seriously ill with pneumonia. (6 March) Josephine Kipling dies at the age of six. (June) The Kiplings return to England. RK refuses a knighthood but receives the honorary degree of LL.D. from McGill University. *Stalky & Co.* and *From Sea to Sea* published.

1900   (20 January) The Kiplings set sail for Cape Town, arriving back in London on 28 April. In December they leave for South Africa again. RK completes *Kim* during the summer and publication begins later in the year.

1901   (December) The Kiplings leave for South Africa again.

1902   (September) The Kiplings move to Bateman's, Burwash, Sussex. *Just So Stories* published.

1903   RK again refuses a knighthood and declines to join the royal party for the Prince of Wales's visit to India. *The Five Nations* published.

1904   *Traffics and Discoveries* published.

1906   *Puck of Pook's Hill* published.

1907   RK receives the Nobel prize for Literature and honorary degrees from Durham and Oxford. His *Collected Verse* is published in New York (London Edition, 1912).

1908   RK receives an honorary D.Litt. degree from Cambridge.

1909   *Actions and Reactions* published.

1910   *Rewards and Fairies* published. (November) Death of RK's mother.

1911   (January) Death of RK's father.

1915   (August) RK visits the front line in France; (September) he visits ships of the Royal Navy. (2 October) John Kipling, aged 18, a subaltern with the Irish Guards, reported missing.

1917   *A Diversity of Creatures* published. RK begins to write a history of the Irish Guards and becomes a member of the War Graves Commission.

1919   *Rudyard Kipling's Verse: Inclusive Edition* published (further editions, with revisions and additions, in 1921, 1927, 1933).

1920   RK receives the honorary degree of D.Litt. from Edinburgh.

1921   RK declines the Order of Merit (and again in 1924). He receives honorary degrees from Paris and Strasburg.

1922   RK becomes Rector of St Andrew's University. The Kiplings tour the battlefields of France and meet George V, between whom and RK a friendship develops. Later in the year RK is seriously ill; he fears cancer but X-rays reveal no sign of it; (November) he undergoes surgery.

1923   *The Irish Guards in the Great War* published in two volumes.

1924   Elsie Kipling marries George Bambridge. RK receives the honorary degree of Doctor of Philosophy from Athens University.

1926   RK visits South America. *Debits and Credits* published.

1927   Kipling Society founded (accorded to Carrington it is regarded by RK with 'gloomy distaste').

1928   RK acts as a pall-bearer at Thomas Hardy's funeral. He spends a weekend at Balmoral.

1930   RK visits the West Indies; Carrie falls seriously ill there and spends three months in hospital in Bermuda.

1932   *Limits and Renewals* published (stories mainly written in 1927–8).

1936   (18 January) RK dies at the Middlesex Hospital, London; his ashes are laid (23 January) in Poets' Corner, Westminster Abbey.

1937   *Something of Myself* published.

1937–9   Sussex Edition of Kipling's works published.

Kipling's World

Places were always to be of the greatest importance to Kipling: his life was to be punctuated by critical arrivals and departures, each marked by emotions as ambivalent as they were strong. (Louis L. Cornell)

INDIA

During Kipling's childhood, India included not only the country known nowadays by that name but also Pakistan, Bangladesh, and the lower part of Burma (Upper Burma was annexed in 1886). His Indian years extended over the period from 1865 to 1889, with a prolonged absence during 1871–82; or, to put it another way, they fall into two periods, one of five years and three months (1865–71), from his birth to his being taken to live in England, the other of six years and five months (1882–9), from his return after leaving school to his departure for England in quest of a literary career. He paid a short visit to India in 1891, but was summoned back to England by the untimely death of Wolcott Balestier; thereafter he never saw India again. Altogether his Indian experience covers a total residence of less than twelve years. They were, however, years critical to his development as man and artist.

Kipling was born in Bombay, where his parents had settled only a few months earlier. The city was entering on a period of prosperity: the growth of a railway system in India made Bombay the main western outlet, and its importance was further increased with the opening of the Suez Canal in 1869. Kipling's father had been appointed Professor of Architectural Sculpture at a newly founded college of art, with special responsibility for fostering Indian arts and crafts. With the job went a bungalow in the

college compound; and it was in that bungalow and its surround-
ings that Rudyard received his first impressions of the world. He
wrote in his autobiography that 'My first impression is of
daybreak, light and colour and golden and purple fruits at the
level of my shoulder'; and he recalled, nearly seventy years after
the event, 'early morning walks to the Bombay fruit market with
my *ayah*'. The *ayah* was a Goanese Roman Catholic who
sometimes took him with her to pray at wayside shrines. The
other companion of his early childhood was Meeta, a Hindu
bearer, with whom the boy talked Hindustani; when he appeared
before his parents, Rudyard was reminded 'Speak English now to
Papa and Mama' – 'So one spoke "English", haltingly translated
out of the vernacular idiom that one thought and dreamed in.' (K.
Bhaskara Rao states in *Rudyard Kipling's India* that 'No other
Anglo-Indian writer uses Indian words with Kipling's ease and
understanding'.) A fictional allusion to the same experiences is to
be found in the early story 'Tods' Amendment'. Meeta sometimes
took him into the Hindu temples. Angus Wilson comments on this
period of Kipling's life:

> this sense of India as the Garden of Eden, before the Fall, never
> left him, making the Indian peasantry – what most Englishmen
> thought of as 'the Indian people' – his first love, his beloved
> children for the rest of his life, decades after he had lost all
> contact with their land. . . . His Bombay time, too, made
> childhood the sacred age from which all growth was a more or
> less painful lesson of cunning endurance.

By the time Kipling returned to India at the age of sixteen, his
family had moved to Lahore. Outside the art school of which his
father had become principal stood a bronze gun, mentioned in the
opening chapter of *Kim*. In Lahore, Kipling entered fully into the
life of Anglo-India, moving between his home, the newspaper
office, and the clubs, and enjoying the male society at various
army messes and at a freemasons' lodge. From time to time he
travelled on behalf of his paper – in 1885, for instance, he went to
Peshawar on the Afghanistan border, and ventured briefly into
the Khyber Pass – and spent various seasons in Simla, the
summer seat of the Viceroy and the government in the
Himalayan foothills. Simla features prominently in his early
stories of Anglo-Indian life (a sketch-map of the city as it was in

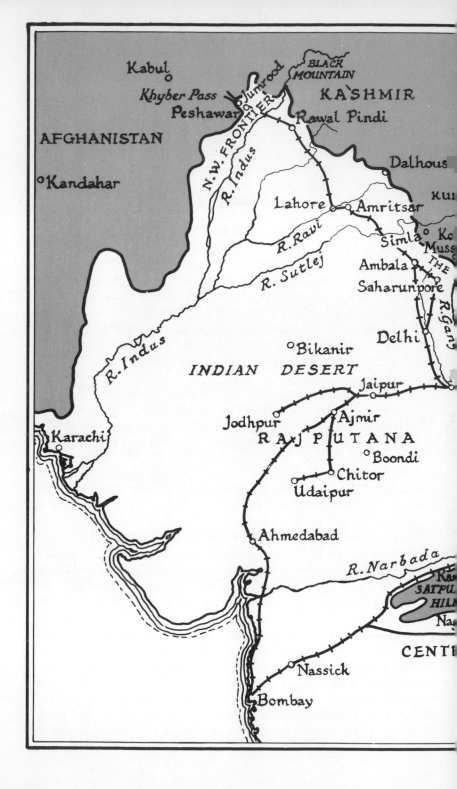

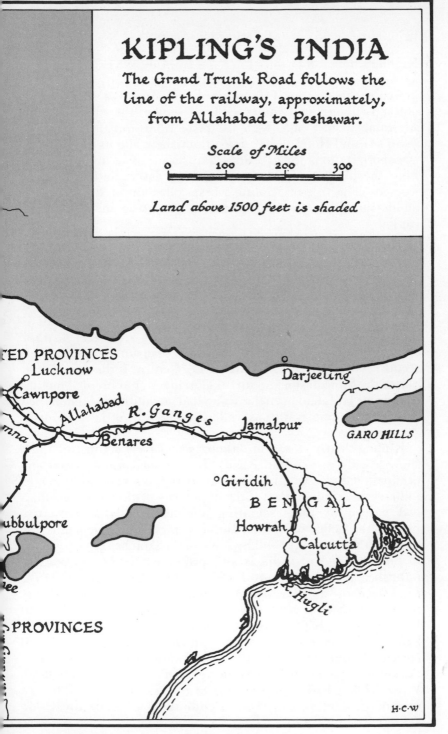

KIPLING'S INDIA

The Grand Trunk Road follows the line of the railway, approximately, from Allahabad to Peshawar.

Scale of Miles

0   100   200   300

Land above 1500 feet is shaded

TED PROVINCES

Lucknow

Cawnpore

Allahabad

R. Ganges

Jamalpur

Darjeeling

GARO HILLS

Benares

°Giridih

BENGAL

Howrah

Calcutta

ubbulpore

R. Hugli

PROVINCES

H·C·W

Map 1   Kipling's India

Source: Based on Charles Carrington's map in *Rudyard Kipling* (Macmillan, 1978) pp. 122–3.

Kipling's time can be found in *KJ*, xxiv, July 1957). The elegant, artificial society of Simla provided excellent copy for a young journalist making his first attempts at fiction: as Martin Fido notes, Kipling's early tales tellingly evoke 'the misty, muddy environment of Simla, with its dusty rides and furtive teas in Peliti's Grand Hotel while *affaires* flourished, and its dismal hired transport stations for greetings and farewells as lovers arrived from the plains, eloped to Europe, or deserted their helpless women'. The title of Kipling's first collection of stories was to allude punningly to the scandalous goings-on in the summer capital.

In 1887 he moved south again, to Allahabad. His work on the *Pioneer* took him to Calcutta, Benares and other cities; and in 1888 he was again in Simla. Kipling's Indian travels made him aware of the two aspects of the country, the ancient and the modern; in 'The Man Who Would Be King' he was to write of the native states that 'They are the dark places of the earth, full of unimaginable cruelty, touching the Railway and the Telegraph on one side, and, on the other, the days of Harun-al-Raschid.' He seems never to have visited the part of Central India in which he places the Mowgli stories; but, as Carrington has pointed out, his friends the Hills had been there and had no doubt shown him their collection of photographs as well as giving him verbal accounts of the country.

Kipling's early stories are almost exclusively set in India and show a wide acquaintance with Indians of various social and occupational classes and with Anglo-Indians male and female, military and civilian. Part of the popularity of his early collections was earned by the fascinating and apparently authoritative picture they offer of British India, a picture supplemented by much of the early verse and by some of the sketches later collected in *From Sea to Sea*. India is still prominent in *Life's Handicap*, published after the move to London, as well as in the novels *The Light that Failed* and *The Naulahka*. In the later collections of stories the Indian element gradually fades. But like Joyce writing about Dublin in exile, Kipling went on writing about India long after he had left it for good. *The Jungle Books* and *Kim* – the latter by general consent the finest as well as the most ambitious of his evocations of the sub-continent – belong to the years in America and England. When Kipling had an opportunity to go back to India in 1903 as a member of the Prince of Wales's entourage, it was declined.

ENGLAND

Kipling saw England for the first time in 1868, when he was two years old. The shock of the alien northern land that his parents called 'home' – its houses and inhabitants, its social customs, and not least its skies and climate – must have been considerable to a child brought up among the sights and sounds of Bombay and accustomed to the deference of native servants; and in his autobiography Kipling recalls 'a dark land, and a darker room full of cold, in one wall of which a white woman made naked fire, and I cried aloud with dread, for I had never before seen a grate'.

He was there again in 1871, this time with both parents and with his sister. At the end of the year the parents departed, leaving the children in the care of the Holloways at Lorne Lodge, 4 Campbell Road, Southsea – a narrow brick dwelling of three storeys, with a tiny front garden protected by a low wall. There Kipling remained for a little more than five years, during which he never saw his parents. The Holloways were paid foster-parents, and this kind of arrangement was a perfectly normal one in Anglo-Indian families; there is also evidence that the Kiplings' relatives living in England were not eager to undertake responsibility for two young children of whom one, Rudyard, had the reputation of being something of a handful. During this period the boy attended a small private school, Hope House, in Somerset Place, Southsea. During school holidays he was sometimes allowed to escape to The Grange, Fulham, the spacious and elegant home of his Burne-Jones relatives; in *Something of Myself* he refers to it as a 'paradise'.

In the spring of 1877 Alice Kipling arrived from India, removed her children from Southsea, and spent the summer and autumn with them, first in 'a little farm-house on the edge of Epping Forest' in Essex and then in 'a tiny lodging-house in the semi-rural Brompton Road' that was handy for the South Kensington Museum. At the beginning of the next year Kipling, now aged twelve, went to the United Services College at Westward Ho!, a seaside resort near Bideford, Devon, and overlooking Barnstaple Bay. He remained there until he left school in the summer of 1882.

The United Services College was a recently opened school accommodated in what had been a terrace of five-storey seaside boarding-houses (in 'A School Song' Kipling calls them, not quite

accurately, 'Twelve bleak houses by the shore'). At first the boy
was miserably unhappy. There was a good deal of bullying, some
of it of a hair-raising kind; and since most of the boys came from
army families and were intended for army careers he was very
much the odd one out. Conditions were spartan and the boys seem
to have been permanently hungry. But as time went on the picture
acquired a brighter side. When the opportunity presented itself,
especially in summer, Kipling and his friends broke bounds and
enjoyed the freedom of the Devon countryside; and the headmaster, Cormell Price, gave him the run of his library. *Stalky & Co.* and
the other stories of school life utilize the settings and personalities
of these years but present an obviously retouched and idealized
account: as a highly successful author in his thirties the creator of
Stalky was in no danger of being sent back to school. During the
holidays Kipling was joined by his sister (still at Southsea) and
they stayed with 'three dear ladies who lived off the far end of
Kensington High Street over against Addison Road'. By the time
he sailed for India in September 1882, he had spent eleven and a
half years in England. He left it as one who had only just ceased to
be a schoolboy; he was to return, seven years later, as a
professional author.

Now nearly twenty-four, he arrived back in England in the
autumn of 1889 and settled in small and dingy third-storey rooms
in Villiers Street, which runs beside Charing Cross Station from
the Strand to the Embankment. In his autobiography Kipling
offers a discreet but sufficiently vivid description of Villiers Street
in that period as 'primitive and passionate in its habits and
population'. His rooms were 'above an establishment of Harris
the Sausage King' and overlooked the Thames; Gatti's Music
Hall, a favourite haunt of Kipling's, was just across the street; and
the full tide of humanity passed along the Strand a few yards
away. *The Light that Failed* belongs to this phase of his experience,
and there are other reflections of it in such stories as 'Brugglesmith' and 'The Record of Badalia Herodsfoot'.

 Kipling made his way rapidly in metropolitan literary circles,
and was elected to the Savile Club. Late in 1890 he visited Italy to
recuperate after a breakdown in health. He was away again on a
world tour from August 1891 to January 1892, and a few days
after his return he married Caroline Balestier at All Souls',
Langham Place. A fortnight later he was off again on the abortive
wedding tour that terminated in Japan; and it was to be four and a

half years before he again resided in England, though he paid brief visits in 1894 and 1895 and stayed with his parents, who had retired to Tisbury, Wiltshire. This second period of Kipling's life in England (1889–92) saw his rapidly growing fame.

When he returned from America with his wife and children in August 1896 he was thirty years old and was to remain in England – though with many absences abroad, some of them prolonged – until his death almost forty years later. At first (1896–7) the Kiplings lived at Rock House, Maidencombe, near Torquay. Lord Birkenhead quotes from a revealing letter that indicates the reactions of this citizen of the world to the prim gentility of Torquay:

> I have been studying my fellow-countrymen from the outside. . . . We are a rummy breed – and O Lord the ponderous wealthy society. Torquay is such a place as I do desire acutely to upset by dancing through it with nothing on but my spectacles

The house, in which three old ladies had previously lived, appears in 'The House Surgeon'. In May 1897 the Kiplings fled from its aura of overpowering depression, and after a short time in a London hotel settled at Rottingdean, then a fishing-village near Brighton, where they were to spend more than five years – first at North End House, which belonged to Lady Burne-Jones, and then (from September 1897) at The Elms, a gracious house on the village green and opposite the church.

In September 1902 the Kiplings, who had grown tired of the trippers who increasingly invaded Rottingdean, moved into Bateman's, a Jacobean stone house on a small estate of thirty-three acres half a mile south of Burwash in Sussex (now the property of the National Trust and open to the public). This remained Kipling's home until his death. His delight in the Sussex countryside and its villages, his respect and affection for its people, and his interest in its history are reflected in many of his later writings – among other examples, in the stories 'They', 'An Habitation Enforced', 'Friendly Brook' and 'The Wish House', the poem 'Sussex', and the children's books *Puck of Pook's Hill* and *Rewards and Fairies*. The England he celebrates is traditional, almost feudal, and it is not difficult to bring against Kipling the charge that has been brought against some of the Georgian poets –

that his view of the villager or the farm labourer, of cottage and church, landscape and history, is the idealized and sentimental-ized one of the weekend visitor. On the other hand, he *did* make Sussex his home for almost forty years; and his feeling for the beauty of the English scene is genuine, though it is perhaps perceived in a way that comes most naturally to one whose deepest roots are elsewhere. For there was a sense in which, with India and America behind him, and with his frequent globe-trotting, Kipling remained permanently an outsider in England. In 1892, having made his home in America, he had nevertheless put a brash American firmly in his place in the story 'A Matter of Fact':

'How old is that farmhouse?'
'New. It can't be more than two hundred years at the most.'
'Um. Fields, too?'
'That hedge there must have been clipped for about eighty years.'

Kipling's boastful pride in the antiquity of the English scene seems self-conscious and very near the surface: the points he insists on are those that impress a visitor rather than a native. Even after settling in England, he did not altogether shake off this attitude: there is something proprietorial and overinsistent in his presentation of English country life in, for instance, 'An Habita-tion Enforced' – as if a Sussex village were a sort of freemasons' lodge or perhaps a public school with its own rites of initiation and codes of behaviour. As late as 1902 he wrote to Charles Eliot Norton that 'England is a wonderful land. It is the most marvellous of all foreign countries that I have ever been in'; and he repeated the point to Rider Haggard: 'I am slowly discovering England, which is the most wonderful foreign land I have ever been in.' Perhaps it was his early journalistic training as well as his Indian childhood and his American wife that made Kipling fall permanently and instinctively into the roles of observer and outsider. It is significant that in his stories English country life is often seen through the eyes of visitors or tourists; even the richly savoured setting of 'They' is encountered by chance in the course of a journey by motor-car.

Kipling began to use English backgrounds in his stories from the early nineties. Thus, *Life's Handicap* (1891) contains only one story with an English setting, 'On Greenhow Hill', and even that places its picture of life in the Yorkshire dales within an Indian frame (Carrington notes that Lockwood Kipling's knowledge of Yorkshire may have been drawn on). But in the next collection, *Many Inventions* (1893), nearly half the stories involve English settings. England is not prominent in *The Day's Work* (1898), which is mainly a product of the Vermont years (though 'My Sunday at Home' is a notable exception to this generalization). In the later collections, however, English settings are very frequent. There is a monograph on *Kipling's Sussex* (1921) by R. Thurston Hopkins.

AMERICA

Kipling first visited the USA in 1889, when he landed at San Francisco and crossed the continent to New York, en route for England. Some of his impressions of that time are recorded in the journalistic sketches collected in *From Sea to Sea*. He paid another brief visit in 1891, and after his wedding in London early in the following year he sailed with his American-born wife to New York, visited her family in Vermont, and traversed the continent again, this time crossing into Canada for the latter part of the journey. They saw something of Chicago, St Paul and Winnipeg, and sailed from Vancouver for Yokohama. After the loss of their money in Japan, they returned to Vermont and remained there until the summer of 1896. This period of four years' residence in the USA was interrupted by occasional absences, including a cruise to Bermuda in 1894, visits to England in 1894 and 1895, and a visit in 1895 to Washington, DC, where Kipling met President Cleveland and Theodore Roosevelt. Kipling seems to have considered taking out American citizenship, and by 1896 he is said to have acquired something of an American accent. But his bitter quarrel with his brother-in-law put an end to this phase of his life, and after quitting Vermont for England in 1896, he paid only one further visit to the USA – the tragic trip to New York at the beginning of 1899, when the six-year-old Josephine Kipling died and Kipling himself was gravely ill.

In Vermont his time was spent in the neighbourhood of Brattleboro, a small country town near which the Balestier family owned an estate and a family house, Beechwood. When the

Kiplings returned from Japan in the summer of 1892 they lived at first at Bliss Cottage, a labourer's dwelling not far from Beechwood. The cottage was isolated (Kipling wrote to W. E. Henley that it was 'three miles from anywhere'), and conditions were spartan; but the cottage lived up to its name, the couple were happy, and it was there that their first child, Josephine, was born. In *Something of Myself* Kipling describes the house and its setting:

> The country was large-boned, mountainous, wooded, and divided into farms of from fifty to two hundred barren acres. Roads, sketched in dirt, connected white, clap-boarded farmhouses, where the old members of the families made shift to hold down the eating mortgages. The younger folk had gone elsewhere. . . . The cottage was of one storey and a half; seventeen feet high to the roof-tree; seventeen feet deep and, including the kitchen and wood-shed, twenty-seven feet wide over all. Its water-supply was a single half-inch lead pipe connecting with a spring in the neighbourhood.

During his first visit to Vermont, in February 1892, Kipling had spent a few days at Maplewood, a seventy-acre farm near Beechwood that had become the home of his brother-in-law Beatty Balestier, who had recently married; and on that occasion Beatty had conveyed to the Kiplings about ten acres of land. On this land Kipling later built a house, Naulakha, named in memory of Wolcott Balestier (the name, incorrectly spelt in the title of the novel they had written together, now used in its correct form). Construction began in the spring of 1893, and by the end of the summer they had moved in. Over the mantelpiece was inscribed a quotation suggested by Lockwood Kipling: 'The Night cometh when No Man can Work' (from John 9:4). In his autobiography Kipling describes the building of the house and includes a photograph of it.

There the Kipling family lived happily, their number increased to four with the birth of Elsie early in 1896. But a quarrel with Beatty Balestier reached a climax when he threatened Kipling with violence and Kipling retaliated by bringing a charge against him. Beatty was arrested, Rudyard had to appear in court, and the case received widespread publicity that Kipling found highly distasteful. As a result he took his wife and children to England, quitting Naulakha on 29 August 1896. His decision to leave may also have been influenced by the dispute in 1895–6 between Britain and the USA over the frontier between British Guiana and Venezuela; for a time it even looked as though the two countries might go to war with each other, and Kipling was much concerned.

He left Vermont with evident regret. On 4 June he had written to William Dean Howells: 'I don't think quite of quitting the land permanently. It is hard to go from where one has raised one's kids, and builded a wall and digged a well and planted a tree'; and he is reported to have said on the day before he left Naulakha for ever that 'there are only two places in the world where I want to live – Bombay and Brattleboro. And I can't live at either.' On this turning-point in Kipling's personal life, Carrington comments: 'Never again was Rudyard so happy, never so sure of himself, as in the honeymoon years at "Naulakha".' While Kipling undoubtedly enjoyed and valued the tranquillity of rural Vermont, however, his attitude to American public life was ambivalent. Birkenhead quotes an American informant, Chalmers Roberts, as saying that

Kipling's attitude to America and Americans was always curious, not to say touchy and explosive. One minute he would load us down with compliments; in the next, attack with vicious precision. If I said something about the ruthless measures which produced the British Empire, he would turn on me like a bull, and bellow that Americans had no cause to boast.

Kipling made several American friends, including Dr James Conland, Charles Eliot Norton and Frank Doubleday. At Naulakha he entertained a number of visitors, including Arthur Conan Doyle, William James, his old editor Kay Robinson, and his father Lockwood Kipling, with whom he made a trip into Canada.

The American period saw Kipling's growing success as a professional writer. In 1894, for instance, his income was about $25,000, a large sum at that time. In Vermont he wrote the *Jungle Books* and many of the stories later included in *The Day's Work*, the title of which recalls the inscription above the mantelpiece at Naulakha. *Captains Courageous* was also a product of these years, and specifically of his friendship with Dr Conland (see p. 24). Angus Wilson's verdict is that 'the material that Kipling got from

America . . . is thin', and it is true that there is little use of American characters or settings in the stories (Kingsley Amis notes that the only story in which Kipling employs a Vermont setting is 'A Walking Delegate', in which the characters are horses). Kipling's American characters are usually presented satirically or as living in exile (or both). Those in 'My Sunday at Home' and 'The Prophet and the Country', for instance, are depicted unsympathetically both as individuals and as representatives of American civilization. More sympathy is accorded to the expatriate Americans in 'An Habitation Enforced' who have the wisdom to renounce American values and settle in England.

For three studies of Kipling's American sojourn, see p. 195.

SOUTH AFRICA

Kipling saw South Africa for the first time in 1891, in the course of his abortive voyage round the world. At the beginning of 1898 – now a married man with three children – he took his family to South Africa (his father accompanying them on this occasion) and remained there until April. It was on this visit, the first of many that enabled him to escape the worst of the English winter, that Kipling met Cecil Rhodes (see p. 32). According to *Something of Myself*, the Kiplings lived 'in a boarding-house at Wynberg [near Cape Town], kept by an Irishwoman'. At the beginning of 1900, in spite of the Boer War, they were back again for what was to become a regular series of annual visits lasting until 1907. Rhodes made available to them a house called The Woolsack at Rosebank, on the Groote Schuur estate at the Cape; this became during these years their second home, and it is vividly described in Kipling's autobiography.

The visits to The Woolsack continued after Rhodes' death in 1902; but after Jameson lost his position as Prime Minister in 1908 and was replaced by a Boer, Kipling never visited South Africa again. (Groote Schuur had been bequeathed by Rhodes to the nation as a prime ministerial residence, and Jameson made it his home during his tenure of office.)

Chapter VI of *Something of Myself* is devoted to South Africa, and very largely to Kipling's wartime experiences there. He recalls that 'During the South Africa War [1899–1902] my position among the rank and file came to be unofficially above that of most Generals.' M. Van Wyk Smith has recently commented that the war put Kipling's imperialist ideology to the test in an acute form, since it involved a struggle between members of the white races. (See *Drummer Hodge: The Poetry of the Anglo-Boer War* (Oxford, 1978), which contains an interesting chapter on Kipling.)

Kipling wrote much verse about the Boer War. The most celebrated piece was 'The Absent-Minded Beggar', which was taken up by Harmsworth's *Daily Mail* and set to music by Sullivan; it helped to raise a quarter of a million pounds for a fund to aid soldiers and their families. Earlier, he had written of South Africa in *Barrack-Room Ballads* (in which, as Smith notes, his imperialism begins to show): see, for example, 'The English Flag', which refers to the war of 1884. Stories with a South African setting include 'Judson and the Empire', 'The Captive', 'A Sahib's War' and 'The Comprehension of Private Copper'. There is a reference to Cape Town in 'A Matter of Fact', and South African settings are also used in 'Mrs Bathurst'. *Just So Stories* was written in South Africa and shows the influence of Kipling's experiences there: as Angus Wilson has pointed out, 'How the Leopard Got Its Spots' evokes the veldt land and the rain forests, 'The Elephant's Child' the jungle and the Limpopo River.

A Kipling Who's Who

BALDWIN, STANLEY (1st Earl Baldwin) (1867–1948). Son of Alfred and Louisa Baldwin: the former was a wealthy ironmaster who became a Member of Parliament and Chairman of the Great Western Railway; the latter was a maternal aunt of Kipling's, known as 'Aunt Louie' – hence he and Stanley Baldwin, who became Prime Minister, were cousins. When the Kiplings lived at Rottingdean, Sussex, the Stanley Baldwins were among their neighbours.

BALESTIER, BEATTY, younger brother of Caroline Balestier and hence Kipling's brother-in-law. His feud with Kipling led to the latter's departure from America. He died in 1936.

BALESTIER, CAROLINE STARR: see Caroline ('Carrie') Kipling.

BALESTIER, JOSEPHINE, sister of the above.

BALESTIER, WOLCOTT, elder brother of Caroline Balestier. Educated at Cornell University, he became a journalist and in 1888 settled in London as agent for a New York publisher. He was introduced to Kipling by Edmund Gosse in 1889, and they collaborated on *The Naulahka* (see p. 146). According to the testimony of Henry James and others, Wolcott Balestier was a young man of charm, talent and promise. He died of typhoid in Dresden on 5 December 1891. See Edmund Gosse's tribute in *Century Magazine* for April 1892, reprinted in his *Portraits and Sketches* (1912).

BEERBOHM, MAX (1872–1956). Wit, author and caricaturist, and a consistently hostile critic of Kipling. J. G. Riewald speaks of his 'lifelong aversion to Rudyard Kipling', and Carrington says that Beerbohm 'hated' Kipling and 'set out to destroy [his] reputation'. What he regarded as the other's brashness and stridency irritated him, as no doubt did Kipling's remarkable success (when the latter received an honorary degree from

Oxford – Beerbohm's own university – in 1907, he complained that 'the idols of the market-place need no wreaths from an university'). Beerbohm executed 26 caricatures of Kipling, six of which are reproduced in J. G. Riewald, *Beerbohm's Literary Caricatures* (1977). Beerbohm also reviewed Kipling savagely and parodied his prose and verse: see, for instance, 'P.C. X. 36' in *A Christmas Garland* (1912).

BERESFORD, GEORGE CHARLES (1865–1938). An Irish boy who was a contemporary and friend of Kipling's at the United Services College (1877–82). He later became a civil engineer in India. As M'Turk he appears in the Stalky stories. Beresford published *Schooldays with Kipling* (1936).

BUCHANAN, ROBERT (1841–1901). Poet, novelist and reviewer who published a major attack on Kipling under the title of 'The Voice of the Hooligan' (*Contemporary Review*, LXXVI, December 1899). R. L. Green has described it as the 'first major attack on Kipling for brutality, war mongering and illiberalism'. It elicited a reply from Walter Besant defending Kipling (*Contemporary Review*, LXXVII, 1900). The two essays, with a further contribution by Buchanan, were published in a small volume (New York, 1900), and both are reprinted in *Kipling: The Critical Heritage*. For a representative quotation, see the section 'Points of View' below.

BURNE-JONES, GEORGIANA (née Macdonald) (1840–1920) was Kipling's maternal aunt ('Aunt Georgie'). She married Edward, later Sir Edward, Burne-Jones (1833–1898), the well-known artist and friend of William Morris and Dante Gabriel Rossetti. He was created baronet in 1894. During Kipling's Southsea years, 'Each December I stayed with my Aunt Georgie . . . at The Grange, North End Road, Fulham . . . and arriving at the house would reach up to the open-work iron bell-pull on the wonderful gate that let me into all felicity' (*Something of Myself*). They also had a house at Rottingdean, Sussex (North End House); the Kiplings lived there briefly in 1897 before moving into The Elms.

BURNE-JONES, PHILIP (later Sir Philip) (1861–1926), son of the above, was also an artist and painted a portrait of Kipling, now in the National Portrait Gallery, in 1899.

BURTON, MRS F. C. The real-life prototype of Mrs Hauksbee (see p. 36), and the putative dedicatee of *Plain Tales from the Hills*.

CAMPBELL, REVD J. C. Chaplain at United Services College

during Kipling's early years there; in 1879 he was succeeded in that post by the Revd C. Willes. A harsh man, of whom L. C. Dunsterville wrote that he could 'never recall his face without an expression of ferocity on it, nor his hand without a cane in it'. When Campbell left the school, some of the boys, under the influence of an affecting farewell sermon, wanted to give him a leaving present; but Kipling objected that 'two years' bullying is not to be paid for with half an hour's blubbering in a pulpit'.

CONLAND, DR JAMES. The Kiplings' family physician during their years in Brattleboro, Vermont; he became a close friend of Kipling. As a young man Conland had seen service with the fishing fleet off the Grand Banks, and it seems to have been his yarns of fishing that in 1896 gave Kipling the idea for *Captains Courageous*. He accompanied Kipling on visits to collect material for that novel. (Kipling writes in *Something of Myself*: 'Conland took large cod and the appropriate knives with which they are prepared for the hold, and demonstrated anatomically and surgically so that I could make no mistake about treating them in print.') Conland also attended the Kiplings when they fell ill in New York in 1899. Kipling wrote many letters to him.

CROFTS, WILLIAM CARR (1846–1912). A master at the United Services College, he taught Kipling Latin and English Literature and became the model for King in *Stalky & Co.* and other stories (though some aspects of King may be derived from F. W. Haslam, another master who taught Kipling Latin and introduced him to Horace, but who left the school at the end of Kipling's second year). Crofts was an Oxford man (Merton and Brasenose); in *Something of Myself* Kipling describes him as 'a rowing-man of splendid physique, and a scholar who lived in secret hope of translating Theocritus worthily. He had a violent temper . . . and a gift of schoolmaster's "sarcasm" which must have been a relief to him and was certainly a treasure-trove to me. . . . Under him I came to feel that words could be used as weapons.' Kipling adds that he had 'tried to give a pale rendering of his style when heated in a "Stalky" tale, "Regulus" '. It was Crofts who applied to Kipling Browning's phrase 'Gigadibs, the literary man' and threw a copy of *Men and Women* at his head. There is an article on Crofts by R. A. Maidment in *KJ*, XLVIII, June 1981.

DOUBLEDAY, FRANK N. (1862–1934), American publisher;

Kipling met him in 1895, when Doubleday was working for the New York firm of Scribner's and visited him in Vermont with a proposal for a collected edition (the 'Outward Bound' Edition, as it became). Later Doubleday set up his own publishing firm and became one of Kipling's publishers and also a lifelong friend (Kipling writes in *Something of Myself* that he 'handed over the American side of my business to him'). They exchanged many letters, and Doubleday visited Kipling in England.

DUNSTERVILLE, LIONEL CHARLES (1865–1946). A schoolfellow of Kipling's at United Services College (1875–83), where he was nicknamed Stalky. From 1880 he, Kipling and G. C. Beresford (see above) shared a study and were known in the school as 'Stalky & Co.' In the school stories he is renamed Arthur Lionel Corkran and, of course, nicknamed Stalky. Dunsterville went on to Sandhurst, served in Malta, Egypt, China, and on the Northwest Frontier, and met Kipling in India in 1886. He rose to the rank of major-general and retired in 1920: on his later career, see Carrington, pp. 565–6. He became the first president of the Kipling Society, founded in 1927, and published *Stalky's Reminiscences* (1928) and several other books, as well as articles in *KJ* (XXII, June 1932; LX, December 1941; LXXIII, April 1945).

EVANS, HERBERT ARTHUR (born 1847). A master at the United Services College and the model for 'Hartopp' in *Stalky & Co.*, he formed a natural history society at the school and organized school plays (Kipling appeared in *The Rivals* in December 1881). He was educated at Balliol College, Oxford.

FLEMING, ALICE. See KIPLING, ALICE.

GARRARD, FLORENCE. Kipling met her in 1880 when he went to visit his sister at the Holloways' home in Southsea (Florence was a fellow-boarder there). He fell in love with her and they became unofficially engaged; but in the summer of 1884 she wrote to him in India to break off their engagement. He met her again by chance in London in 1890, and visited her in Paris shortly afterwards, but she seems not to have reciprocated his feelings at this time. It seems reasonable to detect the influence of this unhappy relationship on Kipling's depiction of women in many of his early stories and in *The Light that Failed* (on 'Flo' Garrard as the prototype of Maisie in the latter work, see p. 142.

GOSSE, EDMUND (1849–1928). Author and critic; he met Kipling in London and introduced him to Wolcott Balestier in 1889. He was one of the three friends who attended Kipling's wedding. Gosse wrote various reviews of Kipling's work, including a long and important early appreciation published in the *Century Magazine* in October 1891 and reprinted in his *Questions at Issue* (1893) and in *Kipling: The Critical Heritage*.

HAGGARD, HENRY RIDER (1856–1925), popular novelist and authority on agricultural problems. His name was linked with Kipling's in J. K. Stephen's satirical verses (see p. x); even earlier Henry James had written to R. L. Stevenson of Kipling as 'your nascent rival. He has killed one immortal – Rider Haggard' (21 March 1890). The two men became close friends: indeed, he has been described as Kipling's closest. Their correspondence has been edited by M. N. Cohen (*Kipling to Rider Haggard: The Record of a Friendship*, 1965); see also Cohen's *Rider Haggard: His Life and Works* (1960) and A.D., 'A Note on Rider Haggard and Kipling', *Notes & Queries*, XII, November 1949. The biography of Rider Haggard by his daughter, Lilias Rider Haggard (1951), includes references to Kipling. The Mowgli stories have been said to owe their origin to a scene in Rider Haggard's romance *Nada the Lily* (1892).

HARDY, THOMAS (1840–1928), novelist and poet, notes in his autobiography that he met both Kipling and 'Miss Balestier' (later Mrs Kipling) in 1890; Hardy records that at what was probably their first meeting Kipling told 'curious details of Indian life'. Hardy was one of his sponsors when he applied for membership of the Savile Club, and the Kiplings visited the Hardys in Dorset in 1897; according to Hardy, he 'passed a few pleasant days in bicycling about the neighbourhood with Mr Rudyard Kipling who had an idea just at that time that he would like to buy a house near Weymouth'. Kipling was one of the pall-bearers at Hardy's funeral. In 1890 Hardy had been one of the signatories of a letter (the others were Sir Walter Besant and William Black) published in the *Athenaeum* (22 November), supporting the American publishing firm of Harper's whom Kipling had accused of pirating his work; Kipling thereupon wrote the satirical ballad 'The Rhyme of the Three Captains', published in the *Athenaeum* on 6 December, in which Hardy is referred to as 'Lord of the Wessex coast, and all the lands thereby'. For further references to Hardy, see under

'My Sunday at Home' (p. 111) and 'A Conference of the Powers' (p. 78).

HASLAM, F. W. See under CROFTS.

HENLEY, W. E. (1849–1903), poet and critic. As editor of the *Scots Observer* (retitled the *National Observer* in November 1890) he published during 1890 poems by Kipling later collected in *Barrack-Room Ballads*, including 'Danny Deever' (22 February), 'Tommy' (1 March), 'Fuzzy-Wuzzy' (15 March), 'The Widow at Windsor' (26 April), 'Gunga Din' (7 June), and 'Mandalay' (22 June). The two men met in March 1890, and Kipling called Henley 'a jewel of an editor'. On 3 May 1890 Henley reviewed *Soldiers Three*, *Plain Tales from the Hills* and *Departmental Ditties* favourably in the *Scots Observer*; the review is reprinted in *Kipling: The Critical Heritage*.

HILL, EDMONIA ('Ted'). An American from Beaver, Pennsylvania, and about eight years older than Kipling, she was the wife of Professor S. A. (Aleck) Hill (died 1890), who was Professor of Science at Muir Central College, Allahabad, when Kipling met them in 1887. Kipling saw her frequently during 1888 and for a time lived with the Hills in their bungalow. At various times he wrote many letters to her. The Hills were Kipling's fellow-travellers when he sailed from Calcutta in 1889, and he spent several weeks at Mrs Hill's family home in Pennsylvania, where he had a brief romance with her younger sister, Caroline Taylor. There is a photograph of Professor and Mrs Hill in *KJ*, XXXI (March 1964) p. 13, where they are described as 'Kipling's closest friends during his last two years in India'. Mrs Hill is said to have suggested the names of the characters in Kipling's story 'The Man Who Would Be King'. On the Hills as a source of information concerning Central India used in the *Jungle Books*, see p. 12. Mrs Hill published 'The Young Kipling: Personal Recollections' in the *Atlantic Monthly*, CLVII (April 1936), and another article on Kipling in *The Classmate*, XLV (17 September 1938); extracts from both may be found in *Kipling: Interviews and Recollections*, ed. Harold Orel (1983).

HOLLOWAY. Captain Pryse Agar Holloway and his wife Sarah became foster-parents to Kipling and his sister from the end of 1871. After the Captain's death his widow seems to have treated the Kipling children unsympathetically or worse, and her son Henry Thomas Holloway seems to have bullied Kipling (according to Carrington, 'Harry was the villain of the piece'). Harry later became a bank clerk. Captain and Mrs Holloway figure in 'Baa Baa, Black Sheep' as Uncle Harry and Aunty Rosa; other accounts of the Southsea years may be found in *The Light that Failed* and *Something of Myself*, as well as in an account by Kipling's sister Alice.

JAMES, HENRY (1843–1916), novelist, became a friend of Kipling and gave Caroline Balestier away when they were married. He was one of the first men of letters in England to register Kipling's remarkable qualities, referring to him privately as 'the star of the hour' and 'the great little Rudyard'. His enthusiasm later waned. For other Jamesian tributes, see p. ix. There is a selection of passages referring to Kipling from James's letters in *Kipling: The Critical Heritage*, pp. 67–70. James wrote a preface for Kipling's *Mine Own People* (New York, 1891) and reprinted it in his *Views and Reviews* (1908). Kipling refers to James in his story 'The Janeites'. There has been speculation whether the complexity and obscurity of Kipling's later manner involved a degree of imitation of James.

JAMESON, DR L. S. (1853–1917), South African statesman of Scottish birth; created baronet in 1911. Kipling was introduced to him by Cecil Rhodes in South Africa, and Jameson visited the Kiplings in England in October 1909. The poem 'If——' is said to have been based on him.

KIPLING, ALICE (née Macdonald) (1837–1910), mother of Rudyard and wife of John Lockwood Kipling. She was the eldest daughter of the Revd George Macdonald (1805–68), a Methodist minister, and his wife Hannah (1809–75). The Macdonald sisters were a remarkable group: one married the painter Edward Burne-Jones; another married another artist, Edward Poynter; yet another married a well-known public figure and became the mother of a prime minister, Stanley Baldwin. See A. W. Baldwin, *The Macdonald Sisters* (1960). With her daughter Alice Fleming, Alice Kipling published *Hand in Hand: Verses by a Mother and Daughter* (1902).

KIPLING, ALICE ('Trix') (1868–1948), sister of Rudyard. She was born in England on 11 June 1868 and spent her early childhood in Bombay. At the end of 1871 she was left, together with her brother, with the Holloways at Southsea; she remained there after Kipling was removed early in 1877, only later returning to India. Her marriage to John Fleming (1858–1942) was childless. As Alice Fleming she published various recollections of her brother; see *KJ* (XLIV, December 1937; XIV, December 1947; XIV, April 1948), also 'Some Childhood Memories of Kipling' and 'More Childhood Memories of Kipling' in *Chambers' Journal* (March & July 1939). She also published a novel, *The Pinchbeck Goddess* (1897), and under the pseudonym of Beatrice Kipling, *The Heart of a Maid* (1891). For the book of verse published jointly with her mother, see under Alice Kipling.

KIPLING, CAROLINE ('Carrie') (née Balestier) (1862–1939), wife of Rudyard. She was the daughter of Joseph Balestier of Brattleboro, Vermont, a wealthy lawyer of Huguenot origin who died in 1888, and his wife Caroline. (For details of her brothers and sister, see under Balestier.) She met Kipling in London in 1890 and they were married on 18 January 1892 – somewhat hurriedly, after Kipling's sudden termination of his world trip as a result of Wolcott Balestier's death (Carrington suggests that 'There is little doubt that . . . Wolcott on his death-bed commended the care of his family to his friend Rudyard'). She became a devoted, protective, and somewhat possessive wife: 'the two were inseparable and her services to him indispensable' (Carrington). Her diary, kept from the date of her marriage, is a valuable source of information. See separate entries for her children Elsie, John and Josephine. For further information, see Hesketh Pearson, *Pilgrim Daughters* (1961), and V. Milner, 'Mrs. Rudyard Kipling', *National Review*, CXIV (February 1940).

KIPLING, ELSIE (1896–1976), second child of Rudyard and his wife Carrie. In October 1924 she married Captain George Bambridge (*d.* 1943). Her home, Wimpole Hall, was left to the National Trust after her death, together with a large and important Kipling archive, now deposited at the University of Sussex.

KIPLING, JOHN (1897–1915), third child and only son of Rudyard and his wife Carrie. Educated at Wellington College, he was offered a naval cadetship but was unable to accept it on account of poor eyesight. He enlisted in the Irish Guards in September 1914, went to France in August 1915, and was reported missing after the Battle of Loos in October of that year.

KIPLING, JOHN LOCKWOOD (1837–1911), father of Rudyard, was the son of a Wesleyan minister, the Revd Joseph Kipling (1805–62) and his wife Frances (née Lockwood) (*d.* 1886). He

was born in Pickering, Yorkshire, and educated at Woodhouse
Grove School, a Methodist boarding school near Bradford.
After working in Staffordshire as a potter, he studied art at
South Kensington and became an artist and sculptor. On 18
March 1865 he married Alice Macdonald at St Mary Abbots'
Church, Kensington, and sailed to India with his new wife
immediately after the marriage. There he became Principal of a
new school of art in Bombay and later (1880) moved to a similar
post at Lahore with which was combined the curatorship of the
Lahore Museum (see the opening chapter of *Kim*). He retired to
Tisbury, Wiltshire. John Lockwood Kipling illustrated some of
his son's work and was himself the author of *Beast and Man in
India* (1891). There is an essay on him by A. W. Baldwin in John
Gross's collection (see Select Bibliography).

KIPLING, JOSEPHINE (1892–9), eldest child of Rudyard and Carrie
Kipling. She was born in Brattleboro, Vermont, on 29
December 1892 and died in New York on 6 March 1899.
Kipling's feelings about her death find expression in the story
'They'.

LANG, ANDREW (1844–1912), poet, critic and folklorist, was one of
Kipling's earliest reviewers. His review of *Departmental Ditties* in
Longman's Magazine in October 1886 was the earliest of the
English reviews. (This and other items are reprinted in *Kipling:
The Critical Heritage*.) The two men met a few days after
Kipling's arrival in London in 1889, and Lang became one of
his earliest literary acquaintances. He later wrote a preface for
an edition of *The Courting of Dinah Shadd* (1890). In an article
published in the *Atlantic Monthly*, CLVII, in April 1936, Mrs
Edmonia Hill quotes from a diary entry of 1888 in which she
wrote:

> I shall never forget the glee in which RK came in one
> afternoon saying, 'What do you suppose I just came across in
> reading the proof of this week's English letter? Andrew Lang
> says, "Who is Mr Rudyard Kipling?" ' He was so pleased
> that they really had heard of him in England, for in all
> modesty he intends to make his mark in the world.

MACDONALD, REVD JAMES MACDONALD (1761–1833) was
Kipling's maternal great-grandfather; his wife was Anne, née
Browne (1763–1815). On his son, the Revd George Mac-

donald, see under Alice Kipling. For Agnes Macdonald, see Agnes Poynter; for Alice Macdonald, see Alice Kipling; for Georgiana Macdonald, see Georgiana Burne-Jones; for Louisa Macdonald, see Louisa Baldwin.

MALCOLM, G. H. A schoolfellow of Kipling's at the United Services College: see *KJ*, xxxv (September 1935), where Malcolm is quoted as saying:

> Kipling hated cricket and football and the other compulsory games and all the to-do there was over them. . . . It is Dunsterville, to tell you the truth, whom I remember best. He was the head and guiding spirit of Stalky, McTurk and Beetle. Kipling was chiefly remarkable as Stalky's closest chum.

MORRIS, WILLIAM (1834–96), author and artist. Kipling encountered him in childhood at the home of his Burne-Jones relatives, where Morris was known to the children as 'Uncle Topsy'. See also under Cormell Price.

NORTON, CHARLES ELIOT (1827–1908). American man of letters and a friend of Kipling when the latter lived in America. They exchanged many letters, and Norton published *Kipling: A Biographical Sketch* (New York, 1899). When he published an article on Kipling's poetry in the *Atlantic Monthly* (LXXIX, January 1897: reprinted in *Kipling: The Critical Heritage*), Kipling wrote to him that 'the notion that *you* should have reviewed me rather makes me gasp'.

POYNTER, EDWARD (1836–1919), artist, later Sir Edward Poynter and President of the Royal Academy (1896). He married Agnes Macdonald, a sister of Kipling's mother known to the Kipling children as 'Aunt Aggie'. Kipling visited their home during his childhood and their son Ambrose (1867–1923), known as 'Ambo', became one of his closest friends. He and Kipling met often during the latter's early years in London, and he was best man at Kipling's wedding. 'Ambo', who had poetic ambitions, became an architect. HUGH (1882–1962) was another Poynter cousin.

PRICE, CORMELL (1835–1910) was Headmaster of the United Services College during Kipling's time there. He was educated at King Edward's School, Birmingham, and at Brasenose College, Oxford, where his friends included Edward Burne-

Jones and William Morris. Later he became friendly with Swinburne and D. G. Rossetti. After periods spent as a medical student, as tutor in a Russian nobleman's family, and as a master at Haileybury College, he became the first head of the United Services College, founded in 1874 by a group of army officers to provide a public school education and coaching for the army entrance examination for their sons. He was a friend of Kipling's parents and was known to Kipling as 'Uncle Crom'. 'Bates' in *Stalky & Co.* is not a close portrait of Price. When he retired in July 1894, Kipling was the guest of honour at a presentation and made a speech on behalf of the Old Boys. See Kipling's 'An English School', published in 1893 and later collected in *Land and Sea Tales*; also H. A. Tapp, *United Services College, 1874–1911* (Aldershot, 1933) and two articles on the school by the same author in *KJ*, xvi (October and December 1949).

PUGH, M. H. Kipling's housemaster at United Services College and the prototype of 'Prout' in *Stalky & Co.* Carrington describes him as 'a suspicious, humourless, well-meaning man'.

RHODES, CECIL (1853–1902), statesman, was born in England, settled in South Africa, and acquired great wealth from the diamond mines. Kipling met him in South Africa in 1891 and in London in 1897. A friendship developed when Kipling visited South Africa in 1898, and every year from 1900 to 1908 the Kiplings stayed at The Woolsack, a house Rhodes had built on his estate under Carrie Kipling's supervision. The Kiplings contributed to the discussions that led to the establishment of the Rhodes Scholarships in Rhodes's will. They were in South Africa when Rhodes died, visited him frequently during his last days, and Kipling composed verses which he recited at the funeral and of which part was engraved on Rhodes's memorial. In *Something of Myself* Kipling writes of his first meeting with Rhodes:

> He was as inarticulate as a school-boy of fifteen. Jameson and he, as I perceived later, communicated by telepathy. But Jameson was not with him at that time. Rhodes had a habit of jerking out sudden questions as disconcerting as those of a child – or the Roman Emperor he so much resembled. He said to me à propos of nothing in particular: 'What's your

dream?' I answered that he was part of it, and I think I told him that I had come down to look at things.

ROBINSON, E. KAY, journalist. He began his career in Fleet Street, then went to India and became assistant editor of the Allahabad *Pioneer*. He and Kipling met in the spring of 1886, when Robinson spent several weeks with the Kipling family during a visit to Lahore. From the summer of 1886 he was editor of the Lahore *Civil & Military Gazette* with Kipling as a member of his staff. *Life's Handicap* (1891) is dedicated to him. Robinson visited the Kiplings in Vermont in 1895 and published several articles containing reminiscences of Kipling: see *McClure's Magazine*, VII (July 1896); *Academy*, L (28 November 1896); *Literature*, IV (18 March 1899).

SCHOFIELD, GEORGE (1839–1907). He served in the army in India, retiring in 1879 and joining the staff of the United Services College as School Sergeant. He appears as 'Foxy' in the Stalky stories.

STEVENS, H. C. An assistant master at the United Services College, said to be the 'original' of Macrea in the Stalky stories.

STEVENSON, ROBERT LOUIS (1850–94), author. Kipling had planned to visit Stevenson in Samoa during his wedding tour in 1892, but the tour was abandoned after the failure of his Japanese bank. In the event the two writers never met, though they corresponded. R. L. Green has stated that Kipling was 'a devoted reader of Stevenson by 1888'; there is a reference to him in 'Black Jack' (*Soldiers Three*), early editions of which include an opening paragraph, later deleted, that contains a reference to Stevenson (see p.71). Green has shown that there are many other references to Stevenson in Kipling's writings ('Kipling and R. L. Stevenson', *KJ*, XXXI, June 1964). *The Wrong Box* (1889), a comic novel by Stevenson and Lloyd Osbourne, is referred to in *Something of Myself* and in the story 'The Vortex'. Stevenson's letters to Henry James contain references to Kipling, usefully assembled in *Kipling: The Critical Heritage*, pp. 65–7.

TAYLOR, CAROLINE. An American girl, younger sister of Mrs Edmonia Hill and daughter of a clergyman. Kipling met her at her father's home in Beaver, Pennsylvania, in 1888. The letters he subsequently wrote to her are, according to Carrington, 'beyond question love-letters', and the prospect of marriage was evidently discussed, though it is not clear whether they were ever actually engaged. In any case, nothing came of the relationship; Carrington suggests that the family's strict religious views would not have made Kipling a welcome addition to their circle.

TWAIN, MARK (Samuel Langhorne Clemens) (1835–1910), American author. Kipling met him in 1889 in Elmira, New York, while travelling to England, and interviewed him for the *Pioneer* (the interview was later included in *From Sea to Sea*). Twain's recollections of the occasion are to be found in *Mark Twain in Eruption* (1940). During Kipling's American years the two authors met often; they saw each other for the last time at Oxford in 1907, when they both received honorary degrees (a photograph of the procession, reproduced in Kingsley Amis's book, shows them both clearly). According to Howard G. Baetzhold, 'their mutual esteem was great' (*Oxford Magazine*, LXXV, 28 February 1957). Kipling described Twain as 'the master of us all' and often refers to his writings. See also 'Mr Kipling and Mark Twain', *Academy*, LVIII (17 March 1900) p. 237.

WILDE, OSCAR (1854–1900), writer, critic and wit. He referred to the young Kipling in an essay published in *The Nineteenth Century* in 1890 (reprinted, with important revisions, in his volume *Intentions* in 1891), and makes there the famous remark that 'As one turns over the pages of his *Plain Tales from the Hills*, one feels as if one were seated under a palm-tree reading life by superb flashes of vulgarity.' The revised version added the tribute that Kipling 'has seen marvellous things through keyholes, and his backgrounds are real works of art'. In a letter to *The Times* (23 September 1891), answering a criticism of his observations, Wilde wrote that 'There is no reason why Mr Rudyard Kipling should not select vulgarity as his subject-matter, or part of it. For a realistic artist, certainly, vulgarity is a most admirable subject.' There seems to be no record of the two writers ever having met. In *Something of Myself* Kipling refers to 'the suburban Toilet-Club school favoured by the late Mr Oscar Wilde'. See H. Montgomery Hyde, 'Wilde and Kipling', *KJ*, XXIX (March 1962).

WILLES, REVD GEORGE (*b.* 1844) was Chaplain at the United Services College during Kipling's later years there, and seems to have been notably more easy-going than his predecessor, the

Revd J. C. Campbell (see separate entry). A Christ Church man, he appears as the Revd John Gillett ('the Padre') in *Stalky & Co.*

The Short Stories

PLAIN TALES FROM THE HILLS

'Plain Tales from the Hills' was the title of a series of 39 unsigned short stories published in the *Civil & Military Gazette* (Lahore) from 2 November 1886 to 10 June 1887. At the end of his life, Kipling wrote in *Something of Myself*: 'I forget who started the notion of my writing a series of Anglo-Indian tales, but I remember our [family] council over the naming of the series.' He used the same title for a volume of stories – his first – published in Calcutta and London in January 1888; a second edition, incorporating revisions, appeared in the following year; and the volume was reissued by Macmillan of London and Lovell of New York in 1890 (the American edition gives the author's name on the title-page as 'Kudyard Kipling').

Kipling's preface is misleading. It states that 'eight-and-twenty' of the forty stories appeared originally in the *Civil & Military Gazette*, and that the rest were 'more or less new'. Actually 29 of the original series of 39 'Plain Tales' were included in the collection; three others had appeared in the *Gazette* but had not formed part of the original series; and eight were now printed for the first time. Of the original series of 39, it seems that six were possibly not (or not wholly) by Kipling: on the problems of authenticity raised by his early work, see p. 64.

The volume was dedicated 'To the wittiest woman in India', and the dedicatee has been convincingly identified as Mrs Burton, wife of Major F. C. Burton. Kipling had known her in 1886–7, and they had acted together in amateur theatricals. Mrs Burton is also regarded as the prototype of Mrs Hauksbee, who appears in a number of the stories: E. Kay Robinson said that 'Everyone in the Punjab knew who Mrs. Hauksbee was', but did not betray the secret. Kipling is said by his sister to have given a copy of the book to his mother with the inscription: 'To the lady of the dedication, from her unworthy son'.

It has been suggested that a favourable review in the influential London weekly, the *Saturday Review* (9 June 1888; reprinted in *Kipling: The Critical Heritage*), probably by W. H. Pollock, helped to make the collection popular in England. Andrew Lang's somewhat later review (*Daily News*, 2 November 1889; reprinted in *Critical Heritage*) is, however, more critically penetrating. A measure of the speed with which Kipling's work became familiar to readers in England is the appearance in October 1890 of a parody of a 'plain tale' by Barry Pain in the *Cornhill Magazine* (also in *Critical Heritage*).

In his *Kipling in India* Louis L. Cornell has suggested that the book was written by an Anglo-Indian for Anglo-Indians: 'we may assume that when Kipling wrote for either of the two Anglo-Indian papers he was acutely concerned with the impression he was making upon the Punjab Club [of Lahore]'. However, the novelty and exoticism of the subject-matter evidently made a strong appeal to readers far away from the subcontinent. T. S. Eliot remarked that in this collection Kipling 'has given the one perfect picture of a society of English, narrow, snobbish, spiteful, ignorant, and vulgar, set down absurdly in a continent of which they are unconscious' – a verdict slightly reminiscent of that delivered by Oscar Wilde (see p. 34). But this would hardly have been a typical contemporary reaction to Kipling's crisp and colourful vignettes of Anglo-Indian and Indian life; nor is it an adequate account of the book we read today: it does not allow, for instance, for the concerned and wholly serious treatment of the difficulties of relationships between white men and natives in stories such as 'Beyond the Pale', which anticipate not only such later stories as 'Without Benefit of Clergy' but Forster's *A Passage to India*.

A more appreciative reader was James Joyce, who wrote to his brother Stanislaus in January 1907: 'If I knew Ireland as well as R. K. seems to know India, I fancy I could write something good.' Later Joyce told a friend that '*Plain Tales from the Hills* shows more promise, I believe, than any other contemporary writer's youthful work. But [Kipling] did not fulfil that promise'; he went on to name d'Annunzio, Tolstoy and Kipling as the three nineteenth-century writers with 'the greatest natural talents'. Henry James's

initial enthusiasm for this volume was recalled long afterwards by
Sir Arthur Quiller-Couch in a letter to *The Times* (10 February
1932):

> It was on an evening of those days, as I sat by the wine listening
> reverently, that Henry James suddenly and irrelevantly stop-
> ped an involved sentence with an 'Oh, by the way! Have you
> heard of a wonderful new man who calls himself, if I remember,
> Kipling, and seems to me almost, if not absolutely, a portent?'
> Next morning, following the master's directions, I found the
> emporium of Messrs Thacker and Spink in the City, and dug
> out from behind piles of cinnamon, aloes, cassia, and other
> products of the East, a collection of grey paper-bound pam-
> phlets, together with *Plain Tales from the Hills* in cloth.

The coherence of the volume has won praise. Randall Jarrell
suggested that 'Only six or eight of the forty *Plain Tales from the
Hills* are very good stories, and yet somehow the whole book is
better than the best of the stories, and gives the reader a
surprisingly vivid and comprehensive feeling of the society that
produced it' (Introduction to *In the Vernacular*, New York, [1963]).
Kingsley Amis says that 'Kipling was to write better stories than
any of these, but no subsequent volume so consistent in quality',
and J. I. M. Stewart also praises the freshness and variety of the
Tales.

> Collections of this sort are often not to their writer's advantage,
> since what may have seemed reasonably diversified and
> resourceful when read over a period of time in newspapers
> reveals sameness and repetitiveness when brought together
> within the covers of a book. But this is not true of *Plain Tales*; one
> can read the volume through from start to finish and be chiefly
> impressed by the range and variety of what is presented.

This range and variety is not purchased at the expense of the
coherence noted earlier. The settings are more unified than in
most of Kipling's subsequent volumes; on the other hand, the
themes range widely, including love, flirtation and marriage;
children; crime and death; the supernatural; hoaxes perpetrated
by men, and tricks played by fate. Mrs Hauksbee makes her
appearance in several stories, as do those other recurring figures,

Mrs Reiver and Strickland, not to mention the 'soldiers three'. Stories such as 'Pig' and 'A Friend's Friend' initiate a long series of revenge-tales; others such as 'A Germ-Destroyer' are early instances of Kipling's lifelong addiction to farce.

Kipling's narrative technique does not woo or buttonhole the reader: it takes him by storm. His narrator is often a man of self-confidence, even audacity, as well as being possessed of much worldly-wisdom – not the fatigued, bored and cynical worldliness of Somerset Maugham's tales, but a brisk, energetic, take-it-or-leave-it variety:

> Now, much of this story . . . you must fill in for yourself, because there are reasons why it cannot be written. If you do not know about things Up Above [i.e., in viceregal circles], you won't understand how to fill in, and you will say it is impossible.   ('Consequences')

and again: 'I have not time to explain why just now' ('The Bisara of Pooree'). The reader is sometimes hectored even more grossly than this, as in a story that begins threateningly ('Understand clearly . . .') and concludes: 'Of course, you don't believe it. . . . A little bit of sober fact is more than you can stand' ('The Broken-Link Handicap'). The reader is also drawn into the fictional situation by being assumed to belong to the same society as the characters (here, of course, we recall that the stories originated in a newspaper with a specialized readership). Thus, in 'The Conversion of Aurelian McGoggin', the reader is told: 'If ever you come across Aurelian McGoggin laying down the law'.

The society is almost exclusively Anglo-Indian, and the stories are concerned in the main with the relationships of the Anglo-Indians among themselves and, to a lesser extent, with the natives. 'A peculiar point of this peculiar country', writes Kipling in 'On the Strength of a Likeness', 'is the way in which a heartless Government transfers men from one end of the Empire to another'; and these transfers help to spin the plot. A man comes to India leaving his wife in England; or a woman goes away, to England or to Simla, leaving her husband a temporary bachelor; or in various other ways the stage is set for temptations, flirtations, infidelities and betrayals. The *Plain Tales* convey many discreet hints of sexual irregularities, as when a young subaltern disguised as a woman turns up in the comic story 'His Wedded Wife' and demands 'Where's my husband?':

> I do not wish in the least to reflect on the morality of the 'Shikarris'; but it is on record that four men jumped up as if they had been shot. Three of them were married men. . . . The fourth said that he had acted on the impulse of the moment.

This is, of course, light-hearted cynicism; but the youthful author's grasp of the emotional realities of certain kinds of marriage can be impressive. Take, for example, the account in 'The Bronckhorst Divorce-Case' of

> the queer, savage feeling that sometimes takes by the throat a husband twenty years married, when he sees, across the table, the same face of his wedded wife, and knows that, as he has sat facing it, so must he continue to sit until the day of its death or his own. Most men and all women know the spasm. It only lasts for three breaths as a rule, must be a 'throw-back' to times when men and women were rather worse than they are now, and is too unpleasant to be discussed.

In the last two sentences of this passage, there is an onset of knowingness that almost amounts to self-parody ('Most men and all women', 'three breaths', 'too unpleasant to be discussed'). But the earlier part has a disturbing realism rare in late-nineteenth-century fiction: consider, for instance, the effect of the unobtrusive phrase 'its death'. Such passages should be read in the light of the fact that *Plain Tales from the Hills* appeared in the same year as Barrie's *Auld Licht Idylls*, Morris's *A Dream of John Ball*, Quiller-Couch's *Troy Town*, and Stevenson's *Black Arrow*. The author of this collection deserves the same tribute that Wordsworth paid to Chatterton when he called him 'the marvellous boy'.

The order of the previously published stories as they appear in this volume does not follow that of original publication: Kipling presumably had some other principle than chronology in mind. For the convenience of those who may wish to read them with a view to tracing the development of Kipling's art, the following list places them in the order in which they first appeared:

1884
26 Sept.   'The Gate of the Hundred Sorrows'

1886
30 Apr.   'In the House of Suddhoo'
 8 Sept.   'The Story of Muhammad Din'
13 Nov.   'The Other Man'
17 Nov.   'Three and – an Extra'
20 Nov.   'The Rescue of Pluffles'
23 Nov.   'The Arrest of Lieutenant Golightly'
29 Nov.   'Lispeth'
 4 Dec.   'Venus Annodomini'
 7 Dec.   'Yoked with an Unbeliever'
 9 Dec.   'Consequences'

1887
10 Jan.   'On the Strength of a Likeness'
24 Jan.   'In Error'
25 Feb.   'His Wedded Wife'
 4 Mar.   'The Bisara of Pooree'
11 Mar.   'The Three Musketeers'
21 Mar.   'Kidnapped'
25 Mar.   'Watches of the Night'
 2 Apr.   'His Chance in Life'
 6 Apr.   'The Broken-link Handicap'
11 Apr.   'The Taking of Lungtungpen'
14 Apr.   'A Bank Fraud'
16 Apr.   'Tods' Amendment'
25 Apr.   'Miss Youghal's Sais'
28 Apr.   'The Conversion of Aurelian McGoggin'
 2 May   'A Friend's Friend'
 5 May   'In the Pride of his Youth'
11 May   'The Daughter of the Regiment'
17 May   'A Germ-Destroyer'
20 May   'Wressley of the Foreign Office'
 3 June   'Pig'
10 June   'By Word of Mouth'

The following were published for the first time in *Plain Tales from the Hills*: 'Beyond the Pale', 'The Bronckhorst Divorce-Case', 'Cupid's Arrows', 'False Dawn', 'The Madness of Private

Ortheris', 'The Rout of the White Hussars', 'Thrown Away' and 'To Be Filed for Reference'.

SOLDIERS THREE

During 1888 A. H. Wheeler & Co., publishers of the *Pioneer* of Allahabad, issued seven booklets in paper wrappers at the price of one rupee each, with the collective title 'The Indian Railway Library'. The first six of these were by Kipling, as follows:

1. *Soldiers Three*
2. *The Story of the Gadsbys*
3. *In Black and White*
4. *Under the Deodars*
5. *The Phantom Rickshaw*
6. *Wee Willie Winkie*

Each booklet contained from four to nine short stories. After being subjected to various revisions, the first three of these booklets were later conflated in a collection published in two volumes and comprising 24 stories; the fourth, fifth and sixth booklets, containing a total of fourteen stories, formed another collection (see below).

The original booklet *Soldiers Three* contained seven stories, six of which had already appeared in *The Week's News* during 1888. A second edition appeared in Allahabad in 1888, an English edition in 1890, and an American edition in the latter year. In the first edition the title-page bears the subtitle: 'Done into type and edited by Rudyard Kipling'.

The two-volume collection was published in London in 1892 by Sampson Low (the English publisher of the Indian Railway Library) under the title *Soldiers Three, The Story of the Gadsbys, In Black and White*. It was reissued by Macmillan in London and New York in 1895, the US edition containing two additional, previously uncollected stories ('Of Those Called' and 'The Wreck of the Visigoth'; both had appeared in the *Civil & Military Gazette*).

Soldiers Three was the subject of one of the earliest Kipling reviews, published in the *Spectator* on 23 March 1889; the review is unsigned, but R. L. Green has suggested that its author may have been John St. Loe Strachey, who was a friend of Kipling's father. Certainly the review is highly favourable. It concludes:

> The perusal of these stories cannot fail to inspire the reader with the desire to make further acquaintance with the other writings of the author. . . . Mr Kipling is so gifted and versatile, that one would gladly see him at work on a larger canvas. But to be so brilliant a teller of short stories is in itself no small distinction.

In his *Essays in Little*, published at the beginning of 1891, Andrew Lang, who established himself very early as a Kipling critic, suggested that 'future generations will learn from Mr Kipling's works what India was under English sway', and added:

> Among Mr Kipling's discoveries of new kinds of characters, probably the most popular is his invention of the British soldier in India. . . . Nobody ever dreamed of telling us all this, till Mr Kipling came.

THE STORY OF THE GADSBYS

Published in Allahabad in 1888 as Number 2 of 'The Indian Railway Library' (see above). The first edition bears the subtitle: 'A Tale without a Plot'. A second edition followed in 1888 and a London edition in 1890, 10,000 copies of the latter being printed. *The Story of the Gadsbys* was subsequently included in the same collection as *Soldiers Three* and *In Black and White*.

Of the eight stories assembled under this title, six had already appeared in *The Week's News* and one in the *Civil & Military Gazette* during 1888. For further details, and for discussion of their content, see p. 122. Kipling's letters reveal that the 'original' of Captain Gadsby was a Captain Beames of the 19th Bengal Lancers.

IN BLACK AND WHITE

Published in Allahabad in 1888 as Number 3 of 'The Indian Railway Library' (see above). A second edition followed in 1889 and a London edition in 1890, 10,000 copies of the latter being printed. The text was subjected to revisions and further minor revisions were incorporated in an edition of 1891. Of the eight stories, seven had already appeared in *The Week's News* during 1888; only 'On the City Wall' was previously unpublished. The group of stories was later included in the same collection as *Soldiers Three* and *The Story of the Gadsbys* (see above).

Reviewing *In Black and White* together with *Under the Deodars* in the *Saturday Review* (10 August 1889), Andrew Lang commented that 'Mr Kipling's least cynical stories are those in *In Black and White*, studies of native life and character'. In the following year, Charles Whibley wrote in the *Scots Observer* (20 September) that

> *In Black and White* exhibits the same glaring inequalities to which Mr Kipling has accustomed us. When the two stories are set side by side it is difficult to believe that the author of 'In Flood-Time' also wrote 'The Sending of Dana Da'. The latter is perhaps worthy to beguile a railway journey; the former is one of the finest examples of its genre in the language.

UNDER THE DEODARS

Published in Allahabad in 1888 as Number 4 in 'The Indian Railway Library' (see above). A second edition followed in 1889 and a London edition in 1890. From 1895 the group of stories was included in *Wee Willie Winkie, Under the Deodars, The Phantom Rickshaw, and Other Stories*. Of the six stories in *Under the Deodars*, all except 'At the Pit's Mouth' had already appeared in *The Week's News*. In the *Saturday Review* (10 August 1889; reprinted in *Kipling: The Critical Heritage*) Andrew Lang wrote that 'Mr Kipling's *Under the Deodars* is more conventional and less interesting than his studies of native life.'

THE PHANTOM RICKSHAW

Published in Allahabad in 1888 as Number 5 in 'The Indian Railway Library' (see above). A second edition followed in 1889 and a London edition in 1890. From 1895 the group of stories was included in *Wee Willie Winkie, Under the Deodars, The Phantom*

Rickshaw, and Other Stories. Of the four stories in *The Phantom Richshaw*, two had appeared in *Quartette* (see p. 3) and one in *The Week's News*; 'The Man Who Would Be King' had not been previously published. 'My Own True Ghost Story' is a slight piece, but the other three items – 'The Strange Ride of Morrowbie Jukes', 'The Man Who Would Be King' and the title-story – are among the best of Kipling's early tales.

WEE WILLIE WINKIE

Published in Allahabad in 1888 as Number 6 in 'The Indian Railway Library' (see above). A second edition followed in 1889 and a London edition in 1890. From 1895 the group of stories was included in *Wee Willie Winkie, Under the Deodars, The Phantom Rickshaw, and Other Stories.* Of the four stories in *Wee Willie Winkie*, the title-story and 'His Majesty the King' had previously appeared in *The Week's News.* Three of the stories live up to the expectations created by the title and deal with childhood; the harrowingly autobiographical 'Baa, Baa, Black Sheep' is particularly notable. Edmund Gosse, however, judged 'The Drums of the Fore and Aft' to be 'By far the most powerful and ingenious story . . . which Mr Kipling has yet dedicated to a study of childhood' (strictly speaking, perhaps, the boys in that tale are not exactly children). Gosse's long essay (*Century Magazine*, October 1891; reprinted in *Kipling: The Critical Heritage*) makes several shrewd points in discussing this volume – including the observation that six years old is Kipling's 'favourite age' (perhaps significantly, it was just before his own sixth birthday that Kipling was left in England by his parents).

LIFE'S HANDICAP

This volume, published in London and New York in 1891, contains 27 stories. Fourteen of them had previously appeared in a variety of magazines (details under individual entries); five others in the unauthorized collection *The Courting of Dinah Shadd* (New York, 1890); and five in the collection *Mine Own People* (New York, 1891). The remaining three were published here for the first time.

The subtitle is 'Being Stories of Mine Own People', and there is a dedication to 'E. K. R.' (no doubt E. Kay Robinson, editor of the *Civil & Military Gazette* of Lahore, and Kipling's old chief). A preface states that the tales 'have been collected from all places, and all sorts of people' and also describes conversations purporting to have taken place between the author and an old native who is waiting for death in a monastery, the topic of their discussions being the nature of story-telling. The volume ends with a poem ('L'Envoi').

Reviewing the book in the *Academy* on 17 October 1891, Lionel Johnson remarked that the title indicated Kipling's view of life: 'You start with your chances and make the best of the race, sure to be tripped up half-way by the irony of the fates and powers, or baulked at the very finish.'

Among the contents of this collection is a group of stories dealing with the 'soldiers three' (Mulvaney, Learoyd and Ortheris): 'The Incarnation of Krishna Mulvaney', 'The Court-ing of Dinah Shadd' and 'On Greenhow Hill'. There is also a group of horror stories ('The Return of Imray', 'The Mark of the Beast', 'The End of the Passage', 'Bertran and Bimi' and 'Bubbling Well Road') as well as three impressive stories about Indians ('Without Benefit of Clergy', 'Georgie Porgie' and 'Little Tobrah'), the fine descriptive sketch 'The City of Dreadful Night', and one of the earliest of Kipling's tales, 'The Dream of Duncan Parrenness'. Most of the stories have an Indian setting, though 'On Greenhow Hill' makes effective and detailed use of a Yorkshire background.

Lionel Johnson took the book seriously, and his substantial discussion of it in the *Academy* has already been referred to. Johnson found it 'characteristic, for good and bad, of its author' and attempted to sort the contents into groups according to quality, judging eight of the stories (plus the preface) 'excellent', and at the other extreme five mediocre and six not worthy of publication. For Johnson's nomination of the best story in the volume, see p. 79, his essay is reprinted in *Kipling: The Critical Heritage*. Another substantial review, published a couple of weeks later, was that by the well-known novelist and critic Mrs Margaret Oliphant (*Blackwood's Magazine*, November 1891; also in *Critical Heritage*). She was obviously struck by the boldness and frankness of Kipling's treatment of his subject, and she warns the squeamish reader that 'Those . . . who wish to avoid pain must not go to Mr Rudyard Kipling for pleasure.' She has high praise for the volume and for its author, finding him 'superlative in the art . . . of the short story'.

MANY INVENTIONS

This collection was published in London and New York in 1893 and comprises fourteen stories, a prefatory poem ('To the True Romance'), and a concluding poem ('Envoy', later retitled 'Anchor Song'). Eleven of the stories had already appeared in various periodicals in India, England and America. The source of the title is Ecclesiastes 7:29.

Six of the stories deal with India or other parts of Asia, and six are set wholly or partly in England; one, 'Judson and the Empire', is set in South Africa; and 'The Children of the Zodiac' is an allegory. Of the Indian stories, two involve the well-known 'soldiers three', 'Love-o'-Women' being narrated by Mulvaney and 'His Private Honour' concerning Ortheris. 'In the Rukh' is a story of the Mowgli of the *Jungle Books*. The English stories are notably varied in theme and setting. Among them, 'The Finest Story in the World' is a tale of reincarnation in a contemporary setting; 'Brugglesmith' is the first of Kipling's elaborate farces; 'A Conference of the Powers' deals with the role of the artist in relation to that of the man of action; and 'The Record of Badalia Herodsfoot' is a highly original exercise in slum fiction.

George Saintsbury found the collection 'not only good, but very good', and Andrew Lang (*Cosmopolitan*, September 1893) noted that 'Among books of fiction' it was 'by far the most popular, and deserves its popularity'. R. L. Green makes apt use of the reception of *Many Inventions* to illustrate the very varied ways in which different critics could respond to the same story. Thus Saintsbury gave high marks to 'Brugglesmith' and 'Judson and the Empire' while another reviewer (Percy Addleshaw in the *Academy*, 1 July 1893) found them among 'the worst things Mr Kipling ever wrote'.

THE JUNGLE BOOK

In *Many Inventions* (1893) Kipling included 'In the Rukh', a story that recounts the last of Mowgli's adventures though it was the first of the Mowgli stories to be published. *The Jungle Book*, which includes seven stories each followed by a poem, appeared in London and New York in 1894. All the stories had been previously published in magazines during the latter part of 1893 and the early part of 1894.

˙ There had been numerous earlier accounts of abandoned or stolen children reared by wolves or other wild animals, and Kipling certainly knew Robert Sterndale's *Natural History of the Mammalia of India and Ceylon* (1884), which contains a reference of this kind.

Carrington says that *The Jungle Book* and its sequel are 'the best-sellers among [Kipling's] works'. Tompkins describes 'the fusion of three worlds' in these stories: first, there is 'the child's play-world' in which 'the good beasts have prototypes in the child's daily life'; second, 'the world of the fable', the purpose of which is didactic; third, and most important of all, 'the world of the wild and strange, the ancient and the far. It includes myth, but extends beyond it.' It is not given to many writers to increase the world's stock of widely familiar myths, but Kipling has achieved this in the Mowgli stories. Not only through the printed versions but through their absorption into the rituals and nomenclature of the Wolf Cub movement, they have become familiar to millions in many countries. Primarily, however, the stories have succeeded by being compellingly readable (or listenable). As one of the early critics observed (*Macmillan's Magazine*, 1898), 'Everybody felt that there was symbolism or allegory, involved in the two *Jungle Books*, but nobody resented it, for the stories were fundamentally interesting.' On Kipling's source of information concerning Central India, see p. 12. On translation of this work, see p. xiv.

THE SECOND JUNGLE BOOK

Like its predecessor, this collection was written in Vermont. It seems to have been completed in March 1895 and was published in London and New York before the end of the year, with illustrations by John Lockwood Kipling. The eight stories had all appeared previously. The original title of 'Red Dog' was 'Good Hunting'; that of 'The Spring Running' 'Mowgli Leaves the Jungle for Ever'; and that of 'The Miracle of Puran Bhagat' 'A Miracle of the Present Day'. Each story was accompanied by a poem. In a letter of 3 November 1895, Kipling writes: 'That ends up Mowgli and there is not going to be any more of him.'

THE DAY'S WORK

This collection was published in New York and London in 1898, the English edition incorporating revisions. On the origin of the title, see p. 19. Many of the stories were written during Kipling's sojourn in Vermont.

All twelve stories (or eleven, if the two parts of 'William the Conqueror' are counted as a single story) had previously appeared in magazines. Several illustrate Kipling's keen interest in technology: 'The Bridge-Builders' is about the work of an engineer, '.007' about locomotives, and three stories deal with ships ('The Ship that Found Herself', 'The Devil and the Deep Sea', 'Bread upon the Waters') – thus to some extent justifying Henry James's observation concerning Kipling in a letter to Grace Norton (25 December 1897):

> In his earliest time I thought he perhaps contained the seeds of an English Balzac; but I have given that up in proportion as he has come down steadily from the simple in subject to the more simple – from the Anglo-Indians to the natives, from the natives to the Tommies, from the Tommies to the quadrupeds, from the quadrupeds to the fish, and from the fish to the engines and screws.

At the same time about half the stories contain an element of fantasy or allegory. 'A Walking Delegate', an animal fantasy, is set in America, and 'An Error in the Fourth Dimension' also deals with American life. Other stories are set in England (e.g., the farcical 'My Sunday at Home') or India (e.g., 'The Tomb of his Ancestors'). 'William the Conqueror' is exceptional in having a female protagonist. 'The Maltese Cat' is about polo. Probably the most interesting stories in the volume are the last two, 'My Sunday at Home' and 'The Brushwood Boy'. The latter, though not completely successful, makes striking use of recurrent dreams; its placing at the end of the collection is perhaps intended to suggest that 'the day's work', however important in a man's life, does not constitute the whole of his significant experience.

A contemporary reviewer in *Macmillan's Magazine* (December 1898) praised 'The Bridge Builders', 'The Tomb of his Ancestors' and 'William the Conqueror', but complained of 'an abuse of technical jargon' and 'an abuse of symbolism' in the volume as a whole. More recently, Kingsley Amis has made the challenging assertion that 'there is not a single first-rate story in the collection'.

STALKY & CO.

Published in London and New York in 1899, the volume includes nine stories, all of which had previously appeared in *McClure's Magazine* in 1897–9 (and simultaneously or within a few months in various other periodicals). 'Stalky', which had appeared in December 1898, was not included in the volume but was collected much later in *Land and Sea Tales for Boys and Girls* (1923). Kipling subsequently wrote four other Stalky tales: 'Regulus' (magazine publication 1917; collected in *A Diversity of Creatures*); 'The United Idolaters' (magazine publication 1924; collected in *Debits and Credits*); 'The Propagation of Knowledge' (magazine publication 1926; collected in *Debits and Credits*); and 'The Satisfaction of a Gentleman' (magazine publication 1929). All fourteen of the above were brought together in *The Complete Stalky & Co.* (1929). Some of the characters also make an appearance in other stories, sometimes in minor roles (e.g., 'A Conference of the Powers', 'A Deal in Cotton', 'The Honours of War').

Kipling, who had left the United Services College in 1882, revisited his old school in the summer of 1890 and spent a week with Cormell Price, who was still headmaster. He was back again on 25 July 1894, when he spoke on behalf of the Old Boys on the occasion of a ceremony to mark Price's retirement. In October 1893 he had published in an American magazine, *Youth's Companion*, an article titled 'An English School' (later collected in *Land and Sea Tales*), which depicts the United Services College; and in December 1895 the story 'The Brushwood Boy' appeared (later collected in *The Day's Work*). The magazine version of this story makes it clear that the school attended by the hero, George Cottar, was USC.

Towards the end of 1896, while Kipling was living near Torquay, there came to him (as he recalls in *Something of Myself*) 'the idea of beginning some tracts or parables on the education of the young. These, for reasons honestly beyond my control, turned themselves into a series of tales called *Stalky & Co.*' Cormell Price visited the Kiplings at the end of December, 'and we discussed school things generally'. 'Slaves of the Lamp' was begun on 14 January 1897; by the end of the following month Kipling was at work on the second part of the story; and the two parts were published in *Cosmopolis* in April and May. According to Mrs Kipling's diary, her husband was 'working at a Stalky story' again in July. In October of the same year Price was a guest of the Burne-Joneses at Rottingdean, and again met his old pupil, who was also living in the village by that time. According to Carrington, Kipling 'was working steadily at his schoolboy stories, and there was a day when he read some of them aloud to Price and "Uncle Ned" [Edward Burne-Jones] and their young friend Sydney Cockerell. "Do you remember that, sir?" he would say to "Crom" Price, after each uproarious incident, and "Crom" would reply, "Yes, I remember that".' Work on the stories continued during 1898, and piecemeal publication into 1899.

Neither Westward Ho! nor the United Services College is actually named in *Stalky & Co.*, but other Devon place-names are mentioned and the setting clearly draws on Kipling's memories of his schooldays. Of the boys, Arthur Lionel Corkran, better known as Stalky, is based on L. C. Dunsterville, and William M'Turk on G. C. Beresford, while 'Beetle' is a self-portrait. Among the masters, King is based largely on W. C. Crofts, with some touches derived from Kipling's memories of F. W. Haslam; Prout on M. H. Pugh; Hartopp on H. A. Evans; Macrea on H. C. Stevens; and the Revd John Gillett on the Revd George Willes, while Foxy, the school sergeant, is based on George Schofield. Kipling had of course known all these prototypes during his schooldays twenty years earlier. Further information about them will be found in 'A Kipling Who's Who' earlier in this volume. The Head is not a very close portrait of Price: perhaps Kipling's particularly close and continuing relationship with the latter made him chary of putting Price into the book, which is dedicated to him.

The staple material of the Stalky tales is the running battle of wits conducted in the isolated, inward-looking world of a boarding-school, especially between masters and boys. There is much emphasis on practical jokes, with a good deal of hysterical mirth (at one point, for instance, Beetle is shown 'literally biting the earth in spasms of joy', which sounds distinctly unpleasant). School, which exists as a form of work, is transformed by Stalky and his friends into a kind of game. But 'work' and 'game' are not simple concepts for Kipling, and the escapades beyond the school's bounds and the plots and hoaxes turn out on closer inspection to be as important and as serious as the Head's moral influence or King's teaching of Horace. On the conscious level, the world of school may be inward-looking, but the reader is frequently reminded that these boys, or most of them (for Kipling himself is the conspicuous exception), will in a very short time be serving – and some of them dying – on the frontiers of the Empire. Scouring the Devon countryside is a rehearsal for active service, and the military overtones in the title of the opening story ('In Ambush') are not accidental. The College teaches mathematics and classics not just for their own sake but as a means to passing the entrance examination for the Army: this was the purpose for which the school had been established, and it is prominent in some of the stories. In a wider sense it instructs its pupils in how to run an Empire: 'They were learning, at the expense of a fellow-countryman, the lesson of their race, which is to put away all emotion, and entrap the alien at the proper time' ('In Ambush'). The limited world of the school story is thus given another dimension by the awareness, shared by narrator and reader, of what lies just beyond – or, in another sense, across the world from – the school.

There is a passage in 'A Little Prep.' where this extra dimension opens up quite suddenly:

> 'By gum!' quoth Stalky, uncovering as he read. 'It's old Duncan – Fat-Sow Duncan – killed on duty at something or other Kotal. *"Rallyin' his men with conspicuous gallantry."* He would, of course. *"The body was recovered."* That's all right. They cut 'em up sometimes, don't they, Foxy?'
>
> 'Horrid,' said the sergeant briefly.
>
> 'Poor old Fat-Sow! I was a fag when he left. How many does that make to us, Foxy?'
>
> 'Mr Duncan, he is the ninth . . .'
>
> The boys went out into the wet, walking swiftly.
>
> 'Wonder how it feels – to be shot and all that,' said Stalky, as they splashed down a lane. 'Where did it happen, Beetle?'
>
> 'Oh, out in India somewhere.'

Several times in 'The Flag of their Country' Kipling abruptly shifts the time-perspective by noting, briefly and parenthetically, the subsequent fates of some of the boys: 'not foreseeing that three years later he should die in the Burmese sunlight outside Minhla Fort', and again, '(This is that Perowne who was shot in Equatorial Africa by his own men.)'. This aspect of the book, sober and even, proleptically, tragic, is not simply a contrast to the exuberant japes but connected with the high spirits; for Kipling's theme is education in both its narrower and its wider senses. (See also the comments on 'Regulus', p. 118.)

In the final story of the volume, the ex-schoolboys are shown as serving in India, to which they have brought the world of school even to the extent of using school slang to describe a killing. Stalky's exploits are a repetition of what he has done at the College, except that the stakes are now higher. In an illuminating essay, Jon Stallworthy has said that a writer such as Newbolt (in, for example, his poems 'Clifton Chapel' and 'Vitai Lampada') celebrates 'the imperialist officer and gentleman, carrying to his country's battlefields a sporting code acquired on the playing-fields of his public school' ('Death of the Hero: Poets at War', in *Essays by Divers Hands*, XLI, 1980). Kipling goes beyond this and shows that the Latin lesson and the dormitory prank no less than – indeed, much more than – the playing-fields have their place in instilling something that is more than merely a 'sporting code'.

Steven Marcus has written an interesting introduction to a modern edition of *Stalky & Co.* (New York, 1962); his essay is reprinted in *Kipling and the Critics*, ed. Elliot L. Gilbert (1966). R. L. Green's 'The Chronology of *Stalky & Co.*' will be found in *KJ*, XXI (December 1954) and XXII (April 1955). Contemporary reviewers were divided on the merits of the collection, which Green has described as 'the most controversial of Kipling's books'. A reviewer in the *Academy* (14 October 1899) complained of the 'piling on of youthful brutality beyond all need' and pronounced it Kipling's 'least satisfactory work', while the *Athenaeum* reviewer on the same day deferred to the opinion of a schoolboy reader: 'the total verdict, in which the higher criticism can but acquiesce, was "Spiffing!" '. Robert Buchanan, in his well-known attack on Kipling at the end of the same year (see p. 23), wrote that 'Only the spoiled child of an utterly brutalized public could possibly have written *Stalky & Co.*'; and a later critic (*Anglo-American Magazine*, December 1902) found it necessary to

confront the questions: 'Is the effect of *Stalky & Co.* on the mind of
the schoolboy reader bad? Does it set before him a low moral
standard, and is it lacking in ideals?' Further evidence of how it
struck a contemporary can be found in the once-popular *Upton
Letters* (1905) of A. C. Benson, who describes it as 'an amazing
book' and admits that he was left 'gasping' by 'the cleverness, the
freshness, the incredible originality of it all', but could not accept
it as a realistic picture of school life (Benson had been at Eton as
boy and master). 'The chief figures . . .', he adds, 'are highly
coloured, fantastic, horribly human and yet, somehow, grotesque'. Kipling's dialogue quickly attracted the specialized attention of a philologist: see F. Schmidt, 'A Study in English
School-life and School-boy Slang, as Represented by Kipling's
Stalky & Co.', *Englische Studien*, xxxix (1908). Edmund Wilson's
opinion, expressed in his well-known essay (1941), is that this is in
artistic terms 'certainly the worst of Kipling's books'.

JUST SO STORIES

The volume, published in London and New York in 1902,
contains twelve stories and twelve poems. The full title is *Just So
Stories for Little Children*. All the stories except 'How the Alphabet
was Made' had previously appeared in various magazines during
the period 1897–1902. There are in addition two other stories with
a claim to belong to this group: 'The Tabu Tale' was included
with the *Just So Stories* in Scribner's Collected Edition but in the
Sussex Edition is included with the *Land and Sea Tales*; and 'Ham
and the Porcupine', which is subtitled 'A Just So Story', was
published in *The Princess Elizabeth Gift Book* (1935) but never
collected (it was reprinted in *KJ*, xxv, December 1958).

The illustrations are by Kipling – this is the only one of his
books that he illustrated – and show the influence of Aubrey
Beardsley. It has been suggested that some of them contain
cryptograms. The original manuscript, together with the draw-
ings in Indian ink, is now in the British Library (Add. MS.
59840); it bears the inscription 'Caroline Kipling to Elsie
Bambridge, July 1936'.

The stories were written at The Woolsack, the house on Cecil
Rhodes's estate that was regularly occupied by the Kipling family
during their South African visits, and were read aloud to John and

Elsie Kipling. (The latter, later Mrs Bambridge, states in a short memoir appended to Carrington's biography that they were 'first told to my brother and myself during those Cape winters'; rather confusingly, she seems to have stated to Lord Birkenhead that they were told to a group of children during a voyage to South Africa at the end of 1900.)

Angus Wilson declares that 'the first seven of the *Just So Stories* are without doubt the cream of the collection', and that each of the seven is 'a triumph in the special art of communicating with young children'; moreover, 'they are all united by the same little joke', namely 'the pleasing little Darwinian send-up'. As with *The Jungle Books*, different levels of intention seem to be in question. Wilson also has some good comments (p. 230) on the language of the stories, an element likely to be relished by anyone who has ever read aloud, for instance, 'The Elephant's Child', with its ritualistic repetitions.

G. K. Chesterton published a notably enthusiastic review of the *Just So Stories* (*Bookman*, November 1902; reprinted in *Kipling: The Critical Heritage*) in which he referred to Kipling as 'a most extraordinary and bewildering genius' and praised the stories as 'really unique':

They are not fairy tales; they are legends. A fairy tale is a tale told in a morbid age to the only remaining sane person, a child. A legend is a fairy tale told to men when men were sane. . . . The peculiar splendour . . . of these new Kipling stories is the fact that they do not read like fairy tales told to children by the modern fireside, so much as like fairy tales told to men in the morning of the world.

TRAFFICS AND DISCOVERIES

The eleven stories in this volume, which was published in London and New York in 1904, had all previously appeared in various magazines. This is the first of Kipling's adult collections in which the stories are interspersed with poems – a regular habit of his later years, the poems often throwing light, directly or obliquely, on the stories they accompany. In this collection each story is preceded by a poem.

According to Edmund Wilson, *Traffics and Discoveries* marks

'the beginning of the more sombre later Kipling'. It also contains
the first of his exercises in mystification and bafflement, the
notorious and fascinating 'Mrs Bathurst'. Angus Wilson has
singled out for praise 'They' and 'Wireless', stories which 'point to
directions in which he will later excel', and has also put in a
special plea for 'Below the Mill Dam'. The three stories about the
South African War, on the other hand ('A Sahibs' War', 'The
Captive' and 'The Comprehension of Private Copper'), Angus
Wilson finds 'insignificant' and 'spoiled by muddle, because
Kipling's social and political ideas were at this time increasingly
confused by the contradictions in a complex world that would not
arrange itself according to his simplistic vision'. 'Their Lawful
Occasions' and 'Steam Tactics' are the first two of a group of
stories involving Pyecroft, who also makes an appearance in 'Mrs
Bathurst'; 'Steam Tactics' is the first fictional outcome of
Kipling's enthusiasm for the new game of motoring, which also
plays an important role in 'They' and was to reappear in many of
the later stories. For many readers the volume is likely to be
memorable for three stories: 'Mrs Bathurst', the obscure power of
which exercises a perennial fascination; 'Wireless', which has a
central idea of compelling imaginative ingenuity; and 'They',
haunted and haunting, which derives an additional dimension of
poignancy from its personal origins.

PUCK OF POOK'S HILL

The volume was published in London in 1906, and an edition with
illustrations by Arthur Rackham appeared in New York in the
same year. All ten stories had appeared in the *Strand Magazine*
during the first ten months of 1906, and simultaneously four had
appeared in the *Ladies' Home Journal* and six in *McClure's Magazine*.
Some of the sixteen accompanying poems are notable.

   Composition of the stories seems to have been begun before the
end of 1904. Late in that year Kipling organized a play for his
children involving the characters Puck and Titania from Shakespeare's *A Midsummer Night's Dream*. Birkenhead relates that:

> Their theatre was an old grass-grown quarry near the brook,
> and with John as Puck, Elsie as Titania, and Rudyard as
> Bottom, rehearsals and performances were happily carried out.

The theatre lay at the foot of a grassy slope which they called Pook's Hill.

Pook's Hill appears to be a fairly common Sussex place-name, and the Kipling family borrowed it for the hill, more correctly known as Perch Hill, that was visible from the windows on the west side of their home, Bateman's. In the book, two children, Dan and Una (i.e., John and Elsie Kipling), meet Puck, who provides a framework for a series of stories drawn from various periods of English history. Mary Lascelles has high praise for this narrative framework; she writes that 'The device of successive short stories, separated by intervals of oblivion as dreams are sometimes separated by intervals of sleep, makes *Puck of Pook's Hill* and *Rewards and Fairies* a singularly happy invention'.

Kipling's theme is the presence of the past in English rural life, and his hero is Hobden the Hedger, an old yeoman who represents the persistence of traditional values. The old man has 'thirty generations' of ancestors laid in the churchyard; the stories reach back through the French Revolution and the Renaissance to the Normans, the Saxons, and the Roman invaders. Kipling's imagination was powerfully stimulated by the sense of the past evoked by the Sussex countryside and by archaeological and historical sites in the immediate vicinity of Bateman's: near his property, for instance, was the site of a forge said to have been used continuously from the time of the Phoenicians and the Romans until the eighteenth century. He did some conscientious research, consulting the relevant portions of Domesday Book and historical works such as Mommsen's *History of Rome*, as well as drawing on the resources of the Sussex County Record Office and the Cape Town Public Library. There is evidence of the influence of E. Nesbit, whose children's stories such as *The Treasure Seekers* (1899) and *The Phoenix and the Carpet* (1904) enjoyed a great popularity. In *Something of Myself* Kipling describes how he began by writing a story about Daniel Defoe and James II, 'overloaded with verified references, with about as much feeling to it as a walking-stick'. This was abandoned, together with another historical tale about Dr Johnson; and he thereupon 'fell first upon Normans and Saxons. Parnesius came later, directly out of a little wood about the Phoenician forge; and the rest of the tales in *Puck of Pook's Hill* followed in order.'

According to R. L. Green, contemporary reviewers were

unimpressed by this volume and its sequel, *Rewards and Fairies*. Angus Wilson has some good comments (p. 292) on the collection as an illustration of Kipling's cyclical view of history, and also notes that the arrangement of the stories is significant:

> The first story, 'Weland's Sword', tells of the old heathen god's adaptation to a Christian world, and the next three stories show the return of law to the land after the Norman conquest; only then does he go back to the fading-out of law and order with the Roman legions on the Wall in the fifth century. Thus renewal is asserted from the start.

Wilson has high praise for this collection and its sequel, which are also well discussed by Tompkins and by Green in his *Kipling and the Children*.

ACTIONS AND REACTIONS

This collection, published in London and New York in 1909, brings together eight stories all of which had appeared in various magazines between 1899 and 1909. Each story is followed by a poem.

J. M. S. Tompkins comments that 'the air of the book is genial and untroubled', with the political allegory of 'The Mother Hive' as the only exception to the prevailing serenity. There is no tale of revenge (a favourite sub-genre of Kipling's), and the theme of healing, to become so prominent in his later work, makes its appearance here. In these respects the volume contrasts both with its predecessor, *Traffics and Discoveries*, which bears the imprint of the South African War, and its successor, *A Diversity of Creatures*, published during the Great War.

'With the Night Mail' is a remarkable piece of science fiction, and 'The Puzzler' one of Kipling's characteristic farces. The two most interesting stories in the book, 'An Habitation Enforced' and 'The House Surgeon', are both set in England, are both about houses, and are both stories of psychological healing.

REWARDS AND FAIRIES

This sequel to *Puck of Pook's Hill* was published in London and New York in 1910. The title comes from Bishop Corbet's charming seventeenth-century poem, 'The Fairies' Farewell', which begins 'Farewell, rewards and fairies' (Kipling had quoted the opening stanza of the poem in 'Weland's Sword' in *Puck*). The volume contains eleven stories, each accompanied by one or more poems (22 poems in all). All the stories except 'Marklake Witches' had appeared in various magazines in 1909 and 1910.

As in *Puck*, the children Dan and Una are used to provide a frame; and again the stories were originally written for Kipling's own children. John and Elsie Kipling were by now a little older (fourteen and thirteen respectively when this volume appeared; they had been ten and nine at the time of *Puck*), and so a different level of story-telling is not altogether surprising. However, some of these stories (for example, 'Cold Iron' and 'The Tree of Justice') are distinctly difficult, highly concentrated, even obscure, and Carrington has judged them to be 'best suited to adult readers'. In his autobiography Kipling makes an oft-quoted statement about the different levels on which he was attempting to write:

> since the tales had to be read by children, before people realised that they were meant for grown-ups . . . I worked the material in three or four overlaid tints and textures, which might or might not reveal themselves according to the shifting light of sex, youth and experience.

A DIVERSITY OF CREATURES

Published in London and New York in 1917, the volume contains fourteen stories and fourteen poems. Kipling's preface states: 'With three exceptions, the dates at the head of these stories show when they were published in magazine form. "The Village that Voted the Earth was Flat", "Regulus", and "My Son's Wife" carry the dates when they were written.' It is not quite clear why he, untypically, should have taken pains to attach dates to the stories in this collection: possibly he wished to indicate that only the last two were written after the outbreak of war.

An anonymous review in the *Athenaeum* (May 1917; reprinted in *Kipling: The Critical Heritage*) had high praise for the book:

> If we had any misgivings, strengthened by some recent excursions in journalism [presumably a reference to the contents of *Sea Warfare*], that decadence had set in with Mr Kipling, this new book puts them to rest. He has never shown himself a greater master of the art of story telling, never combined creative imagination with more triumphant realism, or handled his own English prose with more ease, economy, and certainty of effect.

Angus Wilson's verdict is that the volume 'contains one or two of Kipling's finest serious stories'.

The title is alluded to in the story 'The Honours of War' ('to return thanks yet once more to Allah for the diversity of His creatures in His adorable world'), and the volume certainly offers considerable thematic variety. There are two stories of healing ('The Dog Hervey' and 'In the Same Boat'), one of conversion ('My Son's Wife'), one science fiction story ('As Easy as A.B.C.') of striking originality, one school story that returns to the world of *Stalky & Co.* ('Regulus'), and – perhaps a little disconcertingly in this wartime volume – several farces, of which the best are 'The Vortex' and 'The Village that Voted the Earth was Flat'. 'The Dog Hervey' has the doubtful distinction of being, in the opinion of many readers, Kipling's most obscure story. The collection ends with two stories of war from the point of view of civilians: 'Swept and Garnished' is about a German woman, 'Mary Postgate' about an English spinster. The latter in particular is a work of extraordinary economy and power. The two stories ought probably to be read in relation to one another; Tompkins has described them as 'dreadful tales [that] assault the mind' and 'utterances of deep outrage'.

DEBITS AND CREDITS

Each of the fourteen stories in this volume is followed by one or more poems, and all the stories had previously appeared in magazines. When the volume was published in London and New York in 1926, nine years has elapsed since the publication of

Kipling's previous collection (*A Diversity of Creatures*) – a longer period than he had ever allowed to elapse between the appearance of two major collections. Carrington notes that it was 'at first received coolly by the critics, though rapturously by the Kipling fans'. The same writer comments on the oddity of Kipling's decision to open the volume with a story as deficient in popular appeal as 'The Enemies to Each Other' – and, one might add, to follow it with a story as nearly unreadable as 'Sea Constables'. Kipling took pains with the arrangement of his collections and such a decision is not easily explained, unless we assume that he was intent on showing a defiant indifference to popularity.

Carrington also suggests that the title hints at a recurring theme in Kipling's work, that of love and loyalty, especially where (as, very clearly, in 'The Wish House' and 'The Gardener') one party to a relationship makes a sacrifice for the other or maintains a devotion in the face of death. (Kipling had already touched on this theme in the enigmatic 'Mary Postgate'.) This explanation of the significance of the title seems to me considerably more plausible than Bodelsen's suggestion that it indicates on Kipling's part 'a stock-taking of his work, where the "credits" are presumably the results obtained by his late technique'.

Amis sums up the volume as containing 'some self-indulgent fantasy, some exercises in the supernatural, evidence of a preoccupation with disease, and three good stories' – though he also concedes that 'it is hard to find anything by Kipling that is without its successful moments'. Amis's three good stories are 'The Wish House', 'A Madonna of the Trenches' and 'The Eye of Allah'; but many would insist on including 'The Gardener' on their short list, and perhaps even placing it at the top. Its position at the end of the volume may help to account for the placing of 'The Enemies to Each Other' at the beginning: the volume that starts with Adam and Eve and the Fall ends with Christ forgiving a sinner.

By any criteria this is one of the richest and most varied of all Kipling's collections. War and its aftermath, especially in the persons of those bodily or psychologically maimed by their experiences, are prominent ('A Madonna of the Trenches', 'A Friend of the Family', 'Sea Constables', 'The Gardener', 'The Janeites'), while 'On the Gate' is an eschatological fantasy based on the wholesale slaughter of the Great War. 'The Bull that Thought' and 'The Eye of Allah' are successful allegories that have won the respect and provoked the interpretative ingenuity of modern critics. Kipling's longstanding interest in freemasonry finds renewed expression in 'The Janeites' and 'In the Interests of the Brethren', and his preoccupation with cancer in 'The Wish House' and 'A Madonna of the Trenches'. 'The Wish House' and 'The Gardener' contain memorable studies of older women by a writer who has often been charged with misogyny, or at least with an inability to depict women characters sympathetically and effectively. In quite a different vein, 'The United Idolaters' and 'The Propagation of Knowledge' are school stories that return to the manner of *Stalky & Co.* The best stories in the book tackle the major themes of love and death: a tall order for a writer of short stories, but one that Kipling is capable of discharging triumphantly.

LIMITS AND RENEWALS

Published in London and New York in 1932, this is Kipling's last collection of stories. It contains fourteen stories and nineteen poems. Some of its themes make it very much an old man's book, and Carrington suggests that 'the strength of the book lies in the stories about doctors and disease, topics which now meant more to him than the life of soldiers and sailors that he had written about in his youth'. The stories referred to include 'The Tender Achilles', 'Unprofessional' and 'Fairy-Kist'. On the other hand there is also to be found a group of stories of quite a different kind and equally successful in their own way: the revenge-stories 'Beauty Spots' and 'Dayspring Mishandled', though it is true that the two categories overlap to the extent that disease and death are to be found in the latter story. ('The Tie' is another, less successful, revenge-story.) And, in 'Aunt Ellen', Kipling concludes his long series of riotous, saturnalian farces ('The Miracle of Saint Jubanus' is another, less notable farce).

A recurring theme, hinted at in the title, is the extent to which a man can be subjected to strain before breaking down completely. Dobrée notes that this is a long-standing preoccupation of Kipling's, and cites for comparison the very late poem 'Hymn of Breaking Strain' (1935). Carrington observes, not with approval, the appearance of a shift in Kipling's technique: 'While he reached out continually to master new technologies and to bring them within the scope of his art, he seemed less able to visualize a scene in a few unforgettable words. We are given situations rather than scenes, conversations rather than characters.' For Amis the volume shows 'a sad but not strange decline' – a somewhat grudging comment on a collection that contains a story as distinguished and moving as 'Dayspring Mishandled'.

'The Tie', 'Aunt Ellen' and 'Uncovenanted Mercies' appeared here for the first time; all the other stories had been previously published.

A Guide to Kipling's Short Stories

The following alphabetical listing includes entries for nearly two hundred stories contained in Kipling's collections from *Plain Tales from the Hills* (1888) to *Limits and Renewals* (1932). It does not include the school stories in *Stalky & Co.* or the contents of the five volumes of stories for children (the historical tales in *Puck of Pook's Hill* and *Rewards and Fairies*, and the animal stories in the two *Jungle Books* and *Just So Stories*): these volumes, which possess a greater degree of homogeneity than most of the other collections, are discussed above.

There is a considerable number of uncollected stories and sketches by Kipling, notably from his early years in India. Since most of his youthful journalism was published either anonymously or under a variety of pseudonyms (not all of which can be confidently or consistently identified with Kipling), the problems of authenticity and attribution are complex; and the matter is further complicated by the habit of various members of Kipling's family of collaborating with him. Louis L. Cornell's *Kipling in India* contains two valuable appendixes: 'A Chronological List of Kipling's Writings from October 1882 to March 1889', comprising both collected and uncollected pieces, and an essay on 'Kipling's Uncollected Newspaper Writings'. (Cornell suggests, for instance, that the very first of the 'Plain Tales' published in the *Civil & Military Gazette* on 2 November 1886 and entitled 'Love-in-a-Mist' may well be by Kipling.) J. McG. Stewart's bibliography also contains an appendix on Kipling's uncollected prose and verse. The *Reader's Guide* lists 270 uncollected stories and prints the texts of some, and over the years the *Kipling Journal* has reprinted many uncollected items.

AMIR'S HOMILY, THE.   No magazine publication; *Life's Handicap*
(1891). A slight piece concerning an Afghan ruler who, in
executing summary justice on a thief, recalls his own early days
of hardship. The opening paragraphs contain some generalizations on the Afghan people, to whom, 'when they choose to
rebel', 'neither life, property, law, nor kingship are sacred'.

ARMY OF A DREAM, THE.   *Morning Post*, 15–18 June 1904; *Traffics
and Discoveries* (1904). Written on the voyage to South Africa at
the end of 1900: 'a vision of England trained and prepared for
war by freely offered service' (Carrington). Angus Wilson cites
a letter written by Kipling to Mrs Hill in March 1905, telling
her that *Traffics and Discoveries* had been put together in order to
accommodate this political pamphlet.

ARREST OF LIEUTENANT GOLIGHTLY, THE.   *Civil & Military
Gazette*, 23 November 1886; *Plain Tales from the Hills* (1888).
Golightly is immensely vain of his personal appearance and
prides himself on looking like 'an Officer and a Gentleman'. By
a series of misfortunes in the course of a solitary journey, he
ends up resembling a tramp, is mistakenly identified as a
deserter, and is arrested. His protestations are ignored until at
last he is rescued by a major who recognizes him. But the
humiliation, and the story that goes the rounds, is too much for
him, and he quits India to return home. This is an early
example of a type of story to which Kipling was to become
addicted, involving the physical humiliation of the morally
objectionable. For a much later example, compare 'The Tie'.
The present story is discussed by Gilbert (pp. 52–60), who finds
it, for all its apparent lightweight quality, 'a wonderfully artful
piece of work'.

AS EASY AS A.B.C.   *Family Magazine*, February–March 1912;
London Magazine, March–April 1912; *A Diversity of Creatures*
(1917). According to Carrington, the first draft of this story was
written in 1907. A reviewer in the *Athenaeum* described it in 1917
as 'perhaps the finest short story of the future ever written';
sixty years later Angus Wilson called it 'one of the best
science-fiction stories of all time' and 'one of [Kipling's] very
best short stories'. The story offers a vision of the year 2065, by
which date nationalism and politics, wars and democracy, have
all become extinct. The A.B.C. (Aerial Board of Control), an
international company of radio technicians, has taken over
administration of the earth and is called in to deal with trouble

in Chicago, where there has been a democratic outbreak. A sequel to 'With the Night Mail', it has been described by Bonamy Dobrée as a 'major attack upon democracy'.

AT HOWLI THANA. *The Week's News*, 31 March 1888; *In Black and White* (1888). The story consists of the monologue of a smooth-tongued Delhi Pathan who has been dismissed from the police service and now seeks employment as a messenger. When asked why he was sacked, he resorts to an elaborate and evidently mendacious self-vindication. At the end, even though the 'Sahib' he is addressing recognizes that he is 'a scamp', he obtains the post he is after.

AT THE END OF THE . PASSAGE. *Boston Herald*, 20 July 1890; *Lippincott's Magazine*, August 1890; *Mine Own People* (1891); *Life's Handicap* (1891). Four Englishmen serving in India meet to play whist in the sweltering heat. One, employed by the Indian Survey, has come 130 miles from 'his lonely post in the desert'; one, a civil servant in the political department, has also travelled far for this brief meeting with men of his own race; one is a doctor who has briefly absented himself from 'a cholera-stricken camp of coolies'; the fourth, Hummil, is an assistant engineer at an isolated railway station. All show signs of strain, and the monotony of their lives and the gruelling nature of their work in very trying climatic conditions are stressed. After the others have left, Hummil tells the doctor he has been unable to sleep of late; he is evidently suffering from strain brought on by overwork and heat. The doctor's drugs have no effect on him, and he is plagued by hallucinations, seeing a double or image of himself. The doctor has to depart; when he returns a week later he finds Hummil dead, apparently of terror. He photographs the dead man's staring eyes; then, having developed the film, hastily destroys the pictures. The story begins as a vivid picture of the harshness of the Anglo-Indian's lot and ends as a somewhat obscure horror-story. Carrington describes it as 'a problem-story in the same mode as the problem-pictures which were so popular at the Academy in Kipling's younger days'. There is an analysis by Jeffrey Meyers in *KJ*, xxxviii, June 1971; Meyers suggests that, by introducing the supernatural element, Kipling 'nearly destroys the total effect of the story'. See also 'The Mark of the Beast'.

AT THE PIT'S MOUTH. No magazine publication; *Under the Deodars* (1888). A story, set in Simla, of 'A Man and his Wife and a Tertium Quid'. The wife, during her husband's absence in the plains, carries on an affair with another man. They meet in a cemetery and notice that a fresh grave is being dug ('Each well-regulated Indian Cemetery keeps half-a-dozen graves permanently open for contingencies and incidental wear-and-tear'). When they ride along a narrow mountain track the man's horse slips, and animal and rider fall to their deaths; the man is buried in the grave he has watched being dug. Kipling's irony is genuinely chilling, and the story is told with economy and well-controlled drama.

AT TWENTY-TWO. *The Week's News*, 18 February 1888; *In Black and White* (1888). Janki Meah is a blind man who for thirty years has worked down the mines at the Jimahari Collieries. When the mine floods, his unrivalled knowledge of it enables him to lead a number of his fellow-workers to safety. Among those he saves is his young wife's lover, who promptly elopes with her. The *Athenaeum* described the story as 'a gem of the first water'.

AUNT ELLEN. No magazine publication; *Limits and Renewals* (1932). The narrator, motoring from the country to London, promises to deliver to an old servant an eiderdown that has been rolled up and in which various gifts have been stowed. He is involved in a collision with some undergraduates and a rather forced farce ensues, in which the eiderdown is run over and mistaken for the mangled body of an old lady. A final scene shows a London policeman covered with the contents of the burst eiderdown. Dobrée describes this as 'the most purely farcical of all Kipling's tales'. The poem that follows it, 'The Playmate', casts light on Kipling's views on the comedy of human misadventure.

BAA BAA, BLACK SHEEP. *Wee Willie Winkie* (1888); subsequently reprinted in the Christmas Supplement of *The Week's News*, 21 December 1888. This powerful story of two children left by their Anglo-Indian parents in the care of foster-parents in England fairly closely follows Kipling's own experiences at 'the House of Desolation' in Southsea, where he and his sister were left in the care of the Holloways (see p. 27). Punch, the boy, is subjected by the woman to a long course of harsh treatment; his personality undergoes a change, becoming sullen and deceitful, until at last his mother arrives to rescue him (as Mrs Kipling had done) – but the happy ending is qualified by a final paragraph that declares that 'when young lips have drunk deep

of the bitter waters of Hate, Suspicion, and Despair, all the
Love in the world will not wholly take away that knowledge'.
An early reviewer, Edmund Gosse, suggested that 'Mr Kipling
has looked inside his own heart and drawn from memory', and
the story has often been taken as unretouched autobiography.
On the other hand, it has been pointed out that, after taking her
son away from the Holloways, Mrs Kipling left her daughter
there, and would hardly have done so if the household had been
the grim place it is painted in the story. Comparison may be
made with Kipling's non-fictional version of the events in
question in the opening chapter of *Something of Myself*, with
another fictional version in the opening chapter of *The Light that
Failed*, and with the account given by Kipling's sister. J. I. M.
Stewart points out that it is likely that there was 'some
manipulating of fact in the interest of dramatic effect': to take
an obvious instance, Punch does not enjoy, as the young
Kipling did, the relief afforded by periodic visits to kind
relatives. When the story was written Kipling was staying with
his friends the Hills in Allahabad, and Mrs Edmonia Hill later
described it as 'a true story of his early life. . . . When he was
writing this . . . he was in a towering rage at the recollection of
those days' (*Atlantic Monthly*, 1936). Louis L. Cornell has said
that it is 'not so much a "true story" of Kipling's early life as an
intense and bitter work of art'; at the same time he points out
that it 'cannot be set aside' and 'remains a document of the
greatest importance for understanding some of the early
experiences that helped to shape Kipling as an Anglo-Indian
author'. Carrington's 'Baa Baa Black Sheep: Fact or Fiction',
KJ, xxxix, June 1972, includes a chronology of Kipling's
childhood.

BANK FRAUD, A.   *Civil & Military Gazette*, 14 April 1887; *Plain
Tales from the Hills* (1888). The young English manager of a
bank in India is sent an accountant who proves thoroughly
disagreeable. The latter is found to be suffering from consump-
tion and, unknown to himself, is given three months to live; at
the same time, official notice of his dismissal arrives. The
manager heroically conceals the truth, patiently fosters the
fiction that the dying man's work is recognized by his superiors,
pays his salary out of his own pocket, and endures his
self-righteous reproofs, until the man dies, happily ignorant of
the real state of things to the very end.

BEAUTY SPOTS. *Strand Magazine*, January 1932; *Limits and Renewals* (1932). A revenge-story-cum-farce set in an English village. A retired major, 'bung-full of public-spirit and simian malignity', spreads a malicious rumour about the son of a self-made man who has settled in the village. (Since snobbery enters largely into his motivation, the social origins of hero and villain are relevant: the victim of the slander is a research chemist whose father is a *nouveau riche* industrialist.) The major is punished by a hoax involving a pig, and the final emphasis is on his humiliation. As a revenge-tale in a village setting, the story can be compared with 'The Village that Voted the Earth was Flat'. The major's gratuitous persecution of the newcomers provokes a kind of war to which the young man (who has seen active service and been gassed) responds in kind: see the poem 'The Expert', which follows the story and comments on the post-war setting. Kipling discreetly evokes the England of the period: it is the age of the charabanc and of 'State-aided summer sunlight'. Although the revenge element is at the centre of the story (it is the last of Kipling's exercises in the tale of revenge) there is some pleasant comedy surrounding the pig Angelique; moreover, although the major's final humiliation is total and unsparing, one has the sense that it is in no way disproportionate to his deserts. The young man's plan of revenge results in the restoration of tranquillity to the rural scene.

BELOW THE MILL DAM. *Monthly Review*, September 1902; *Traffics and Discoveries* (1904). A fable in which the chief characters are a black rat and a grey cat. Angus Wilson finds this story 'excellent' and unjustly neglected by present-day readers, though 'it was the subject of much discussion in right radical political circles when it first appeared' two months after Balfour became Prime Minister. Wilson interprets it as

> a political fable expressing Kipling's alarm and dismay at England's apparent inability to address herself socially, imperially, culturally and technologically to the future. It embodies his antipathy to the traditional elitist, conservative, but, at the same time, *laissez-faire* cultural and political outlook of Balfour's country-house world.

BERTRAN AND BIMI.   No magazine publication; *Mine Own People*

(1891); *Life's Handicap* (1891). Hans Breitmann (see also 'Reingelder and the German Flag') narrates the story of Bertran, a Frenchman, whose pet orang-utan Bimi lives with him almost as a friend and equal, dining at his table, smoking a cigar, and sleeping in a bed. When Bertran takes a wife, Bimi murders her; Bertran kills the animal with his bare hands but is himself killed in the struggle. The *Edinburgh Review* said that it was 'a kind of thing that ought never to have been written' and described it as 'nightmare literature'; another contemporary reviewer in the *Spectator* called it 'detestable, and . . . not in the least saved by being extremely cleverly written'.

BEYOND THE PALE.   No magazine publication; *Plain Tales from the Hills* (1888). Trejago, an Englishman serving in India, by chance meets an Indian girl, Bisesa, 'a widow, about fifteen years old'. He talks to her through the window of the room in which she is confined by her family, and then regularly visits her. But her relatives discover what is going on, the girl's hands are cut off, and Trejago is slightly wounded. He never sees the girl again. The story carries the epigraph (identified as a Hindu proverb): 'Love heeds not caste nor sleep a broken bed. I went in search of love and lost myself', and opens: 'A man should, whatever happens, keep to his own caste, race and breed.' Kingsley Amis describes it as 'one of the most terrible stories in the language'. Cornell notes that 'Kipling maintains a nearly perfect control of the contrary impulses towards conventionality on the one hand, and anonymity on the other'; he also notes that the wound Trejago receives in the groin is reminiscent of the punishment of Abelard. For other stories by Kipling dealing with a similar theme, see 'In the House of Suddhoo', 'Kidnapped', 'Without Benefit of Clergy'.

BIG DRUNK DRAF, THE.   *The Week's News*, 24 March 1888; *Soldiers Three* (1888). Mulvaney recalls how he helped a young and inexperienced officer lick into shape an undisciplined group of soldiers. In this story Kipling 'discharged Mulvaney from the Army and wrote . . . about him as a civilian on the Indian Railways' (Carrington).

BISARA OF POOREE, THE.   *Civil & Military Gazette*, 4 March 1887; *Plain Tales from the Hills* (1888). The Bisara of Pooree is a tiny silver box studded with rubies and containing a carving of 'a little eyeless fish'. It possesses supernatural powers: if stolen, it brings luck to the thief. A 'nasty little man' steals it and an attractive woman promptly promises to marry him – only to drop him abruptly when the love-charm is in turn stolen from him.

BLACK JACK. No magazine publication; *Soldiers Three* (1888). Mulvaney overhears and outwits a plot to steal his rifle and to kill an unpopular officer with it so that the blame falls on him. The Indian Railway Library Edition has an opening paragraph omitted from later editions:

> There is a writer called Mr Robert Louis Stevenson, who makes most delicate inlay work in black and white, and files out to the fraction of a hair. He has written a story about a suicide club ['The Suicide Club', in *New Arabian Nights* (1882)], wherein men gambled for Death because other amusements did not bite sufficiently. My friend Private Mulvaney knows nothing about Mr Stevenson, but he once assisted informally at a meeting of almost such a club as that gentleman has described, and his words are true.

BONDS OF DISCIPLINE, THE. *Windsor Magazine* and *Collier's Weekly*, August 1903; *Traffics and Discoveries* (1904). The story was written in 1900 and, according to Carrington, reflects 'a short anti-French phase' through which Kipling passed. It is narrated largely through dialogue and shows how a French spy disguised as a Portuguese castaway on a ship of the Royal Navy falls a victim to the crew's taste for spoofing once they discover his identity.

BREAD UPON THE WATERS. *The Graphic*, Christmas Number, 1896; *McClure's Magazine*, December 1896; *The Day's Work* (1898). (A different story with the same title appeared in the *Civil & Military Gazette* on 14 March 1888 and was collected in *The Smith Administration* [1891].) A Scots ship's engineer relates how he was dismissed by his employers after twenty years' service, but contrived to get the better of them in the end. Carrington suggests that Kipling derived the idea for the story from his Atlantic crossing in a German ship in the summer of 1895.

BRIDGE-BUILDERS, THE. *Illustrated London News*, Christmas Number, 1893; *The Day's Work* (1898). Findlayson of the Public Works Department, an engineer who has laboured long to construct a bridge over the Ganges, finds his almost completed work threatened with destruction when the river floods. He refuses to leave his post, but takes opium for medicinal purposes at the urging of his native servant and is plunged into a dream in which the Indian gods discuss man's presumption in bridging the great river and dismiss his vast labours as petty: 'It is but the shifting of a little dirt . . .'. Contemporary reviewers were quick to spot the symbolism and allegory: 'The spanning of the Ganges is not merely an engineering achievement: it stands for a type of the losing battle which the old gods of the East fight against new and spiritual forces' (*Macmillan's Magazine*). According to Mrs Kipling's diary, the story was written in the autumn of 1893. There is a long discussion of this complex story by Gilbert (pp. 127–57), who draws attention to the contrasts between its first and second halves. Angus Wilson describes it as 'one of the most splendid of the Indian administrative stories'.

BROKEN-LINK HANDICAP, THE.   *Civil & Military Gazette*, 6 April 1887; *Plain Tales from the Hills* (1888). The race-horse Shackles, hitherto unbeatable, loses a race when his jockey is the victim of a trick, and the arrogant owner is duly humiliated. An early instance of Kipling's favourite theme of the punitive practical joke.

BRONCKHORST DIVORCE-CASE, THE.   No magazine publication; *Plain Tales from the Hills* (1888). This is the story promised in 'Miss Youghal's Sais'. Bronckhorst is a thoroughly disagreeable man who subjects his wife to mental cruelty and at last wrongfully accuses her of infidelity. Strickland (see 'Miss Youghal's Sais') is called in and again resorts to a disguise: by mixing with the native servants he discovers that the witnesses to the supposed misconduct have been bribed to give false evidence. The case is dismissed and Bronckhorst is horse-whipped, whereupon his wife weeps over him and nurses him back to health.

BRUGGLESMITH.   *Harper's Weekly*, October 1891; *Many Inventions* (1893). The narrator becomes involved by chance with a drunken character who gives his address as Brook Green, Hammersmith (his slurred speech corrupting it to 'Bruggles-smith'), and involuntarily accompanies him on a nocturnal odyssey first down the Thames and then through the streets of London. There is much forced hilarity. George Saintsbury said that he 'would not wish for a better farce', and Bonamy Dobrée cites it as an example of 'the healing laughter of farce'; but other critics, including several contemporary reviewers, have been less enthusiastic – though Carrington classes the group of farces that includes this story (together with 'My Sunday at Home', 'The Vortex', 'The Village that Voted the Earth was Flat', and others) 'among his greater achievements', and Angus Wilson cites it as an instance of 'the best of Kipling's comic tales [that are] built on journeys charted like children's games'. These critics do not seem troubled by the implausibility of the story (the narrator had many opportunities of quietly abandoning his old man of the sea before reaching Hammersmith), or by the disproportion between what is described as happening and the somewhat hysterical reaction provoked in the narrator. (For a relevant comment, however, see Tompkins' excellent discussion, pp. 43–5.) In short, this is a good instance of the kind of Kipling story that evokes radically different responses even from Kipling's admirers. Tompkins points out that it is the only one of Kipling's farces in which 'the "I" is a protagonist'. As Carrington notes, Brook Green, Hammersmith, was the address of Charles Whibley, man of letters and early acquaintance of Kipling. In *Something of Myself* Kipling refers to the hand-ambulance kept at the back of St Clement Dane's Church during his early years in London.

BRUSHWOOD BOY, THE. *Century Magazine*, December 1895 (with map by Kipling); *The Day's Work* (1898); separate editions published in 1899 (illustrated by O. Lowell) and 1907 (illustrated by F. H. Townsend). The magazine version was shortened before republication: see R. L. Green in *KJ*, XXII, October 1955. George Cottar – successively presented as child, schoolboy, and the very model of a young army officer – has recurring dreams in which a pile of brushwood on a beach is prominent and which also involve a girl who grows up as he does. On leave in England after service in India, he meets a girl who strikingly resembles his dream-figure and finds that she has had dreams similar to his own. They realize they love each other and precipitately become engaged. The story was written in Vermont in two weeks in the autumn of 1895, and Angus Wilson finds in it 'an embarrassingly sentimental attitude to the mother [Kipling] had left behind'. Bodelsen aptly comments: 'That [Kipling] should have ended a volume called *The Day's*

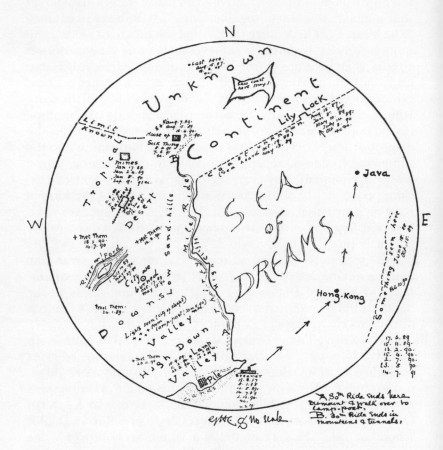

Fig. 1   Kipling's Map for 'The Brushwood Boy'

Source: *Century Magazine*, LI (December 1895) p. 272.

Work with a story about a life half of which is spent in a dream world is surely a very curious thing.' He speculates that 'it is possible that the story reflects [Kipling's] own feeling of having a double life, divided between a daylight and a nocturnal world, with this difference: that the young officer in the story only finds his way to the secret country in dreams, while Kipling entered it awake'. R. L. Green points out (*KJ*, XXII, October 1955) that George Cottar, the hero of the story, was educated at the United Services College and was a contemporary of Stalky and Co.; references to this point were more explicit in the magazine version. 'The Brushwood Boy' bears some interesting resemblances to George Du Maurier's novel *Peter Ibbetson* (1891), in which the hero and heroine relive their childhood by meeting in shared dreams. Kipling's uncle, Edward Burne-Jones, read the novel and wrote to the author about it.

BUBBLING WELL ROAD. *Civil & Military Gazette*, 18 January 1888; *Life's Handicap* (1891). While hunting wild boar the narrator becomes lost in a stretch of high jungle grass and discovers a well, believed by local natives to be haunted, from which disturbing noises and an uncanny echo emerge.

BULL THAT THOUGHT, THE. *MacLean's Magazine*, 15 November 1924; *Cosmopolitan*, December 1924; *Nash's & Pall Mall Magazine*, January 1925; *Debits and Credits* (1926). The story is set in France. The narrator, an Englishman on a motoring holiday, hears from a Frenchman the story of a bull with uncanny intelligence and murderous designs. The climax of the story concerns a bull-fight in which, after it has killed men and horses wholesale, the bull's life is spared. The story has been extensively discussed by Gilbert (pp. 168–87) and Bodelsen (pp. 53–72). Bodelsen's essay argues that there is a 'symbolic structure running parallel with that of the action' and that the underlying theme concerns art and the artist. Gilbert takes a similar line in seeing it as a parable of art: for him it 'explores the relationship of brutality to art', and the story of Apis the bull is 'nothing less than the classic story of the artist's growth'. The bull is named after the Egyptian bull-god.

BY WORD OF MOUTH. *Civil & Military Gazette*, 10 June 1887; *Plain Tales from the Hills* (1888). This was the last of the series of 'Plain Tales from the Hills' to appear in the *Civil & Military Gazette*. Dumvisc, a civil surgeon, is devoted to his wife, but she dies in an outbreak of typhoid. Soon afterwards his servant reports having seen her ghost and brings him the message that she will see her husband the following month in Nuddea – a distant place that he has no plans to visit. Then he is unexpectedly transferred to Nuddea to deal with a cholera epidemic, and in a short time is dead himself.

CAPTIVE, THE. *Collier's Weekly*, 6 December 1902; *Traffics and Discoveries* (1904). Carrington refers to this – one of the three stories in *Traffics and Discoveries* that deal with the Boer War – as one of Kipling's 'most sophisticated, most thoroughly elaborate, stories, packed with allusion and technicality, and making no concession to the casual reader'. The narrator is an American adventurer held prisoner by the British; he tells of the Boer commandant and the British general, professional soldiers who, though enemies, respect each other. The British general refers to the war in South Africa as 'a first-class dress parade for Armageddon'. Compare Carrington's assessment, quoted above, with that of Angus Wilson, who finds in this story 'all the growing faults of Kipling's later work – over-technical language, too elaborate a framework of narration'.

CHILDREN OF THE ZODIAC, THE. *Harper's Weekly*, December 1891; *Many Inventions* (1893). An allegory concerning certain figures among the signs of the zodiac, especially Leo and Virgo, who come down to earth and learn the lessons of human life: 'whatever comes or does not come we men must not be afraid'. Contemporary reviewers did not much care for this story: Saintsbury, for instance, liked it least of those in *Many Inventions*. Carrington finds it baffling but proposes a biographical explanation: 'All that can be said about it with conviction is that it deals with the marriage of a young poet, who dreads death by cancer of the throat, and that in 1891 Kipling was a young poet contemplating marriage, and ill with an affliction of the throat.[1] Tompkins has a good paragraph (pp. 171–2) on the story's astrological symbolism. Angus Wilson interprets it as a parable of the function of art: the poet's songs make men a little happier and better able to endure the pains of life. Wilson sees it as an expression of 'the preaching purpose of the art which was the centre of [Kipling's] life', and which Kipling 'could never quite lay down'. This is the first of Kipling's stories in which is expressed a fear of cancer, which in a letter of 1906 he was to describe as a 'family complaint'.

CHURCH THAT WAS AT ANTIOCH, THE. *London Magazine*, August

1929; *Limits and Renewals* (1932). The story is set in the first century A.D. A young Roman official is involved in maintaining law and order in the city of Antioch, where there is dissension between Christians and Jews, and between Gentile and non-Gentile Christians. St Peter and St Paul appear as characters. The young man is stabbed, and as he dies he pleads for his murderer in words that echo those of Christ ('Don't be hard on them. . . . They don't know what they are doing'). Angus Wilson finds this one of the best of Kipling's later stories. For a source, see Galatians 2:2. See also 'The Manner of Men'.

CITY OF DREADFUL NIGHT, THE. *Civil & Military Gazette*, 10 September 1885; *Life's Handicap* (1891). Kipling borrowed his title from James Thomson, whose poem of the same title had appeared in 1874. A sketch rather than a story, it evokes very powerfully – and, for an author of nineteen, with astonishing confidence and sureness – the atmosphere of the city of Lahore, crowded with humanity on an August night of stifling heat. The narrator, unable to sleep, walks through the streets and sees the sleeping natives who lie everywhere as 'ghosts' and 'corpses'. The final image is of the funeral procession at dawn of a woman who has 'died at midnight from the heat'. The piece no doubt owes something to Kipling's self-confessed habit of nocturnal rambles. Of the spectacle depicted, 'Doré might have drawn it! Zola could describe it', he writes – but in fact Kipling himself does remarkably well:

> a disused Mahomedan burial-ground, where the jawless skulls and rough-butted shank-bones, heartlessly exposed by the July rains, glimmered like mother o' pearl on the rain-channelled soil. The heated air and the heavy earth had driven the very dead upward for coolness' sake.

From this passage there follows the nightmarish vision of a city densely populated by the dead. The *Spectator* found this sketch 'wonderfully vivid and convincing', and *Blackwood's* commented that 'Never was there a more astonishing picture'.

COMPREHENSION OF PRIVATE COPPER, THE. *Everybody's Magazine* and *The Strand*, October 1902; *Traffics and Discoveries* (1904). A story of the Boer War, which had been over for six months by the time it was published. It involves an encounter between a British soldier and an English-speaking settler fighting for the

Boers (the latter's accent is described as 'chi-chi'). Private Copper, the son of a Sussex shepherd, is captured by the renegade son of a Transvaal burgher, but turns the tables on him and takes him prisoner in turn. Angus Wilson comments:

> we are left with the utterly improbable figure of a rich young white South African farmer who speaks and looks like an Indian but also has the drawl and the culture snobbery of a young Etonian squire. Against this the very real and sympathetically realized figure of Private Copper doesn't stand a chance of coming to life. Kipling has too many points to make and too many hang-ups from the past to be rid of.

Bodelsen draws attention to a curious feature of the story: Kipling takes pains first to suggest that the antagonist is a half-caste, then to indicate that he is not. Bodelsen's explanation of this puzzle, via an argument too complex to summarize here, is that this is 'a piece of daring symbolization' and that the story is 'a kind of parable on the chief issue of the Anglo-Transvaal conflict' – namely, the rights of the Uitlanders.

CONFERENCE OF THE POWERS, A. *Pioneer*, 23–4 May 1890; *Harper's Weekly*, 31 May 1890; *The Courting of Dinah Shadd* (1890); *Many Inventions* (1893). Eustace Cheever, a successful middle-aged novelist, meets three young subalterns who are on leave in London after seeing action in Burma. These boys in their early twenties relate to him, a man of the world and professional story-teller, accounts of their experiences; and he comes to realize how much of life he has never seen at first hand. When one of them says 'I haven't seen much – only Burmese jungle', he murmurs 'And dead men, and war, and power, and responsibility.' This encounter between the man of letters and the men of action ends with the former 'blaspheming his art' and with the narrator commenting that he 'would be sorry for this in the morning'. Amis states that this story 'is always cited by those who feel that Kipling betrayed his art'; he might have added that this is a view that hardly makes sufficient allowance for the ambiguity of the conclusion. Cheever bears some resemblance to Thomas Hardy, who was fifty in 1890 (though Cheever has 'big eyes' and a 'gray beard' and is a 'golden talker', none of which applied to Hardy). Angus Wilson suggests that the story expresses Kipling's attitude towards the distinguished men of letters he met soon after his arrival in London, and relevantly quotes from *Letters of Travel* (1892): 'There is no provincialism like the provincialism of London.' Birkenhead comments that 'the "Powers" of the title are the Pen and the Sword, and Kipling makes an abject surrender to the latter', the story revealing him as 'ridiculously ashamed of his sedentary life'; but this is again to identify Kipling too readily with Cheever. One of the young officers in the story is referred to again in a later story, 'A Deal in Cotton'. On Hardy, see also 'My Sunday at Home'.

CONSEQUENCES. *Civil & Military Gazette*, 9 December 1886; *Plain Tales from the Hills* (1888). A slight piece concerning Tarrion, who obtains a lucrative official post with the help of Mrs Hauksbee, largely thanks to the implausibly lucky accident of some important papers falling into her hands. Note that the last three paragraphs of the story follow the conventions of the game of 'Consequences'.

CONVERSION OF AURELIAN McGOGGIN, THE. *Civil & Military Gazette*, 28 April 1887; *Plain Tales from the Hills* (1888). A self-important know-all ('all head, no physique, and a hundred theories'), the student of Comte and Herbert Spencer, bores everyone with his intellectual arrogance. Thanks to overwork in the heat of summer, he has a breakdown and is stricken by aphasia, involving the loss of speech and memory. Although he makes a recovery he is permanently chastened by the experience, for it is something beyond his comprehension.

COURTING OF DINAH SHADD, THE. *Macmillan's Magazine* and *Harper's Weekly*, March 1890; *The Courting of Dinah Shadd* (1890); *Mine Own People* (1891); *Life's Handicap* (1891). A story of the soldiers three, this time showing a tragic side to the picture. Mulvaney tells the narrator of his courtship of Dinah Shadd, a sergeant's daughter; the courtship is almost wrecked by his irresponsible folly in flirting with another girl and becoming trapped by her artful designs. Dinah sticks to him and forgives him; but the other girl's witch-like mother curses them both — and, Mulvaney adds, the curses have all been fulfilled (the death of their only child is particularly stressed). Lionel Johnson, writing in the *Academy*, described it as 'the one story in the book admirable from first to last', and Henry James declared it 'a masterpiece'. Francis Adams in the *Fortnightly*

Review gave more qualified praise: though 'a little masterpiece', it was marred by 'a large allowance of second-rate second-sight prediction'; and the same element was deplored by a reviewer in the *Bookman* in the same month (November 1891): 'Sometimes he stoops to the Supernatural . . .'.

CUPID'S ARROWS. No magazine publication; *Plain Tales from the Hills* (1888). This entertaining anecdote, set in Simla, concerns 'a very pretty girl' whose mother is anxious to marry her off to a rich but extremely ugly middle-aged Commissioner ('the ugliest man in Asia, with two exceptions', as the narrator observes with characteristic knowingness). The suitor arranges an archery tournament for ladies and, knowing that the girl shoots 'divinely', offers a diamond-studded bracelet as a prize. But she deliberately shoots wide of the mark, the prize goes to another, and the girl goes off with the young man she loves, who has 'a handsome face, and no prospects'. The story is based on an incident in George Eliot's *Daniel Deronda* (1876).

DAUGHTER OF THE REGIMENT, THE. *Civil & Military Gazette*, 11 May 1887; *Plain Tales from the Hills* (1888). Mulvaney tells the story of an Irish girl who makes heroic efforts during a cholera epidemic and, after her mother's death, is adopted by the regiment, eventually marrying a corporal. 'In the Matter of a Private' is a sequel to this story.

DAYSPRING MISHANDLED. *McCall's Magazine*, March 1928; *Strand Magazine*, July 1928; *Limits and Renewals* (1932). This remarkable story concerns a highly elaborate and protracted scheme of revenge. The victim's crime is an offensive remark about a dead woman, whom Manallace has loved devotedly but unrequitedly and has nursed to the end. (The remark is undisclosed, and Angus Wilson has argued that this omission weakens the story, 'for we are not allowed to be judge of Manallace's justification, which is a centre to the story'. Wilson suggests that it involved an allegation that the paralysis from which the woman suffered was a symptom of 'syphilis contracted by whoring'.) The slanderer, Castorley, inherits a private income and becomes a man of letters and a scholar of genuine accomplishments, more particularly an authority on Chaucer; meanwhile Manallace, who has genuine literary talents, writes potboilers for a living. To revenge the dead woman's memory, he embarks on a scheme of revenge that involves enormous labours and the acquisition of a considerable expertise: he forges a fifteenth-century manuscript of a spurious Chaucerian fragment and contrives that it fall into Castorley's hands. The latter is deceived, makes a reputation on the strength of his remarkable 'discovery', and receives a knighthood; the other's plan, of course, is to destroy him by disclosing the truth. But Castorley falls ill with cancer, and Manallace discovers that the other's wife, who is having an affair with his doctor, has guessed what he has done and is anxious that her husband should learn the truth, thus hastening his end. His scheme of revenge is therefore abandoned, and he lets Castorley die without telling him what he has done, realizing in the process that his own life has been wasted, since all this has taken many years. The story, one of Kipling's best, has been widely misunderstood. Carrington calls it 'an astonishing performance, a profound, obscure, and singularly unpleasant story', and while his first two epithets are acceptable, his last two are less so. There are also some inaccuracies in the same writer's description of it as concerning 'a vindictive feud between two expert bibliophiles, or rather the vindictive persecution of a sham expert by a genuine expert. Revenge goes so far that the victim is not spared further taunts and triumphings when dying of a painful disease' – an account that hardly does justice to the story's subtlety, complexity and humanity. Distinctly odd, too, is J. I. M. Stewart's view that it involves a 'joke'. Angus Wilson finds it Kipling's 'best late story' and one of his 'best and most original stories', though it is hard to accept his categorization of Manallace's plan, which is motivated by intense bitterness and hatred, as 'a Stalky joke that misfires'. Wilson is on surer ground in describing it as 'a picture of a life wasted in hoarded-up hatred and complicated revenge'. The best account of this story has been given by Tompkins, who points out that it is 'very tightly written . . . every sentence tells and matters' and that the title is both a quotation from the forged Chaucer fragment and a metaphorical allusion to Manallace's wasted life. She has a note (pp. 146–7) on the chronology of the action, which begins in the nineties and extends to a period after the war. The story has some powerful ironies: Castorley, in his interminable monologues showing off his expertise, unconsciously provides Manallace with the information he needs in order to dupe his enemy; Manallace begins in a spirit of revenge and ends by trying to spare the other man the knowledge of the truth. It has provoked very diverse reactions from Kipling's critics: for Amis it is 'a squalid revenge-tragedy, not redeemed by the forger's eventual recognition of the squalor', while for Tompkins it is 'one of Kipling's great achievements'.

DEAL IN COTTON, A. *Collier's Weekly*, 14 December 1907; *Actions and Reactions* (1909). A story of the Arab slave-trade in Africa. According to Carrington, it was begun at the end of 1903; Kipling had recently met Sir George Goldie and Sir Frederick Lugard, the makers of Nigeria. In May 1904 he renewed his acquaintance with Major Dunsterville, and 'Stalky' appears in the frame-story. There are also brief references to Strickland (now in retirement in Weston-super-Mare) and to 'the Infant', one of the young officers who appears in 'A Conference of the Powers'.

DEBT, THE. *Liberty*, 26 April 1930; *Story-Teller*, June 1930; *Limits and Renewals* (1932). The hero of this very late Anglo-Indian tale is six-year-old William, son of 'the Doctor of the Gaol'. During his parents' absence he listens to and joins in the conversation of the native servants, as the young Kipling had no doubt done in his time.

DEVIL AND THE DEEP SEA, THE. *Graphic*, Christmas Number, 1895; *The Day's Work* (1898). The adventures of a British whaling-steamer are recounted: it is seized by a foreign man-of-war but eventually makes its escape, only to founder in the end. Carrington comments that the story 'appears to have been written out of sheer delight in the terminology of marine engineering', and confesses that he has 'never been able to discover what happens in the end'. The ending is certainly abrupt, and Kipling does not choose to disclose the fate of the crew. Angus Wilson, however, refers to it as 'perhaps the most casual-seeming terrible ending of any in his work'.

DISTURBER OF TRAFFIC, THE. *Atlantic Monthly*, September 1891; *Many Inventions* (1893). The idea for this story came to Kipling during a visit to the Isle of Wight with Wolcott Balestier in July 1891. Dowse, a lonely lighthouse-keeper in the Java Straits, becomes mentally deranged and contrives to keep all shipping out of the area. The situation is both absurd and pathetic. The frame-story concerns a lighthouse-keeper on the English coast, who has known Dowse and tells his story to the narrator. Tompkins identifies it as 'Kipling's first full-sized experiment with the imperfect narrator'. Angus Wilson finds it 'a horrible and purposely puzzling tale', notes that it 'introduces the theme of obsession which was to reappear often in his work', and suggests that the relationship of Dowse and the strange, wild native Challong parallels that of Prospero and Caliban in *The Tempest*. The fog that features in the frame-story seems to be a metaphor for the baffling obscurity of the central tale. As the above comments suggest, the story is a strikingly early anticipation of some of the features prominent in Kipling's later work.

DOG HERVEY, THE. *Century Magazine*, April 1914; *Nash's & Pall Mall Magazine*, May 1914; *A Diversity of Creatures* (1917). Tompkins describes this as 'Kipling's most difficult tale', and Carrington declares that it 'presents more puzzles, the more it is examined; it abounds in literary, masonic, psychological, and canine clues which lead nowhere. . . . Like "Mrs. Bathurst" [it] seems to have been made incomprehensible by ruthless cutting.' A similar view is expressed by Angus Wilson, who also finds it 'confused and elliptic' and suggests that it 'might have proved to be a good, longish novel (and might not)'. Bodelsen, on the other hand, claims that 'with the possible exception of "Mrs. Bathurst" ' Kipling 'invariably took care to insert so many clues [in his stories] that the full meaning can *always* be understood if the reader is patient enough to notice them all' and states that 'there are about thirty clues to the witchcraft theme' in this story. He also points out that 'Miss Sichliffe's habit of making people presents of goldfish is mentioned no less than five times': the significance is obscure, but Bodelsen may well be correct in suggesting that

> the most likely reading is that the goldfish (and the bowl in which she presumably sends them) symbolize the spiritual imprisonment of the rich and lonely woman in the sinister house, whose 'reek of varnish' in its turn symbolizes the respectability with which her father covered up the source of his wealth

Tompkins concurs in seeing it as a modern tale of sorcery: 'The desolate longing of a woman makes a vehicle for itself out of the little sickly dog she cherishes, and projects its wraith into the hallucinations of the drunkard who, years before, was kind to her'.

DRAY WARA YOW DEE. *The Week's News*, 28 April 1888; *In Black and White* (1888). The story is told by a Mohammedan whose young wife has been unfaithful to him (the title consists of the opening words of a song sung by her lover and heard by the narrator as he returns unexpectedly from a journey only two months after his marriage). He has murdered her, hacking off her head and breasts and throwing the body into a watercourse, but her lover has escaped. The latter part of the story recounts the quest, as yet unfulfilled, for the man he intends to kill in order to gain peace. 'Does a man tear out his heart and make fritters thereof over a slow fire for aught other than a woman?'

DREAM OF DUNCAN PARRENNESS, THE. *Civil & Military Gazette*, 25 December 1884; *Life's Handicap* (1891). Kipling's second short story; according to a letter written to his aunt in November 1884, it took him three months to write 'and it is only six pages long'. The story is set in the late eighteenth century during the Governor-Generalship of Warren Hastings. A young man is visited in a dream by his own self grown older. Louis L. Cornell comments: 'The action is mechanically allegorical, and the narrator's language is an awkward and self-conscious attempt to suggest the idiom of Hastings' time: these unpromising elements are used to support a Christmas ghost story, an Anglo-Indian version of Dickens's *Christmas Carol*, in which the hero confronts his own future and sees the waste land that lies before him.'

DRUMS OF THE FORE AND AFT, THE. No magazine publication; *Wee Willie Winkie* (1888). The heroes of this story are two ill-disciplined fourteen-year-old boys – they 'smoked and drank . . . swore habitually . . . fought religiously once a week' – who are drummers in a regiment that goes into action for the first time. The men begin to flee before the Afghan horde but rally when the drummer-boys march towards the enemy playing 'The British Grenadiers'. The boys are killed, but their courage produces a victory. As J. I. M. Stewart points out, however, Kipling does not quite leave it at that: the boys have found, and emptied, a bottle of rum on the battlefield and have thus been prompted to heroism by intoxication, so that 'as often in Kipling, what may at first seem very crude is in fact rather subtle'. Kipling may be said to have it both ways, giving the reader both a stirring tale of a conventional kind and, simultaneously, a wry comment on the entire genre that such tales constitute. Contemporary reviewers had high praise for this story; Henry James 'wept copiously' over it and found the 'glamour' of Kipling's 'intense militarism . . . astonishingly contagious, in spite of the unromantic complexion of it – the way it bristles with all sorts of uglinesses and technicalities' (Introduction to *Mine Own People*).

EDGE OF THE EVENING, THE. *Metropolitan Magazine*, December 1913; *Pall Mall Magazine*, December 1913; *A Diversity of Creatures* (1917). Two Germans – the forerunners of an army of invasion – land by aeroplane in the grounds of an English country house and are killed by the occupants and their American guests. For another, richer treatment of a similar theme, see 'Mary Postgate'. The story is discussed by E. N. Houlton, *KJ*, XLVI (December 1979).

EDUCATION OF OTIS YEERE, THE. *The Week's News*, 10 and 17 March 1888; *Under the Deodars* (1888). Inspired by a longing to exert power and influence over another human being, Mrs Hauksbee takes up an insignificant man and, by bestowing attention and flattery on him, fills him with a new-found confidence. But the platonic relationship she has cultivated goes wrong when he declares his love for her, and he is crushed by her indignant rejection. The *Athenaeum* found that the story left 'a disagreeable taste in the mouth'.

ENEMIES TO EACH OTHER, THE. *MacLean's Magazine*, 15 July 1924; *Hearst's International Magazine*, August 1924; *Debits and Credits* (1926). (The title in the magazine versions was 'A New Version of What Happened in the Garden of Eden'. The story also appeared in *Good Housekeeping* in August 1924 under the title 'Adam and Eve: the Enemies of Each Other'.) A story of Adam and Eve written in a style that is a pastiche of Arabic sacred literature. As Carrington observes, it is odd that Kipling should have chosen to open the volume with this piece – unless, indeed, he wished to draw attention to his 'indifference to public opinion'.

ERROR IN THE FOURTH DIMENSION, AN. *Cosmopolitan Magazine*, December 1894; *The Day's Work* (1898). A wealthy young American living in England and aspiring to be 'a little more English than the English' has a train flagged down because he is in a hurry to reach London. He finds that this very unEnglish behaviour involves him in being arrested, imprisoned, fined, and harried by lawyers and doctors. Cured of his enthusiasm for England, he returns to New York. Kipling's satire is directed at the type of American who believes that his wealth and influence place him above the law; and it perhaps expresses, as Angus Wilson suggests, his dislike of the lawlessness of America as well as his disapproval of the invasion of England by wealthy Americans. The story was written, like 'My Sunday at Home' (with which it has some affinities), when Kipling was visiting his parents at their retirement home at Tisbury, a Wiltshire village, in the summer of 1894; he was himself at the time, of course, a resident of Vermont.

EYE OF ALLAH, THE. *McCall's Magazine*, September 1925; *Strand Magazine*, September 1925; *Debits and Credits* (1926). Set in a thirteenth-century English monastery, this story describes various reactions to the arrival of a simple microscope, brought back from Spain by John of Burgos, an illuminator of manuscripts. The instrument's revelation of a hidden world produces different reactions in different members of the community. 'The point . . . is the reactions of four different types of men to the momentous possibilities of the new invention' (Bodelsen). In the struggle between the desire for knowledge and the fear of being accused of heresy and witchcraft, the latter wins the day and the 'Eye of Allah' (the name given by the Moors to a magnifying glass) is destroyed. Gilbert interprets the story plausibly as an allegory of 'the relationship between art and pain'; it has received high praise from both Angus Wilson ('Kipling's finest story of historical conjecture') and Kingsley Amis.

FAIRY-KIST. *MacLean's Magazine*, 15 September 1927; *McCall's Magazine*, October 1927; *Strand Magazine*, February 1928; *Limits and Renewals* (1932). Written in October 1924 and revised in November 1925, this is the story of a mysterious death, clues, a suspect, and amateur detectives (there is a passing reference to 'the Sherlock Holmes business'). But the crime story is less important than a second mystery that is solved: the suspect is a man psychologically disturbed by war experiences (he hears voices and shows signs of obsessive behaviour), and the amateur detectives, who are doctors, succeed in discovering the explanation of his condition. Characteristically this turns on a piece of highly specialized knowledge – an acquaintance with

Mrs Ewing's story *Mary's Meadow*, which has been read to him by a nurse in the hospital. (Mrs Ewing was a favourite author of Kipling's in boyhood, and her *Six to Sixteen* is referred to in *Something of Myself*.) Amis seems to miss the point in describing this as 'a neat detective story', since the real centre of interest is the man's psychological condition. Tompkins is, as usual, a more reliable guide in seeing the detective element as 'only the outer and misdirected envelope': she cites the story as an instance of Kipling's habit of deliberately laying a false trail, and points out that the problem is 'pathological, not criminological'. The main characters also appear in 'In the Interests of the Brethren'.

FALSE DAWN.   No magazine publication; *Plain Tales from the Hills* (1888). Two sisters, who have 'a strong likeness between them in look and voice', set their cap at the same eligible bachelor. They attend 'a moonlight-riding picnic' at which, in the confusion of a vividly-described dust-storm, he proposes to the wrong girl; but after much distress and embarrassment, and with the help of the narrator, the mistake is rectified. The story is discussed at length by Carrington (pp. 131–4), who comments:

> A vulgar, improbable tale, revealed, as Oscar Wilde put it, by lurid flashes, but strangely moving. The desultory talk, the suburban morality, the salacious prying into this very private affair, form the monochrome background against which the lightning reveals the naked will of the lovers in reckless realism. When daylight comes the other jaded picnickers look as unreal as actors bowing before the curtain. . . .
>
> This was the method that Kipling was to elaborate in his maturer works: he would construct a frame about his picture and contrast the picture with the frame.

FATIMA.   See 'The Story of the Gadsbys'.

FINANCES OF THE GODS, THE.   No magazine publication; *Life's Handicap* (1891). A slight anecdote in which a holy man tells a child the story of how a money-lender, in an attempt to cheat an old mendicant whom the gods intended to make rich, was caught in his own trap.

FINEST STORY IN THE WORLD, THE.   *Contemporary Review*, July

1891; *Many Inventions* (1893). The narrator, an author, encounters Charlie Mears, a twenty-year-old City bank clerk who aspires to be a writer but is totally without talent. It turns out that, without realizing it, Charlie can in certain moods conjure up detailed memories of previous incarnations – as an oarsman in a Greek galley, and as a Viking sailor. The narrator encourages his reminiscences in the hope that a masterpiece can be fashioned from them; but Charlie falls in love with a shop-girl and loses interest in the idea of turning his memories of the remote past into a story; 'Charlie had tasted the love of woman that kills remembrance, and the finest story in the world would never be written.' (J. I. M. Stewart suggests, not unreasonably, that Kipling's 'lurking antagonism to women' can be detected in the ending.) The story exploits the contrast between the commonplace, weedy clerk and the romantic and heroic incarnations he can fitfully recall. There is, though, some implausibility in his command of the technical terms relating to seafaring. Kipling conveys effectively the paradox of a man possessing uniquely precious raw *material* for a literary work who is totally without talent to manipulate the literary *medium*. The story is based partly on Kipling's cousin Ambrose Poynter, an architect with unfulfilled (and probably unfulfillable) aspirations to become a poet, of whom he saw a good deal in his early years in London. Tompkins has also pointed to a literary source: Edwin Arnold's *Wonderful Adventures of Phra the Phoenician*, serialized in the *Illustrated London News* from July to December 1890, a romance of reincarnation now forgotten but very popular in its day. Not everyone will agree with Amis's judgement that Kipling's story fails because 'reincarnation is such an intractably dull idea'. In contrast, J. I. M. Stewart and others have praised the power of Kipling's historical imagination. Carrington notes that Kipling 'throughout life was haunted by the notion that buried and even inherited memories reveal themselves in dreams', and that his interest in the subject predates the advent of Freudianism in England.

FRIENDLY BROOK. *Metropolitan Magazine*, March 1914; *Windsor Magazine*, December 1914; *A Diversity of Creatures* (1917). In the conversation of two countrymen, the words of a third are quoted whose field is threatened by flooding from a swollen brook: ' "I ain't going to shift my stack a yard' " he says. "The Brook's been good friends to me . . ." '. Their ensuing reminiscences tell of a London character who has invaded the rural world with threats and blackmail, and whose drowning in the brook has restored peace. Tompkins defines the theme as 'the survival in the mind of a countryman of a vague animistic conception of the brook that has flooded and drowned his enemy for him'. The story is followed by a poem, 'The Land', which expresses Kipling's feelings about the antiquity of the English landscape and introduces the yeoman 'Hobden' who, despite the comings and goings of Roman, Saxon, Norman, and Kipling himself, is the real owner of the land.

FRIEND OF THE FAMILY, A. *MacLean's Magazine*, 15 June 1924; *Hearst's International*, July 1924; *The Storyteller*, August 1924; *Debits and Credits* (1926). A quiet, self-effacing Australian ex-soldier comes to the rescue of a family who have been victimized by unscrupulous business competitors. He throws bombs at the rival establishment in such a way as to create the illusion that an air-raid has taken place. It belongs to Kipling's group of Masonic stories (there is a reference to Lodge No. 5837).

FRIEND'S FRIEND, A. *Civil & Military Gazette*, 2 May 1887; *Plain Tales from the Hills* (1888). The narrator expresses his intense indignation at the behaviour of Tranter, who has sent him a letter introducing a man called Jevon. The latter has become drunk at a ball, and his host's reputation has suffered. As a punishment Jevon has been subjected to physical humiliation by members of the club: 'We corked the whole of his face. We filled his hair with meringue-cream. . . . We put a ham-frill round his neck, and tied it in a bow in front' – thus, and much more, we are reminded, in 'punishment, not play'. As often, there seems to be something excessive, almost hysterical and sadistic, about the punishment: one wonders why, at an early stage of the evening, the drunken man was not simply led off home. Disturbingly, we learn at the end that the man, after being trussed up and dropped on a bullock-cart, is never heard of again ('Perhaps he died and was thrown into the river'). But all this has not satisfied the narrator's desire for revenge on Tranter, whom he wants, in the closing words of the story, 'dead or alive. But dead for preference.'

GARDENER, THE. *McCall's Magazine*, April 1926; *Strand Magazine*, May 1926; *Debits and Credits* (1926). The story was written during a tour of France in 1925. On 14 March Kipling

visited Rouen cemetery, with its 11,000 graves of men killed in
the war, 'and collogued with the Head Gardener' (letter to
Rider Haggard). That same evening he began the story, which
was finished at Lourdes on 22 March. Lord Birkenhead's
biography contains the interesting information that, when
Kipling visited the Flanders battlefields in the autumn of 1920,
he photographed a son's grave for an elderly lady from
Durham, and that when they reached home again Mrs Kipling
wrote in her diary: 'The gardener gives notice – no reason
assigned'. One of the best of Kipling's stories, it concerns an
English spinster, Helen Turrell, who is respected in her village
for doing 'her duty by all the world'. She adopts and brings up a
child who is said to be her nephew; he grows up and is killed in
the war, Kipling rendering very tellingly the arrival of the
telegram that reports him missing, and the ensuing stages of
Helen's grief. After the war she travels to the military cemetery
in France to visit his grave. At first she has difficulty in finding it
among so many, but a gardener comes to her aid with a promise
to 'show you where your son lies'. The reader (though not
Helen) realizes that the gardener is Christ and the episode an
echo of Mary Magdalene's encounter in John 20:15. (The
allusion seems quite clear, though over-ingenious interpreters
have suggested that the gardener was the dead young man, or
his father, or an actual gardener – if so, why does he speak
English? – or even the rector's gardener from Helen's village
who is the young man's father!) The story thus ends with a
double surprise: the truth about Helen's relationship to the
boy, and the revelation of the gardener's identity. Helen
Turrell's situation in some respects resembles that of Mary
Postgate in the story of that name, but the tone and outcome of
the two stories are in strong contrast. In a sensitive and brilliant
analysis Tompkins draws attention to the compression of this
story (it covers twenty years in fifteen pages) and to its
wonderfully delicate, unemphasized irony (she argues that the
implication of the opening paragraph is that everyone in the
village knows the truth about Helen's relationship to the boy,
but that there is a 'general kind conspiracy' to respect the
fiction she has created). There is also a long discussion of the
story by Gilbert (pp. 78–94), who takes a different line from
Tompkins in his analysis of the opening: for him, Kipling's
theme is 'the baleful influence of respectability' and Helen is 'a

woman who has been defeated by a repressive, parochial society and whose only chance of salvation lies in the hope of an act of grace which she is destined not to understand when it comes' – an interpretation perhaps not quite consistent with Kipling's general attitude to English rural society. Edmund Wilson praises this story; Angus Wilson finds it 'brilliantly carried out' but flawed by the ending.

GARDEN OF EDEN, THE. See 'The Story of the Gadsbys'.

GARM – A HOSTAGE. *Saturday Evening Post*, 23 December 1899; *Actions and Reactions* (1909). A dog-story on the typical Kipling theme of deep attachment; it may be found sentimental or over-written by those who do not share Kipling's enthusiasm for dogs. Garm is a bull-terrier of remarkable intelligence; he and his master, an English soldier in India, have a profound love for each other. But the soldier, Stanley, insists on giving him to the narrator, who has done him a good turn, as a 'penance' and a 'hostage . . . for his good behaviour'. Stanley and Garm both sink into a decline, but recover instantly when they are reunited.

GATE OF THE HUNDRED SORROWS, THE. *Civil & Military Gazette*, 26 September 1884; *Plain Tales from the Hills* (1888). The narrator reports a monologue delivered to him by a half-caste opium-addict, who describes the opium den and his own mode of life. Andrew Lang said that the sketch 'defeats De Quincey on his own ground'. Written at the age of eighteen, it was Kipling's first published short story. During the summer of 1884 he had been alone in the family house at Lahore and had taken opiates to relieve gastric pains and insomnia. This is the first of many stories dealing with the moral collapse of Europeans or Eurasians in Asia. Cornell notes that Kipling refrains from political comment, even though there was a long-standing controversy among Anglo-Indians over the official opium monopoly.

GEMINI. *The Week's News*, 14 January 1888; *In Black and White* (1888). Durga Dass and Ram Dass are identical twins (the former, the narrator of the tale, insists that his brother is 'the younger by three full breaths'). Durga Dass complains that his brother has treated him badly: first he was beaten up in mistake for Ram Dass by the servants of a wealthy landowner; then Ram Dass, on the pretence of helping him to obtain justice from the courts, has posed as his brother, obtained false witnesses, and pocketed the substantial damages; finally, he has stolen his brother's savings and decamped. Durga Dass asks the English sahib to see that justice is done. A reviewer in the *Quarterly Review* drew attention to the similarity of the central situation to Shakespeare's *Comedy of Errors*.

GEORGIE PORGIE. *The Week's News*, 3 November 1888; *Life's Handicap* (1891). An Englishman in Burma buys a native 'wife' as a cure for loneliness, and they live together very happily until it occurs to him that marriage to an English girl would be even more agreeable. Without telling the girl of his intentions, he goes to England on leave and marries an English bride, bringing her back to India. Tired of waiting for his return, the Burmese girl sets out to find him, and after much hardship does so; but a glimpse of the English couple through the window of a lighted room informs her of the truth, and she creeps away broken-hearted.

GERM-DESTROYER, A. *Civil & Military Gazette*, 17 May 1887; *Plain Tales from the Hills* (1888). Cornell describes this story as 'a comedy of official manners'. The secretary to a certain Viceroy is an ambitious man anxious to wield power, but his downfall comes when he sends an invitation to a private meeting with the Viceroy to the wrong man. Two men with similar names are staying at the same hotel: one is a rich and self-important man from Madras, the other a crank who claims to have found a method for destroying cholera germs, and both are anxious to see the Viceroy. In error the invitation goes to the crank, who demonstrates his discovery (it involves burning a powder that produces clouds of smoke). The Viceroy enjoys the situation and gratefully seizes on the secretary's error in order to get rid of him. According to John Lockwood Kipling, the secretary is modelled on Lord William Beresford, who was military secretary at Simla. The incident is said to be based on a real-life happening no doubt widely reported at the time and subsequently narrated by Sir John Rivett Carnac in *Many Memories* (1910): a certain Major Lucie-Smith discovered a vein of coal and tried to demonstrate its qualities at Government House in Negpore; the result was 'such a Fifth of November blaze that Government House, the public offices, and the new church nearly all perished in the conflagration'. Rivett Carnac was a friend of the Kipling family.

GOD FROM THE MACHINE, THE. *The Week's News*, 7 January 1888;

Soldiers Three (1888). The version in the original edition of *Soldiers Three*, published as No. 1 of 'The Indian Railway Library', included a dedication (omitted from later editions) to 'that very strong man, T. ATKINS, . . . in all admiration and good fellowship'. Mulvaney tells how, by a stratagem, he frustrated the attempt of a blackguardly captain to elope with the colonel's daughter.

HABITATION ENFORCED, AN. *Century Magazine*, August 1905; *Actions and Reactions* (1909). A young American multimillionaire suffers a breakdown through overwork, and he and his wife embark on an extensive recuperative tour through Europe. At last they find themselves in an English village, where they fall under the spell of a large and beautiful but neglected eighteenth-century house. They buy the house and the surrounding estate, and throw themselves into the task of restoring it. In the process they take their place in the local squirearchy, a son is born to them, and they discover that the wife's ancestors have lived in that spot before emigrating to America. This attractive story, dealing with the intangible but agreeably free from mystification, is perhaps flawed by the injudicious use of coincidence. The Kiplings' own experience of leaving America to settle in England obviously contributed much to this story, with which 'My Son's Wife' may be compared. Angus Wilson, for whom the story 'doesn't convince', suggests that its tone is not uniformly idealized: 'there are more satirical overtones in the Sunday at church . . . than is usually allowed'. Kipling's endorsement of the rural values, scenic, architectural, and even climatic, as well as social, is unmistakable, however. This is the first story in the volume *Actions and Reactions* and introduces the theme of healing which, as Tompkins has shown, is prominent in Kipling's later work. In reviewing the volume in *New Age*, Arnold Bennett reasonably objected that the story relies on 'a terrific coincidence'.

HEAD OF THE DISTRICT, THE. *Macmillan's Magazine*, January 1890; *Life's Handicap* (1891). When the Englishman in charge of a district dies, he is replaced, at the Viceroy's suggestion, by a native administrator, an Oxford-educated Bengali. The idealistic notion misfires, however, and the natives stage an uprising; it is put down by force, with some loss of life, and the Bengali hastily vacates his position when he realizes its perils. The Blind Mullah who has instigated the uprising is murdered by his own people. The *Athenaeum* reviewer declared that the story summed up 'the whole question of Indian administration'.

HILL OF ILLUSION, THE. ˙ *Civil & Military Gazette*, 28 September 1887; *The Week's News*, 21 April 1888; *Under the Deodars* (1888). This story, written in dialogue form, tells of a married woman and her lover who are planning to elope. As they talk, she realizes that he will grow tired of her in the end and that for them there can be no abiding relationship with mutual trust. She withdraws from the scheme. Contemporary reviewers singled the piece out for high praise: *Blackwood's*, for instance, called it 'a masterpiece'.

HIS CHANCE IN LIFE. *Civil & Military Gazette*, 2 April 1887; *Plain Tales from the Hills* (1888). A young telegraph signaller, one-eighth of whose blood is European, wishes to marry a girl whose mother insists that he first earn at least fifty rupees a month. Stationed in a small town, he succeeds in putting down a riot (feeling himself, in a short-lived but crucial fit of courage, to be a representative of white authority), and is promoted and enabled to marry.

HIS MAJESTY THE KING. *The Week's News*, 5 May 1888; *Wee Willie Winkie* (1888). The hero is a small boy whose parents are estranged though continuing to live together, and who have no time for him. He falls ill and comes close to death; over his sick-bed his parents are reconciled and family harmony is restored. For further comments, see under 'Wee Willie Winkie'.

HIS PRIVATE HONOUR. *Macmillan's Magazine*, October 1891; *Many Inventions* (1893). Ortheris, struck on parade by a young officer, finally obtains satisfaction by fighting him and ends by declaring him 'a gentleman all over'. George Saintsbury found this story the 'noblest and most complete' item in the volume.

HIS WEDDED WIFE. *Civil & Military Gazette*, 25 February 1887; *Plain Tales from the Hills* (1888). A subaltern fresh from England obtains his revenge on the Senior Subaltern who bullies him by disguising himself as a woman and passing himself off as the discarded wife of the man, who is engaged to be married. He then discloses his real identity. 'It leaned as near to a nasty tragedy as anything this side of a joke can', as the narrator comments. The final sentence promises another story, of 'a case something like this, but with all the jest left out and nothing in it but real trouble'; see 'In the Pride of his Youth'.

1a

1b

1a   Kipling as a young child
with native servants

1b   Kipling as a small boy

2a   Rudyard Kipling, aged 17, *c.* 1882

2b   Kipling as a young man

3   The Burne-Jones portrait of Kipling, 1899

4a 'Mr Rudyard Kipling takes a bloomin' day aht on the blasted 'eath, along with Britannia, 'is gurl' (Max Beerbohm,

4b 'The Old Self and the Young Self', by Max Beerbohm, 1924. Young Self: 'I *say*! Have you heard the latest about Mrs Hauksbee?'

5a   Kipling and his wife at the Cemetery at Loos

5b   Kipling with George V

6a *(left)* Lorne Lodge

6b *(below)* The United Services College, Westward Ho!

7a Naulakha, Kipling's home in Vermont

7b Bateman's, Burwash

RECESSIONAL.

God of our fathers, known of old—
Lord of our far-flung battle-line—
Beneath Whose awful Hand we hold
Dominion over palm and pine—
Lord God of Hosts, be with us yet,
Lest we forget—lest we forget !

The tumult and the shouting dies—
The captains and the kings depart—
Still stands Thine ancient Sacrifice,
An humble and a contrite heart.
Lord God of Hosts, be with us yet,
Lest we forget—lest we forget !

Far-called our navies melt away—
On dune and headland sinks the fire—
Lo, all our pomp of yesterday
Is one with Nineveh and Tyre !
Judge of the Nations, spare us yet,
Lest we forget—lest we forget !

If, drunk with sight of power, we loose
Wild tongues that have not Thee in awe—
Such boasting as the Gentiles use
Or lesser breeds without the Law—
Lord God of Hosts, be with us yet,
Lest we forget—lest we forget !

For heathen heart that puts her trust
In reeking tube and iron shard—
All valiant dust that builds on dust,
And guarding calls not Thee to guard—
For frantic boast and foolish word,
Thy Mercy on Thy People, Lord !
                              Amen.
                    RUDYARD KIPLING.

8b The first publication of 'Recessional', *The Times*, 17 July 1897

8a Text of manuscript for 'The Rhyme of the Three Sealers'

HONOURS OF WAR, THE. *Family Magazine*, May 1911; *Windsor Magazine*, August 1911; *A Diversity of Creatures* (1917). A young officer, victim of a practical joke that leaves him physically humiliated and passionately determined on revenge, repays the perpetrators in kind, and his equanimity is thereby restored. Stalky appears in this story as a Colonel.

HORSE MARINES, THE. *Pearson's Magazine*, October 1910; *A Diversity of Creatures* (1917). The last of the seven stories featuring Emanuel Pyecroft, the Cockney petty officer: for Angus Wilson's strictures on this mouthpiece, see p. 127 below. A retired colonel is gratified to discover that young men have not changed since the days of his own active service.

HOUSE SURGEON, THE. *Harper's Magazine*, September and October 1909; *Actions and Reactions* (1909). *Actions and Reactions* ends, as it begins, with a story about a house and with the theme of healing (the opening story is 'An Habitation Enforced'). This story is said to have been based on the Kiplings' experience of living at Rock House, Maidencombe, near Torquay, in 1896–7. A psychic detective story, it contains a significant reference to Sherlock Holmes and Dr Watson, and the house is called Holmescroft. The narrator meets a retired Jewish furrier who has a Greek wife and a twenty-year-old daughter. The furrier tells him of the house in the country, built in 1863 and therefore hardly old enough to be haunted, which he has bought and which afflicts its inhabitants with occasional spells of intense depression. The narrator visits him and is quickly overcome by depression (the latter is vividly evoked – as is, in quite a different vein, the *nouveau riche* neighbourhood). He succeeds in tracing the elderly spinsters who were the previous occupants and discovers that their sister was believed by them to have committed suicide by throwing herself out of an upstairs window, and hence to have consigned herself to eternal damnation. (The new owners had purchased the house on the understanding that no deaths had taken place in it; and this is strictly true, since the dead woman had fallen into the garden and died there.) When the spinsters are persuaded that the death was in fact accidental, the mysterious presence is appeased and the haunting ceases.

INCARNATION OF KRISHNA MULVANEY, THE. *Macmillan's Magazine*, December 1889; *The Courting of Dinah Shadd* (1890); *Mine Own People* (1891); *Life's Handicap* (1891). A story of the

Irishman Mulvaney, the Yorkshireman Learoyd, and the Cockney Ortheris, 'three men who loved each other so greatly that neither man nor woman could come between them' (see also under 'The Three Musketeers'). The narrator is a civilian 'admitted to their friendship'. Mulvaney finds a white man, Dearsley, engaged in exploiting coolies; after a fair fight, he and his friends appropriate a gorgeous palanquin in the man's possession. When Mulvaney during a brief leave pays a return visit to Dearsley, the latter renders him drunk and has him put on a train in order that he may be punished as a deserter. Mulvaney finds himself in Benares, and is conveyed in the palanquin to a temple, where he impersonates and is taken for the god Krishna. A priest, aware of the deception but anxious to safeguard the temple's reputation as the scene of a 'miracle', gives him money, and he returns safely to barracks. Some editions add an extra paragraph at the end as follows: 'There is no further space to record the digging up of the spoils, or the triumphal visit of the three to Dearsley, who feared for his life, but was most royally treated instead, and under that influence told how the palanquin had come into his possession. But that is another story.' (Andrew Lang in 1891 not unjustifiably mentioned the expression 'But that is another story' as among Kipling's mannerisms in a list of his faults.) *Blackwood's* described the story as 'rollicking, incomparable, irresistible farce'. Cornell writes:

> At his best, Mulvaney becomes larger than life. Tougher, stronger, more imaginative than any man could be, he takes on heroic size and enters a realm that is outside normal experience; part of the greatness of 'The Incarnation of Krishna Mulvaney' lies in the fact that he becomes, in some mysterious way, equivalent to Krishna, the legendary hero whom he impersonates.

IN ERROR. *Civil & Military Gazette*, 24 January 1887; *Plain Tales from the Hills* (1888). A civil engineer who has been driven to alcoholism by solitude during a period of service in a remote district is cured by his devotion to Mrs Reiver, an evil woman (see 'The Rescue of Pluffles') whom he believes to be an angel. 'Moriarty thought her something she never was, and in that belief saved himself. Which was just as good as though she had been everything that he had imagined.' This is one of a group of stories on self-delusion – here of a beneficent kind. Compare 'Venus Annodomini', 'Wressley of the Foreign Office' and 'In the Pride of his Youth' for other treatments of the same theme, of different degrees of seriousness.

IN FLOOD TIME. *The Week's News*, 11 August 1888; *In Black and White* (1888). A sahib who is unable to ford a river in flood is entertained by an old man who for thirty years has assisted those using the ford. He tells how, in his youth, he loved a girl who lived on the other side of the river; but they concealed their love, for she was a Hindu and he a Mohammedan. He would swim across the river and they would meet secretly 'among the crops'. On one occasion, however, he was 'whirled down-stream' and almost drowned by a flood, only saving himself by using the corpse of a drowned man as a lifebuoy. The drowned man turned out to be a Sikh to whom the girl's relations intended to marry her. Kipling's description of the river in flood is very vivid. He himself had been forced to halt at a flooded river while travelling from Simla to Allahabad, and had written about the incident in an article published in the *Pioneer* on 28 July 1888.

IN THE HOUSE OF SUDDHOO. *Civil & Military Gazette*, 30 April 1886; *Plain Tales from the Hills* (1888). The magazine version bears the title 'Section 420, I.P.C.'. An old man is defrauded by a rogue who claims to practise magic, his ritual involving some ingenious and grisly tricks, including ventriloquism. The white narrator detects the fraud but can see no satisfactory way to deal with the situation. 'The story represents both a liberation from grotesque monologue and a new ability to come to grips with the real queerness of Indian life' (Cornell). Cornell suggests that Kipling has

> penetrated to the heart of the Anglo-Indians' historical dilemma with amazing swiftness and economy. On one level, Western technology . . . has been perverted to the uses of fraud and superstition. On another, Western judicial institu-tions . . . have been made impotent by a conspiracy of custom, ignorance, and malice.

A leading article in *The Times* on 25 March 1890 coupled this story with 'Beyond the Pale' as 'almost the best of Mr Kipling's writings, perhaps because they appear to lift the veil from a state of society so immeasurably different from our own'.

IN THE INTERESTS OF THE BRETHREN. *Story-Teller Magazine* and *Metropolitan Magazine*, December 1918; *Debits and Credits* (1926). The narrator by chance meets a London tobacconist, Mr Burges, who introduces him to a Masonic Lodge ('Faith and Works 5837') frequented by ex-soldiers from all parts of the world, many of them horribly maimed. (Burges's only son has been killed in the war.) Freemasonry is put forward 'certainly not as a substitute for a creed, but as an average plan of life'. For these men, disabled from resuming their normal place in society, it restores some of the camaraderie of service life. The Lodge, which also serves as club and lodging-house, is somewhat irregularly run. The last sentence, in which the narrator speculates whether he can 'inform against' the Lodge for infringement of Masonic law, is puzzling. Compare 'A Madonna of the Trenches' in the same volume. Some of the characters reappear in a later story, 'Fairy-Kist'.

IN THE MATTER OF A PRIVATE. *The Week's News*, 14 April 1888; *Soldiers Three* (1888). A sequel to 'The Daughter of the Regiment'. Private Simmons is persistently bullied by Losson, 'a big gross man', who even goes so far as to buy a parrot and teach it to scream obscenities at him. Driven to desperation in the heat ('running up sometimes to 103° at midnight'), Simmons shoots his persecutor dead; when pursued, in a frenzy he also wounds an officer. He is hanged 'in hollow square of the regiment'. The colonel attributes the crime to drink, and the chaplain blames the devil; newspaper articles deplore 'The Prevalence of Crime in the Army'; only the narrator knows the truth – that the cause is hysteria, which can affect an army as much as a girls' school. The *Athenaeum* praised this story as a 'wonderful study of heat-hysteria'.

IN THE PRESENCE. *Everybody's*, March 1912; *Pearson's Magazine*, March 1912; *A Diversity of Creatures* (1917). After the death of Edward VII in 1911, four Gurkhas are among those on guard at the lying-in-state. Their experience is recounted to a regiment in India.

IN THE PRIDE OF HIS YOUTH. *Civil & Military Gazette*, 5 May 1887; *Plain Tales from the Hills* (1888). This is the story promised at the end of 'His Wedded Wife'. Dicky Hatt marries at twenty-one, then goes out to India, keeping his marriage a secret. He lives frugally, sends money to his wife in London, and saves for the passage that will bring her out to join him after a year. But he is chronically short of money; his wife complains, their baby dies, and at last she writes to tell him she is going off with another man. The story ends with an ironic twist: Dicky is offered promotion at a salary that would have enabled him to maintain a wife and child. He refuses it, and disappears. Cornell points out that Dicky's situation resembles Kipling's in certain respects: the story dramatizes what might have happened to Kipling if he had married Florence Garrard before leaving England. See also 'In Error'.

IN THE RUKH.   No magazine publication; *Many Inventions* (1893); later transferred to *The Jungle Book*. A pendant to the stories in the *Jungle Books*, though published earlier than them: Mowgli appears as a grown man and the story narrates his love, elopement, marriage, and work for the Forestry Service. Tompkins suggests that the Mowgli of this tale 'does not quite tally with the Mowgli of the *Jungle Books*'. Angus Wilson finds it 'moving, if a little disjointed'.

IN THE SAME BOAT.   *Harper's Magazine*, December 1911; *A Diversity of Creatures* (1917). A story of psychological healing. A man and woman are both haunted by terrifying recurring dreams which are eventually explained in terms of their mothers' experiences during pregnancy.

JANEITES, THE.   *The Storyteller Magazine*, May 1924; *Hearst's International Magazine*, May 1924; *Debits and Credits* (1926). Written in April 1923 when Kipling was visiting the French Riviera. In the Masonic Lodge 'Faith and Works No. 5837 E.C.' one day 'in the autumn of '20', Humberstall, a wartime mess-waiter, recalls 'this secret society business' concerning 'this Secret Society woman I was tellin' you of – this Jane' (i.e., the use of allusions to Jane Austen's novels by her devotees as passwords). The climax of his reminiscences occurs when he recalls having been found a place in a crowded hospital-train by a nursing-sister to whom he has casually mentioned Miss Bates, a character in *Emma*: 'You take it from me, Brethren, there's no one to touch Jane when you're in a tight place. Gawd bless 'er, whoever she was.' The theme of the story is the brotherhood enjoyed by initiates in a secret society or those bound by shared experiences, whether Freemasons, admirers of Jane Austen, or survivors of the war.

JEWS IN SHUSHAN.   *Civil & Military Gazette*, 4 October 1887; *Life's*

Handicap (1891). This touching story concerns a Jewish bill-collector who lives with his family in Shushan, a city in North India. The eight of them are the only Jews in the city, and his great desire is for their number to increase to ten in order that they may have their own synagogue in which he may serve as priest. But an epidemic carries off his wife and children, and the remnant quit Shushan for Calcutta, thus abandoning for ever the dream of their own synagogue.

JUDGMENT OF DUNGARA, THE. *The Week's News*, 28 July 1888; *In Black and White* (1888). The magazine version was entitled 'The Peculiar Embarrassment of Justus Krenk'. The Reverend Justus Krenk, 'Pastor of the Tübingen Mission', formerly of Heidelberg, lives at a lonely mission outpost with his wife Lotta. He makes a number of converts, 'a shining band nearly forty strong'. But the crafty priest of Dungara, the local deity, shows the converts how to make cloth for garments to cover their nakedness; and this material turns out to be manufactured from a nettle that stings savagely. In a frenzy of pain, the converts tear off their clothes and leap into the river for relief; their ordeal is interpreted as a visitation of Dungara's anger, and they abandon their short-lived Christianity. The Krenks depart, and 'the chapel and school have long since fallen back into jungle'. Kipling's sympathies are evidently with the young and realistic assistant collector who knows the country and finds 'one creed as good as another'. Edmund Gosse praised the story's 'rattling humour worthy of Lever'.

JUDSON AND THE EMPIRE. No magazine publication; *Many Inventions* (1893). Judson, a British naval lieutenant, deals with an awkward situation in a South African colony. This is Kipling's first naval story and was suggested by his first visit to South Africa in 1891. There is some mild satire at the expense of Portuguese colonists.

KIDNAPPED. *Civil & Military Gazette*, 21 March 1887; *Plain Tales from the Hills* (1888). A young official wishes to make an unsuitable marriage with a girl whose family is of mixed blood. Prompted by Mrs Hauksbee, his friends forcibly carry him off on a hunting trip until the date of the wedding has passed. He comes to his senses, and the matter is smoothed over. The story is told to illustrate the wisdom of arranged marriages. For serious treatments of a similar theme, see 'Beyond the Pale' and 'Without Benefit of Clergy'.

LANG MEN O' LARUT, THE. *Civil & Military Gazette*, 29 May 1889; *Life's Handicap* (1891). An Aberdonian chief engineer recounts an anecdote concerning a bet. Three exceptionally tall Scotsmen lived at Larut, near Penang. An American visitor, himself very tall, said that he was prepared to lay a bet that he was 'the longest man in the island'; however, when he saw the resident giants, he admitted himself beaten and confessed the trick he had kept up his sleeve (his name was Esdras B. Longer). He paid for a drinking bout of epic proportions, and a week-long hangover ensued. A contemporary critic in the *Fortnightly Review* castigated the story as 'unspeakably mediocre and wretched stuff', and another reviewer dismissed it as 'one of the shortest and poorest of Kipling's tales'. For yet another adverse criticism, see 'The Wandering Jew'.

LIMITATIONS OF PAMBÉ SERANG, THE. *St James's Gazette*, 7 December 1889; *Life's Handicap* (1891). A Malay sailor nurses a grievance against a 'big fat Zanzibar stoker' and, obsessed by thoughts of revenge, follows him round the world. In London the Malay falls ill with pneumonia; when the negro happens to pass by he is summoned to the other man's sickbed by a Christian visitor unaware of the relationship between them. When the negro bends over the bed – ' "How beautiful!" said the kind gentleman. "How these Orientals love like children!" ' – he is stabbed to death by the Malay, who is nursed back to health and then hanged 'in due and proper form'. The story's satire exemplifies Kipling's dislike of missionaries (cf. 'The Judgment of Dungara'). According to Carrington, the idea for the story was given to Kipling by 'a lascar from the [London] docks'.

LISPETH *Civil & Military Gazette*, 29 November 1886; *Plain Tales from the Hills* (1888). This stands as the first story in Kipling's first collection. Lispeth is a hill-girl baptized in infancy; when she is orphaned she becomes servant-companion to a chaplain's wife and grows into a beautiful young woman. She finds and carries home a young English traveller hurt in an accident; during his convalescence he flirts with her, and she falls deeply in love with him, believing her feelings to be reciprocated. When he leaves she is convinced that he will return to marry her, and the chaplain's wife encourages this delusion in order to avoid a scene. On learning the truth at last, she casts aside her 'civilized' dress and behaviour and returns to her 'own people'. The final picture of her is a hideous old woman, squalid and drunken but still able to tell of her first love affair in perfect English. A contemporary critic commented rather oddly that the story 'illustrates the truth that a mere dab of Christianity is insufficient to "wipe out uncivilized Eastern instincts" '; actually, Kipling's point is the shallowness of the moral code of the English (the man's heartlessness, the chaplain's wife's cowardly lie), and his irony stresses the superior honesty of the girl's conduct ('Being a savage by birth, she took no trouble to hide her feelings'). According to Carrington, the traditional scene of the story is a house in Simla called Alice's Bower. Lispeth reappears as a minor character in *Kim*.

LITTLE FOXES. *Collier's Weekly*, 27 March 1909; *Actions and Reactions* (1909). The governor of a British colony in Africa imports a pack of hounds and establishes a hunt to deal with the local foxes; natives who do not stop the earths on their land are beaten, and the beatings come to be regarded by them as a kind of legal recognition of their ownership. But an officious politician comes out from England, and, interpreting the governor's behaviour as despotic, determines to put a stop to it. He falls victim to a practical joke and is greeted with ridicule for his pains. J. I. M. Stewart suggests that the story parades 'some of Kipling's most shocking prejudices'; certainly the satire is directed at liberals with high ideals but total ignorance of local conditions.

LITTLE TOBRAH. *Civil & Military Gazette*, 17 July 1888; *Life's Handicap* (1891). In a smallpox epidemic the boy Tobrah has been orphaned and his sister left blind. The children have subsequently been exploited by a rapacious employer and abandoned by their elder brother. For lack of witnesses Tobrah is acquitted on a charge of killing his blind sister by pushing her down a well; but after being given a home by an Englishman he admits that he did it, for 'it is better to die than to starve'.

LOST LEGION, THE. *Strand Magazine*, May 1892; *Many Inventions* (1893). Partly a ghost story, partly an adventure-tale about the capture of an Afghan outlaw and his confederates. According to Carrington, it is based on 'a tradition of 1857 arising out of John Nicholson's punishment of the mutinous 55th Native Infantry'.

LOVE-O'-WOMEN. No magazine publication; *Many Inventions* (1893). Mulvaney tells the story of Tighe, nicknamed 'Love-o'-Women', an unscrupulous seducer who serves in the ranks but is evidently a 'gentleman' and who heartlessly abandons the women he has ruined. At last he is overcome by the tortures of remorse, but cannot find an easy death: dying slowly of a progressive disease, he encounters again a woman with whom he might have had an enduring relationship but who, on being deserted by him, has turned to prostitution. He dies in her arms, and she commits suicide. The frame-story concerns a soldier who, goaded to desperation, has murdered a man who had an affair with his wife, the quick death of this adulterer contrasting sharply with the prolonged agony of 'Love-o'-Women'. This story of immorality and callousness, guilt, remorse and punishment, was praised by some contemporary critics, though Saintsbury found it uneven and Andrew Lang 'rather dully disagreeable'. Amis rightly praises the effectiveness of the opening but criticizes Kipling for 'indulging in his favourite vice of over-mystification': the protagonist is 'a disappointed man, but we never quite find out what disappointed him'. This objection can be countered by suggesting that Kipling is anticipating Conrad's use of the imperfectly informed narrator: Mulvaney's final comment that 'I've tould ut as I came acrost ut – here an' there in little pieces' suggests that the technique of this story anticipates in a minor way that of Conrad's *Lord Jim* a few years later.

MADNESS OF PRIVATE ORTHERIS, THE. No magazine publication; *Plain Tales from the Hills* (1888). Private Stanley Ortheris is overwhelmed by homesickness for London ('orange-peel and hasphalte an' gas comin' in over Vaux'll Bridge'), and laments his lot ('An' I lef' all that for to serve the Widder beyond the seas'). He sinks into a kind of trance of lethargy (as, according to Mulvaney, he has done before), and, in order to shake him out of his depressed state, the narrator offers to exchange clothes with him and to give him money in order to enable him to desert. At first it looks as though he will seize the opportunity, but at last he shakes off his fit and returns to normal. 'Ortheris's madness is too arbitrary, his recovery too wholehearted, to gain our complete credence' (Cornell).

MADONNA OF THE TRENCHES, A. *MacLean's Magazine*, 15 August 1924; *Hearst's International Magazine*, September 1924; *Nash's* and *Pall Mall Magazine*, September 1924; *Debits and Credits* (1926). Another story about the somewhat irregularly-run Masonic

Lodge 'Faith and Works E.C. 5837' (see also, in the same collection, 'In the Interests of the Brethren' and 'The Janeites'). One of the 'unstable ex-soldiers' who come to the Lodge of Instruction after the war is Strangwick, who breaks down hysterically with what turns out to be the significant cry: 'Oh, My Aunt. I can't stand this any longer' (contemporary readers would not have immediately grasped the full import of the words, since 'my aunt' and 'my giddy aunt' were common jocular expressions of the period). He appears to be haunted by memories of frozen corpses creaking in the trenches; but a doctor, through a combination of drugs and cross-examination, gets at the truth. Strangwick's aunt has died of cancer and previously has sent to the sergeant with whom she was carrying on an affair the promise that her ghost would visit him (she has written, with nice ambiguity, 'Tell Uncle John . . . I'm dying to see 'im . . .'). Strangwick sees her ghost, and the sergeant kills himself in the trenches in order to be reunited with his lover. Strangwick's glimpse of another world leaves him deeply disturbed ('there wasn't a single gor-dam thing left abidin' for me to take hold of, here or hereafter. If the dead *do* rise – and I saw 'em – why – why *anything* can 'appen'). There is the implication that acknowledging the true source of his hysteria, in the manner of a Freudian analysis, will effect a cure of his neurosis. This is a good example of the type of story in which Kipling uses, in Tompkins' phrases, 'an imperfect and baffled narrator' to present 'a situation of high intensity'. The story was begun in 1923; in the latter part of the previous year Kipling had been ill with abdominal pains of undiagnosed origin, and he had undergone surgery in November; in the early part of 1923 he was 'very low and depressed' (it seems clear that he believed he had cancer).

MALTESE CAT, THE. *Pall Mall Gazette*, 26 and 27 June 1895; *The Day's Work* (1898). The story of a polo-pony and its success in winning an important match. The conversation of the horses is presented. See also 'A Walking Delegate'.

MAN WHO WAS, THE. *Macmillan's Magazine*, April 1890; *Harper's Weekly*, 15 April 1890; *Mine Own People* (1891); *Life's Handicap* (1891). Limmason, a lieutenant of the White Hussars, has long been a prisoner of the Russians. At last he escapes from Siberia and painfully makes his way back to his regiment. Unrecognizable at first in his squalor and wretchedness, he is mistaken for a thief; but eventually he appears before his brother-officers, who happen to be entertaining a Russian guest, and establishes his identity by showing his familiarity with certain former customs of the mess. Three days later he dies. The *Gentleman's Magazine* hailed the story as a 'glorious masterpiece', and the *Academy* called it 'an admirable story'. A dramatic version was produced in London in 1907.

MAN WHO WOULD BE KING, THE. No magazine publication; *The Phantom Rickshaw* (1888). Two adventurers afflicted by delusions of grandeur decide to travel to a remote region and become kings. Skilfully disguised, they pass safely through the dangers of Afghanistan and establish themselves in Kafristan, one of them being regarded as a god by the natives, who give him a gold crown. But his longing for a wife to perpetuate his dynasty proves his undoing: when the girl bites him, he bleeds, and he is declared to be only human after all. He is killed and his companion crucified; the latter survives, however, and brings back the tale to the narrator, together with the head of his friend in a bag. Cornell regards this as 'the best of the stories Kipling wrote in India'; earlier J. M. Barrie had declared it 'our author's masterpiece . . . the most audacious thing in fiction'. Tompkins praises the effectiveness of the symbolism. The frame-story seems to have been based on Kipling's own experience, and the element of freemasonry is important. There is a discussion of the story by Paul Fussell in *Journal of English Literary History*, xxv (1958) pp. 216–33.

MANNER OF MEN, THE. *London Magazine*, September 1930; *Limits and Renewals* (1932). The magazine version has the subtitle 'A Romance of the Middle Sea'. This is a companion-story to 'The Church that was at Antioch' and concerns the profound effect made by St Paul upon the captain of the ship in which he travels and which is wrecked on the island of Malta. For the source of the title, see I Corinthians 15: 32.

MARK OF THE BEAST, THE. *Pioneer*, 12 and 14 July 1890; *Life's Handicap* (1891). An intoxicated Englishman insults a temple idol, whereupon he is seized and embraced by a hideous leper who serves the god. He develops a ghastly disease diagnosed by a doctor as hydrophobia but actually closer to lycanthropy: he behaves like a wild animal, craving raw meat, and howling. He is at length saved by his friends, who capture the leper and compel him to remove the curse. Kipling described it as 'a rather nasty story'. Andrew Lang, as literary adviser to *Longman's Magazine*, is reported to have refused it with the comment that it had 'left an extremely disagreeable impression on my mind' and that he would have given a fiver never to have read 'this poisonous stuff'; another literary man, William Sharp, hazarded the guess that 'the writer is very young and that he will die mad before he has reached the age of thirty'. Other contemporary critics were divided: the *Pall Mall Gazette* said that 'as a tale of sheer terror' it 'could not easily be surpassed'; but the *Athenaeum* felt that the author had stepped over 'the bounds of decorum', and the *Spectator* found it 'loathsome'. According to Carrington, this story and 'At the End of the Passage' reflect Kipling's mood of 'nervous exhaustion' in the summer of 1890. Amis, on the other hand, offers a different view: 'We might be tempted to see in the two horror stories . . . a reflection of the author's own low spirits at the time of writing, if we did not know how often low spirits in the self produce high spirits on paper.' According to the *Reader's Guide*, a dramatic version of this story was 'frequently played at the Grand Guignol in Paris'.

MARY POSTGATE. *Century Magazine*, September 1915; *Nash's Magazine*, September 1915; *A Diversity of Creatures* (1917). The magazine versions included the heading 'How does your garden grow'. One of Kipling's most powerful stories, it has aroused widely diverse reactions and interpretations. According to Mrs Kipling's diary, it was begun early in March 1915: Carrington pertinently notes that German air-raids on English towns had begun in January. Its prominent position at the end of the volume should be noted, as should its relationship to the story that precedes it, 'Swept and Garnished'. J. I. M. Stewart calls it 'Kipling's most notorious story', and W. W. Robson states that it has been 'more attacked than anything else Kipling wrote'. Stanley Baldwin's son Oliver called it 'the wickedest story ever written', and many early readers saw it as expressing a hatred for the Germans amounting to blood-lust. Bodelsen reminds us, however, that it may be rash to equate the author's attitude too readily with that of his protagonist; he also points out the 'suggestion of a sexual element' in the woman's enjoyment of the dying man's agony, and particularly in the story's remarkable final sentence. Less convincing is Bodelsen's suggestion that the story may be intended as a parable of 'the spiritual harm that Germany has done to the English: this is what it has come to, that a kindly and respectable English spinster finds herself turned into a torturer', for 'kindly and respectable' hardly squares with Kipling's characterization of the repressed and distinctly odd Miss Postgate. Dobrée denies that it is 'a story embodying hatred of the Germans': 'Kipling is not suggesting . . . that this is how people should behave; he is merely telling us "this is what happens".' There has been much speculation about the identity of the airman: Malcolm Page (*KJ*, xxxvii, June 1970) argues that his 'nationality is deliberately unspecified, so that the wounded man may possibly be a Frenchman, an ally, which increases the horror of the tale'. John Bayley (*The Uses of Divison* [1976]) goes further and states that 'the key to the tale is that it remains unclear how much in it, particularly the climactic act of cruelty, happens in fact, and how much in Mary's mind'; Bayley questions the reality of the bomb said to have killed the child, finding in it 'a wholly effective ambiguity'. I would myself go even further and suggest that Kipling intends the reader to see that the airman has never existed outside of Mary's mind, and that he has planted enough clues in the story to support this interpretation. Tompkins, however, accepts the airman as real: 'he is at once the proof that it was indeed a bomb that killed Edna Gerritt and the enemy that Wynn did not live to kill'. For Tompkins, 'the force and horror of the last lines are extreme. . . . Kipling wrote nothing else like this'. A recent essay is Peter E. Firchow's 'Kipling's "Mary Postgate": the Barbarians and the Critics', *Etudes Anglaises*, xxix (1976) pp. 27–39.

MATTER OF FACT, A.   Issued as a pamphlet in 1892 for copyright purposes; *Many Inventions* (1893). Three journalists sailing from Cape Town to Southampton are presented with the scoop of a lifetime when an earthquake on the sea-bed brings to the surface an extraordinary sea-monster and its mate. But when they reach England, its traditional imperturbability is brought home to them and they realize that the story cannot be published – except as fiction. The story is uneven: the sudden crisis at sea and the fantasy of the sea-monster are vividly presented, but the satire on American journalism is unsubtle and unfunny, and the assertion of English superiority embarrassing. Kipling's contemporaries admired it, however, and the *Saturday Review* found it 'the most striking' of all the stories in *Many Inventions*.

MIRACLE OF SAINT JUBANUS, THE. *Story-Teller Magazine*, December 1930; *Limits and Renewals* (1932). One of the last of Kipling's stories. Like 'The Bull that Thought', it is set in France. It concerns a priest, an atheistical schoolmaster, and a peasant afflicted by his war experiences. The young man is restored to health by healing laughter after a ludicrous incident takes place in church.

MISS YOUGHAL'S SAIS. *Civil & Military Gazette*, 25 April 1887; *Plain Tales from the Hills* (1888). Strickland, a policeman with unconventional methods, falls in love with Miss Youghal but fails to win her parents' approval. He thereupon disguises himself as a native servant and enters the family's service (*sais* means 'groom'). His disguise is successfully maintained until, exasperated by witnessing an elderly general's attempt to flirt with the girl, he reveals himself. The general, impressed by his resourcefulness and tickled by the joke, puts in a good word for him, the girl's parents change their minds, and the story ends happily. This is the first of the Strickland stories: he appears also in 'The Bronckhorst Divorce-Case', 'The Mark of the Beast', 'The Return of Imray', 'A Deal in Cotton', and as a minor character in *Kim*. The character has been inconclusively identified with an Afghan police officer, stepson of a British officer, and with an Englishman called Christie who was born in India.

MRS BATHURST. *Windsor Magazine* and *Metropolitan Magazine*, March 1904; *Traffics and Discoveries* (1904). Vickery, a warrant-officer in the navy, jumps ship in Cape Town and disappears. It emerges that he has been visiting the cinema obsessively in order to watch a newsreel in which one of the figures in a crowd filmed at Paddington Station is (or appears to be) Mrs Bathurst, a New Zealand widow and hotel-keeper whom he has formerly known and in some unspecified way has let down. Later, beyond Bulawayo, two corpses turn up: they have been struck by lightning and turned to charcoal, and they disintegrate at a touch, but one has the dentures of Vickery. The other is unidentified. The frame-story involves three men in a railway siding in South Africa; the story is partly told by Pyecroft (see p. 127). The theme of this baffling tale appears to be the destructive power of love. Tompkins describes it as 'one of the earliest and most extreme of [Kipling's] experiments in suppressed narrative'. Angus Wilson finds it 'very pretentious', 'over-complex' and 'over-revised'; Kingsley Amis remarks that 'authorial self-indulgence can leave out too much as well as put too much in'; Carrington says that it 'suffers from too much compression, so that in parts it is unintelligible'. But John Bayley (*The Uses of Division*) has high praise for it, comparing the Kipling of this story to Lawrence and Camus. Bayley comments:

> The backbone of the tale is Kipling's old theme, the preoccupations of men in a team, in this case one of the biggest and most distantly linked that history has seen, the English navy at the summit of its powers and responsibilities, but separated in pre-wireless days by immense stretches of ocean.

Overlaying this theme, he adds, is 'the more sombre and general one of human isolation'. The 'original' of Mrs Bathurst is said to have been a barmaid encountered by Kipling in Christchurch, New Zealand. The use of the new medium of the cinema is striking. The story is discussed by Bodelsen and Gilbert; see also E. L. Gilbert, 'What Happens in "Mrs. Bathurst"?', *Publications of the Modern Language Association*, LXXVII, 1962.

MOTHER HIVE, THE. *Collier's Weekly*, 28 November 1908; *Actions and Reactions* (1909). In the magazine version the story is entitled 'Adventures of Melissa'. This is a political fable based on the social life of bees. The Wax Moth, a 'progressive' villainess, brings corruption and destruction to the hive, but the heroine-bee Melissa leaves and establishes a new colony elsewhere. It shows how society can be reconstructed after a major calamity; or, in Angus Wilson's more specific and topical terms, how, 'if Liberal-ruled England is doomed, then Australia or Canada will save civilization'. Kipling was an enthusiastic bee-keeper at his Sussex home, Bateman's.

MOTI GUJ – MUTINEER. No magazine publication; *Mine Own People* (1891); *Life's Handicap* (1891). The drunkard Deesa is the only man who can handle the magnificent elephant Moti Guj. When Deesa goes off on a ten-day orgy and fails to return, the elephant refuses to work; but eventually master and beast are reunited and all is well.

MUTINY OF THE MAVERICKS, THE. No magazine publication;

Mine Own People (1891); *Life's Handicap* (1891). The story opens in San Francisco, where a group belonging to a Fenian organization resolves to send Mulcahy, a young Irish-American with a 'blind rancorous hatred of England', to India in order to stir up disaffection in Her Majesty's Royal Loyal Musketeers, an Irish regiment familiarly known as the 'Mavericks'. He joins the regiment as a corporal and for six months deals out beer and sedition to the troops, who are well aware what he is up to. When the regiment goes into action, in spite of his attempts to bolt, Mulcahy is thrust into the front line; at last 'the panic excess of his fear drove him into madness beyond all human courage', and 'he went forward demented' and is killed. But he has unwittingly helped to bring about the retreat of the Afghans, and – a final irony – the colonel writes to his mother that her son has fought valiantly for the Queen and 'would have been recommended for the Victoria Cross had he survived'. For another Irish story in the same collection making a similar point, see 'Namgay Doola'.

MY LORD THE ELEPHANT.   *Civil & Military Gazette*, 27 and 28 December 1892; *Macmillan's Magazine*, January 1893; *Many Inventions* (1893). A farcical story of an unruly elephant tamed by Mulvaney, who takes a wild ride on its back that one contemporary reviewer compared to the ride of Tam o' Shanter in Burns's poem. The elephant turns up again long after; and, once again recognizing Mulvaney, it responds to his commands. Angus Wilson makes the interesting suggestion that in this story Kipling 'creates a continuous motion picture in words' that anticipates later developments in the technique of the cinema.

MY OWN TRUE GHOST STORY.   *The Week's News*, 25 February 1888; *The Phantom Rickshaw* (1888). Actually an anti-ghost-story: the narrator passes the night in a strange bungalow that he comes to believe is haunted, but the psychic phenomena turn out to have a simple and matter-of-fact explanation.

MY SON'S WIFE.   No magazine publication; *A Diversity of Creatures* (1917). According to Kipling, the story was written in 1913. It is a tale of conversion and regeneration. A young man involved with the metropolitan left-wing intelligentsia (the 'Immoderate Left') inherits a house in Sussex, where he discovers a completely new mode of life as a landed proprietor and eventually becomes engaged to a local girl who is passionately fond of hunting. The key-word in the opening sentence is 'disease', and the story tells of a psychic cure effected by the healing powers of nature. There is some pleasant satire at the expense of city-dwellers ignorant of the country, as in the letter written by the hero before his enlightenment, in which his wit is implicitly turned back upon himself: 'Their land is brown and green in alternate slabs like chocolate and pistachio cakes, speckled with occasional peasants who do not utter. In case it should not be wet enough there is a wet brook in the midst of it.' The 'wet brook' plays an important role in his change of heart, its flooding – at once realistic incident and potent symbol – bringing forth qualities he did not suspect himself of possessing. (Compare 'Friendly Brook', in which a crucial part is again played by a stream.) Angus Wilson describes the story as putting forward 'the plain man's case against Bloomsbury' and comments: 'As so often, Kipling is stating the same case as Lawrence, but Lawrence, of course, knew intimately the world he attacked.' Kipling stresses the artificiality and immorality of the metropolitan smart set; he shows that there is sexual irregularity in the country too, but of a more spontaneous and endearing, less heartless and mechanical kind. The story has much in common with 'An Habitation Enforced'. The source of the title is Jean Ingelow's once-popular poem, 'The High Tide on the Coast of Lincolnshire', to which Kipling makes explicit reference:

> And sweeter woman ne'er drew breath
> Than my sonne's wife Elizabeth.

The poem commemorates a disaster caused by flooding, whereas in the story the flood brings the lovers together. See also the poem that follows the story ('The Floods'), which describes the benefits brought to the thirsty plains by flooding.

MY SUNDAY AT HOME.   *The Idler*, April 1895; *McClure's Magazine*, June 1895; *The Day's Work* (1898). Kipling described this story in a letter of 17 August 1894 as 'a piece of broad farce . . . which made me laugh for three days'. It was written during a visit to England and completed at Tisbury, Wiltshire, where his parents had retired. It has a Wiltshire setting. The narrator becomes involved in an episode in which an American doctor visiting England falls into the clutches of a drunken navvy, as a result of a series of comic misunderstandings. It belongs to a group of stories in which, in a setting of normality (in this case a railway journey through the English countryside on a hot summer Sunday), a dream-like series of farcical misadventures unfolds. Tompkins sees it as a 'counter-statement' to Hardy's tragic view of life (there is a passing but perhaps significant reference to *Tess of the d'Urbervilles*), intended to show that 'the artifices of chance are not always tragic or life's little ironies deadly'. On Kipling and Hardy, see also 'A Conference of the Powers'. Angus Wilson finds in the story 'the first of those superb impressionistic Constable-like accounts of the English countryside caught in a particular moment of English weather'.

NABOTH.   *Civil & Military Gazette*, 26 August 1886; *Life's Handicap* (1891). For the title, see I Kings 21. 'A shrewd sweetmeat-seller appropriates more and more of the reporter's garden, so that the reporter ends by driving the man from his property; peasant shrewdness forces the Englishman into a state of exasperation' (Cornell).

NAMGAY DOOLA.   *Mine Own People* (1891); *Life's Handicap* (1891). The narrator chances to visit a petty kingdom 'on the road to Thibet, very many miles in the Himalayas', ruled over by a king with 'a standing army of five men'. The king is troubled by a native with flaming red hair who refuses to pay taxes and is generally a disruptive influence. The narrator discovers that the man is the son of an Irish soldier and a native woman ('Doola' being a corruption of 'Doolan'), and solves the problem by persuading the king to make the man chief of his 'army'. (His Irish blood makes him refuse to conform but enables him to work devotedly if his pride is flattered.) For another Irish story in the same collection making a similar point, see 'The Mutiny of the Mavericks'. According to Carrington, the story is based on 'an incident of the Black Mountain campaign'.

NAVAL MUTINY, A.   *The Story-Teller*, December 1931; *Limits and Renewals* (1932). The story was written in Jamaica in 1931, and according to Carrington is based on a scene that Kipling had witnessed in Bermuda. Angus Wilson describes it as 'an elaborate farce that fails'. The uncollected story 'A Sea Dog' is a sequel to it.

ONE VIEW OF THE QUESTION.   *Fortnightly Review*, February 1890; *Many Inventions* (1893). The story presents a satirical view of

England and the English in the form of a letter written by an Indian Moslem visiting London on a diplomatic mission.

ONLY A SUBALTERN. *The Week's News*, 25 August 1888; *Under the Deodars* (1888). A highly promising young officer is admired alike by his superiors and his men. But conditions in India have no respect for this flower of English manhood, and he dies in a cholera epidemic. The *Athenaeum* found this story the 'one redeeming feature' of the volume *Under the Deodars*. But the portrayal of an ideal young Englishman will seem unsubtle to later tastes, and Angus Wilson has found in the story 'a mawkish, Sunday-school-prize tone' that spoils it.

ON GREENHOW HILL. *Harper's Magazine*, 23 August 1890; *Macmillan's Magazine*, September 1890; *The Courting of Dinah Shadd* (1890); *Mine Own People* (1891); *Life's Handicap* (1891). The Yorkshireman Learoyd tells of an early love before he left England. Climbing a wall in the Yorkshire Dales, he falls and breaks his arm and is taken to a nearby house and nursed by 'Liza Rountree, with whom he falls in love. Under her influence he joins the Primitive Methodists, but finds that the minister is his rival in love. In a dramatic scene in a lead-mine, he is tempted to murder the other man, who is physically puny but proves unexpectedly courageous. In the event neither of them wins 'Liza, for she goes into a decline and soon dies. In despair Learoyd enlists, seeing her for the last time just before going away. The recruiting sergeant advises him to forget her – 'And,' comments Learoyd, 'I've been forgettin' her ever since.' The frame-story, set in India, shows the three soldiers, who are encamped 'on a bare ridge of the Himalayas', lying in wait for a native deserter who, at the end of the story, is shot by Ortheris. The English and Indian settings are linked by Learoyd's realization that one of the Himalayan foothills reminds him of Greenhow Hill near Pateley Bridge, where the episode of his youth occurred. Carrington comments (pp. 203–4) on the autobiographical element in this story and on the contribution made to it by Kipling's father, 'who knew Yorkshire and Methodism so much better than his son'. Carrington interprets the story as 'Rudyard's farewell to Caroline Taylor'.

ON THE CITY WALL. No magazine publication; *In Black and White* (1888). Lalun is a well-to-do prostitute with a house on the east wall of the city. (Her membership of what the opening sentence of the story calls 'the most ancient profession in the world' presumably precluded magazine publication.) She holds a regular salon frequented by local intellectuals, and harbours a political prisoner, assisting him to escape during a religious riot. The story was praised by contemporary reviewers in the *Quarterly* ('a masterpiece') and the *Athenaeum*. Cornell (pp. 152–5) offers an interesting interpretation in terms of political allegory.

ON THE GATE: A TALE OF '16. *McCall's Magazine*, June 1926; *Debits and Credits* (1926). The story was begun in April 1916 according to Mrs Kipling's diary, where it is referred to as 'his *St Peter* Story'. It was copyrighted in the USA in June 1916 under the title 'The Department of Death', but ten years elapsed before publication; the magazine version was entitled 'The Gate'. At the entrance to Heaven, St Peter and his assistants are rushed off their feet by the heavy casualties of the War: 'Thanks to the khaki everywhere, the scene was not unlike that which one might have seen on earth any evening of the old days outside the refreshment-room by the Arch at Victoria Station, when the Army trains started' (a quotation that conveys adequately the tone of the story). An elaborate bureaucratic system is developed for dealing with the flood of arrivals. Compare 'Uncovenanted Mercies' for another fantasy of the after-life. The relationship to Byron's *Vision of Judgment* is discussed by Tompkins (pp. 210–11). J. I. M. Stewart finds it 'a deeply serious story'.

ON THE STRENGTH OF A LIKENESS. *Civil & Military Gazette*, 10 January 1887; *Plain Tales from the Hills* (1888). A shallow young man who has been disappointed in love meets a married woman, Mrs Landys-Haggert, who strikingly resembles the girl who has refused him. After pursuing her because she reminds him of his lost love, he discovers to his dismay that he is in love with her for her own sake. When they part, he tells her, 'very earnestly and adoringly', 'I hope to Heaven I shall never see your face again!' A letter from Kipling to Mrs Maunsell (10 June 1887) refers to the story and, according to Cornell, 'identifies her implicitly as the original of Mrs Landys-Haggert' as well as implying that Kipling was 'extremely disconcerted by Mrs Maunsell's resemblance to Florence [Garrard]'.

OTHER MAN, THE. *Civil & Military Gazette*, 13 November 1886; *Plain Tales from the Hills* (1888). A macabre little tale concerning a girl who, though in love with a penniless young officer, is persuaded by her parents to marry a rich colonel much older than herself. The young officer falls ill and is eventually sent to Simla, where the wife is. She goes to meet him and finds him dead on the back seat of his carriage, 'with a grin on his face, as if he enjoyed the joke of his arrival'. She tells no-one of what has happened, and eventually returns to England to die herself.

PHANTOM RICKSHAW, THE. *Quartette*, 1885; extensively revised for republication in *The Phantom Rickshaw* (1888). A story of sexual immorality, the death of a discarded mistress, guilt, haunting, and eventually the death of the narrator. The frame-story introduces the narrative of Pansay, 'dated 1885, exactly as he wrote it'. After conducting an adulterous affair with Agnes Keith-Wessington, he had grown tired of her, brutally turned her away, and became engaged to a young girl. Agnes, broken-hearted at his rejection of her appeals, dies; but her ghost, riding in a rickshaw and accompanied by her former servants (who have all conveniently died of cholera), persistently haunts him until he is reduced to a state in which 'it seemed that the rickshaw and I were the only realities in a world of shadows'. He confesses to his fiancée what he has done, and she breaks off their engagement. He waits for death thereafter, knowing it to be a richly deserved fate. Contemporary critics took a dim view of Kipling's excursions into the supernatural: the *Fortnightly Review* found this and other exercises in the same genre 'distinct failures', and the *Edinburgh Review* objected to the 'crudely material supernaturalism'. A modern critic, Cornell, takes the present story altogether more seriously, pointing out the affinity to Poe but arguing that 'Kipling has improved on his models', for 'instead of taking place in the vaguely Gothic world of the conventional nineteenth-century tale of terror, [it] is firmly based in Kipling's Simla'; 'the Simla milieu and the conventions of an Anglo-Indian flirtation give substance to this tale of a blackguard and his pathetic demon-lover'. The same critic points out that, in one remarkable passage, Kipling 'changes and deepens the tone of the story' and 'foreshadows nearly all of his later excursions into the supernatural'. The passage referred to is that in which the hag-ridden narrator, his life now obsessed by the ghostly ex-lover, says that it was 'a ghastly and yet in some indefinable way a marvellously dear experience', and asks himself whether he 'was in this life to woo a second time the woman I had killed by my own neglect and cruelty?' As Cornell says, this anticipates the 'powerful nostalgia for the unseen world' in the later Kipling. Kipling added the frame-story when he revised the story for republication in 1888 and thus, as Tompkins points out, enriched the ambiguity: is Pansay really afforded glimpses of the spirit-world in which, bizarrely, a dead woman hires dead servants to drive her around Simla; or is there, as the doctor in the story insists, a material explanation for his experiences? Kipling himself said of the story that 'Some of it was weak, much was bad and out of key; but it was my first serious attempt to think in another man's skin' (*Something of Myself*) – a recollection, or claim, that seems to make it a landmark in the development of his art.

PIG. *Civil & Military Gazette*, 3 June 1887; *Plain Tales from the Hills* (1888). Cheated by Pinecoffin over a horse, Nafferton obtains an elaborate revenge: he concocts a scheme for feeding the army in India on pork, and contrives matters so that Pinecoffin, who is a government official, has to supply him with large quantities of memoranda on every aspect of the subject. He also puts Pinecoffin in the position of appearing to perform these duties incompetently, and at the end of the story tells his victim what he has done and why. This is one of the earliest of the numerous stories in which an elaborate revenge is obtained by means of a hoax or practical joke; in this instance the satire on bureaucracy is also notable.

POOR DEAR MAMA. See 'The Story of the Gadsbys'.

PRIVATE LEAROYD'S STORY. *The Week's News*, 14 July 1888; *Soldiers Three* (1888). Mrs DeSussa covets Rip, a fox-terrier belonging to the colonel's wife, and, being on the point of going away, bribes Learoyd to steal the dog for her. Mulvaney and Ortheris hatch a plan whereby another dog resembling Rip in appearance but of very uncertain temper is caught and delivered to Mrs DeSussa at the railway station. She pays up, believing that she has the dog she wants, and the three soldiers divide the 300 rupees between them. The *Athenaeum* reviewer praised the story as 'nothing short of a masterpiece'.

PROPAGATION OF KNOWLEDGE, THE. *Strand Magazine*, January 1926; *McCall's Magazine*, January 1926; *Debits and Credits* (1926). Written in 1925, this is a school story in which the co-operative efforts of a group of boys that includes Beetle and Stalky succeed in impressing a visiting examiner. The deviousness of innocent-seeming youth is demonstrated as they contrive to outwit the system and its representatives. Compare 'The United Idolaters' in the same volume.

PROPHET AND THE COUNTRY, THE. *Hearst's International Magazine*, October 1924; *Nash's and Pall Mall Magazine*, November 1924; *Debits and Credits* (1926). This rather undistinguished comic and satirical story concerns an eccentric American who encounters the narrator by chance on the Great North Road and describes to him his campaign against Prohibition, which has involved the making of a film. The failure of his idealistic efforts has led him to quit America and to conclude that 'Those ancient prophets an' martyrs haven't got much on me in the things a Democracy hands you if you don't see eye to eye with it.' Tompkins suggests that the story expresses Kipling's 'disquietude about America'.

PUZZLER, THE. *North American*, 15 January 1906; *Tribune*, 15–16 January 1906; *Actions and Reactions* (1909). Three distinguished men – a law lord, a Royal Academician, and a famous engineer, who have been at Harrow together – try an experiment to ascertain whether an organ-grinder's monkey is capable of climbing a monkey-puzzle tree in the garden of what appears to be an empty house. The monkey gets into the house, and before it is recaptured a frantic chase ensues. The people who are moving into the house arrive, to be confronted by this bacchanalian scene, and thus providing a comic tableau. There is much masculine hilarity: 'we rolled on the ground . . . and ceased not till we had arrived at the extremity of exhaustion'. The story makes the point that the English ruling classes are capable of such relaxations of dignity, which constitute a kind of celebration of brotherhood (the shared public school background is relevant). This lesson is conveyed to Penfentenyou, a politician from the colonies, who is involved in the frame-story (he reappears in a later farce, 'The Vortex'). The escapade with the monkey may seem childish, but (argues Kipling) it is evidence of a sense of fun that is valued by a wise man as something precious, and that is a distinctive mark of British civilization.

RECORD OF BADALIA HERODSFOOT, THE. *Harper's Weekly*, 15 and 22 November, 1890; *The Courting of Dinah Shadd* (1890); *Many Inventions* (1893). The heroine is a girl of the London slums who marries a drunken ruffian. After two years he abandons her, their baby dies, and she is left alone. She becomes a valued and trusted assistant to the clergy, who are engaged in charitable work in the East End; but her husband returns and in a drunken fit beats her to death. As she dies, she makes an effort to exonerate him. The story is a notable and very early exercise in the highly realistic genre of slum fiction practised a little later in the decade by such authors as Arthur Morrison and (in *Liza of Lambeth*) Somerset Maugham. See P. J. Keating, *The Working Classes in Victorian Fiction* and *Working-Class Stories of the 1890s* (1971). Angus Wilson finds it, though 'a little sentimental', 'the first really successful expression of that deep compassion for lonely and unloved women that ran alongside [Kipling's] superficial misogyny and outlived it to produce some of the finest stories of his last twenty years'. Its quality was not immediately recognized, contemporary reviewers finding it 'cynical', 'brutal', and 'too painful', and J. M. Barrie describing it as 'merely a very clever man's treatment of a land he knows little of'.

REGULUS. *Metropolitan Magazine*, April 1917; *Nash's Magazine*, April 1917; *A Diversity of Creatures* (1917). According to Kipling, the story was written as early as 1908. It employs some of the characters from *Stalky & Co.* and adopts a characteristic strategy of recounting two episodes that seem at first sight unconnected or only very loosely connected, leaving the reader to detect the underlying connection between them. In the first part, King takes a class through the Fifth Ode in Horace, Book III. The relevance of classical literature to modern conduct is implied; King also argues its superiority to science as an educational instrument. In the second part, a boy faces up to punishment manfully. In a prefatory note Kipling reminds the reader that Regulus, celebrated in Horace's ode, went willingly to his death at the hands of the Carthaginians.

REINGELDER AND THE GERMAN FLAG. *Civil & Military Gazette*, 16 April 1889; *Life's Handicap* (1891). Another story narrated, with much rendering of his thick German accent, by Hans Breit-mann, whom Kipling borrowed from Charles Godfrey Leland's collection of humorous verse *Hans Breitmann's Ballads* (1857 and subsequently), and who also appears in 'Bertran and Bimi'. In this story the German tells of a fellow-naturalist anxious to secure a specimen of the 'German Flag', a tropical snake. When he obtains one, he ignores Breitmann's advice and insists on handling it, relying on a statement in the standard handbook that the snake is not poisonous. He is bitten, and dies protesting at the unreliability of the authority in whom he had put his trust. The *Edinburgh Review* found it 'a delightful study of the stolid egotism of the middle-class German *savant*, with his assumption that everyone is ignorant beside himself'.

RESCUE OF PLUFFLES, THE. *Civil & Military Gazette*, 20 November 1886; *Plain Tales from the Hills* (1888). Mrs Hauksbee rescues Pluffles, who is 'callow, even for a subaltern', from the clutches of the predatory Mrs Reiver, who is 'wicked in a business-like way', and ensures that he marries his fiancée. A weak tale, narrated rather than dramatized.

RETURN OF IMRAY, THE. No magazine publication; *Mine Own People* (1891), under the title 'The Recrudescence of Imray'; *Life's Handicap* (1891). Imray, an English official serving in India, unaccountably disappears and 'after three or four months' his bungalow is rented by the policeman Strickland (see 'Miss Youghal's Sais'). The narrator, on a visit to Strickland, observes the strange behaviour of Imray's dog Tietjens. When Strickland looks into the 'dark . . . cavern of the roof' above the ceiling-cloth in order to deal with some poisonous snakes, he finds the remains of Imray, which descend gruesomely into the room. A native servant confesses that he has murdered his master, believing that the latter had put a curse on his child, and then allows one of the snakes to bite him fatally rather than going to the gallows.

ROUT OF THE WHITE HUSSARS, THE. No magazine publication; *Plain Tales from the Hills* (1888). A beloved regimental drum-horse, supposedly dead and buried, appears with a skeleton on its back and causes the Hussars to flee in panic. The trick is played by an Irish subaltern in order to teach a lesson to a choleric colonel who has ordered the horse to be killed. The reference at the end to 'Charity and Zeal, 3709, E.C.' may be the first of Kipling's many references to freemasonry (he had joined 'Hope and Perseverance, No. 782 E.C.' at Lahore in 1885).

SAHIBS' WAR, A. *Windsor Magazine*, December 1901; *Collier's Weekly*, December 1901; *Traffics and Discoveries* (1904). A story of the Boer War consisting of the monologue of an elderly Sikh who has accompanied his master, an English cavalry officer, to South Africa. 'Kurban Sahib' (Captain Corbyn) has been killed by Boer treachery; the old man, who is now making his way home, narrates the incident. Carrington suggests that the story embodies 'Kipling's notion of how the war might have been fought if the Indian Army had been employed'. Tompkins notes that it is 'the last and longest of the unframed dramatic monologues', and suggests that the limitations of the narrator make its emotions more vehement. Angus Wilson comments: 'The violence with which the treachery is answered is shocking, but then Kipling means to shock us and, as always, he knows how.'

SEA CONSTABLES: A TALE OF '15. *Metropolitan Magazine*, September 1915; *Nash's & Pall Mall Magazine*, October 1915; *Debits and Credits* (1926). The story was written in February 1915 – the month in which the German policy of all-out submarine warfare was made known. Four speakers, yarning over dinner in a West End restaurant, are naval officers who recall their pursuit of a neutral ship known to be carrying oil to the enemy, and their refusal to come to the aid of its dying skipper. The story is highly technical in language and far from easy to follow; Carrington finds it 'if not the most obscure, perhaps the most difficult story Kipling ever wrote', and also judges it 'ethically . . . deplorable'. Angus Wilson, on the other hand, discusses it sympathetically and finds the moral, though 'unpleasant', quite consistent with the ethos of the Stalky stories. The *Reader's Guide* defines its theme as 'retributive justice'. There is an extended discussion by Tompkins (pp. 137–40).

SECOND-RATE WOMAN, A. *The Week's News*, 8 September 1888; *Under the Deodars* (1888). A slight anecdote about Mrs Hauksbee. She feels only contempt for the dowdy Mrs Delville, but changes her opinion when the latter, by her presence of mind, saves the life of a dying child in a situation in which Mrs Hauksbee confesses herself 'worse than useless'. She concludes that 'They ought to build her a statue, only no sculptor dare copy those skirts.'

SENDING OF DANA DA, THE. *The Week's News*, 11 February 1888; *In Black and White* (1888). Dana Da exploits a fashionable interest in psychic phenomena and enriches himself by contriving what appears to be a miracle. On his deathbed, 'dying of whisky and opium' but still avaricious, he confesses for a small consideration how the trick was done, then promptly dies.

SHIP THAT FOUND HERSELF, THE. *The Idler*, December 1895;

McClure's Magazine, March 1896; *The Day's Work* (1898). A cargo-steamer is on her maiden voyage to New York, and all the separate parts of her structure and her engines 'talk' with their separate voices until they merge into one voice, signifying that the ship has found her 'soul'. See the poem 'McAndrew's Hymn' for a comparable treatment of the romance of machinery. Tompkins, who finds the story 'ingeniously amusing and straightforwardly moral', interprets it as an allegory of human life: men, like the parts of a machine, must learn to accept their functions and learn to work together, and this can only be achieved in the practical circumstances of the working world. For Angus Wilson, however, 'the fable doesn't work', and in this story, as in the somewhat similar '.007', we have 'information without the illusion of life'.

SOLID MULDOON, THE. *The Week's News*, 2 June 1888; *Soldiers Three* (1888). Mulvaney recalls how he dealt with a jealous husband and with the ghost of a dead soldier. The title seems to be taken from an early nineteenth-century negro minstrel song, 'Muldoon, the Solid Man', by Edward Harrigan.

STEAM TACTICS. *Windsor Magazine*, December 1902; *Saturday Evening Post*, December 1902; *Traffics and Discoveries* (1904). Carrington notes that Kipling became enthusiastic about motor-cars at the end of 1899; in December of that year he hired a car 'which, at times, could cover eight miles an hour' (*Something of Myself*), and the following summer he bought his first car, a steam-driven 'Locomobile'. The latter features in 'Steam Tactics', which has been described as 'a complex tale of sailors ashore, officious policemen, and a private zoo' (Carrington). Pyecroft (see p. 127) makes an appearance. As so often, the action involves a trick that leads to well-deserved punishment: a policeman intent upon catching motorists who exceed the speed limit becomes the victim of a stratagem that lands him in a private zoo (compare 'The Village that Voted the Earth was Flat' for a similar implicit indignation directed at those who restrain motorists from speeding).

STORY OF MUHAMMAD DIN, THE. *Civil & Military Gazette*, 8 September 1886; *United Services College Chronicle*, 18 December 1886; *Plain Tales from the Hills* (1888). Muhammad Din is the small son of Imam Din, the narrator's servant. The narrator finds pleasure in watching him play; but before long the child falls sick and dies of fever, the English doctor remarking that

'They have no stamina, these brats.' The *Edinburgh Review* called it 'a pathetic masterpiece', and the story – written when Kipling was twenty – is tender and touching. Cornell notes that the narrator is 'left conscious of the futility of his good intentions; he becomes symbolic of England's helplessness in the face of India's frailty, her triple curse of poverty, starvation, and disease'.

STORY OF THE GADSBYS, THE.   Published by Wheeler & Co. of Allahabad in 1888 as No. 2 of their 'Indian Railway Library', a series of slim volumes in paper wrappers. A second edition appeared in 1889. When publication in London followed in 1890, 10,000 copies were printed. The work, which bears the subtitle 'A Tale without a Plot', includes eight stories, six of which had appeared in *The Week's News* and one in the *Civil & Military Gazette*. The volume concludes with a poem, 'L'Envoi'. The eight stories are cast in the form of dramatic dialogues, complete with stage-directions and scene-descriptions. All are set in India, either in Simla or on the Plains. They resemble episodes from a continuous narrative – a kind of fragmentary short novel (Carrington, indeed, describes the collection as 'a short sentimental novel') – and the continuity from one story to the next makes it preferable to describe them all under one heading.

'Poor Dear Mama', first published in *The Week's News* on 26 May 1888, is set in Simla. Captain Gadsby, a bachelor cavalry officer of a wealthy and titled family, calls on Mrs Threegan, a middle-aged woman with whom he is in the habit of riding. While she gets ready, her young daughter Minnie talks to him: vivacious and even pert, she drops some telling hints about 'poor dear mamma' ('*You* don't know what rheumatism is . . .'), and the captain finds himself captivated by the daughter and at the same time seeing the mother with new and less eager eyes. An epilogue, two months later, reveals him as engaged to Minnie.

'The World Without' (*Civil & Military Gazette*, 18 May 1888, under the title 'In Gilded Halls') presents a group of young men in a club discussing Gadsby's engagement to Minnie; they suggest that his previous involvement with a Mrs Herriott, a colonel's wife, is likely to prove a source of trouble.

'The Tents of Kedar' (*The Week's News*, 18 August 1888) shows Gadsby and Mrs Heriott seated together at a dinner-party and engaged in a tête-à-tête. By slow degrees he tells her that their affair is over, and that he loves another – not a married woman this time, but 'a girl', so that it will be no brief liaison but will involve abandoning her permanently. The disturbing power of this story (the *Fortnightly Review*'s praise of it as 'drawing-room comedy of a high order' seems very far from hitting the nail on the head) resides in the dramatic situation: the formal and public context precludes either of the participants from giving open expression to their feelings, yet we have a sense of the woman's rage and despair even as she helps herself to asparagus and arranges her gloves and fan. For the source of the title, see Genesis 16, 17, 20 and 25 (Kedar was the son of Ishmael).

'With Any Amazement' (*The Week's News*, 9 June 1888) is set in Simla and deals with Gadsby's wedding. In a state of extreme nervousness, he is encouraged by his friend and best man, Captain Mafflin, who gives him military commands in order to ensure his proper behaviour at the altar. For the title, see I Peter 3:6.

'The Garden of Eden' (*The Week's News*, 16 June 1888) is set three weeks later than the previous story. The Gadsbys are still on honeymoon and talk of their love for each other; she shows a fear of life's impermanence, and asks him not to tell her anything he does not want her to remember for ever (he has confessed an earlier engagement, broken off when he came to India).

'Fatima' (no magazine publication) is set somewhat later in the Gadsby's marriage, which is now beginning to show signs of strain. Minnie is upset that her husband excludes her from the professional interests that mean so much to him. She finds a letter from Mrs Herriott (see above) among his papers, and angers him by reading parts of it aloud. At the end she confesses that she has come to his room to tell him that she is expecting a child.

'The Valley of the Shadow' (*The Week's News*, 23 June 1888): by now a year has passed since the marriage and Minnie's baby has been born and died. Minnie falls seriously ill and is delirious. Gadsby speaks to her for what he believes will be the last time, and they declare their love for each other. Against all expectations she recovers, and the epilogue shows her convalescent five weeks later. Edmund Gosse praised 'the pathos of the little bride's delirium'. The title is a quotation from Psalm 23.

'The Swelling of Jordan' (*The Week's News*, 30 June 1888) is set three years later. The Gadsbys now have a ten-month-old son. Gadsby, who is thirty-three, tells Mafflin that he is thinking of resigning the service and returning to England for the sake of his wife and child; he also confesses that his family responsibilities have rendered him cowardly, or at least conscious of his personal safety, in his soldierly duties. Mafflin reproaches him bitterly for thinking of abandoning his work; but Gadsby's final decision is to leave, though he admits that 'marriage – even as good a marriage as mine has been – hampers a man's work . . . and oh, it plays Hell with his notions of duty!' The concluding poem has the well-known refrain, 'He travels the fastest who travels alone'. As the above comments indicate, these stories throw considerable light on Kipling's attitude in the late eighties to women and their effect upon 'a man's work'. For the title of 'The Swelling of Jordan', see Jeremiah 7:5.

Kipling's letters reveal that the prototype of Gadsby was a Captain Beames of the 19th Bengal Lancers, a friend of Kipling's.

Cornell comments on this collection that it is

> nothing but a series of ordeals, some facetious and some serious. . . . It might have turned out well, for the Gadsbys' marriage has to outlast nearly every strain to which an Anglo-Indian marriage can be subject. But something went wrong, as Kipling realized later. The innocence and good intentions of old Gaddy and his Minnie win victories that seem contrived, and the story keeps descending into troughs of the commonplace: the nervous bridegroom, the compromising letter from an old flame, the tender announcement of pregnancy. Only at the end does Gadsby face a real dilemma and the story take on substance. The carefully built structure of domestic happiness is finally confronted by a moral imperative, the Captain's duty to his regiment; Gadsby's weakness is exposed, and for a moment he becomes real.

STRANGE RIDE OF MORROWBIE JUKES, THE. *Quartette* (1885);

extensively revised for republication in *The Phantom Rickshaw* (1888). This extraordinary tale, written when Kipling was nineteen, is set in a desert region about a hundred miles from Lahore. Jukes, a civil engineer, finds himself trapped in a sandy crater that is an abode of the living dead, those who have been supposed dead but, having revived from a trance or coma, have been expelled from human society. There appears to be no way of escape from the crater, and a power-struggle develops between Jukes and a Brahmin, Gunga Dass, whom he has known formerly.

After savouring the horrors of the situation to the full, Jukes is somewhat implausibly rescued in a conclusion that is curiously and disappointingly rushed. The effectiveness of the central portion of the story is undeniable, however. Gosse and Lang made the obvious comparison with Poe, and Cornell refers specifically to Poe's 'The Pit and the Pendulum'. Kipling's original title was 'The Village of the Dead'. The story was at first intended to be much shorter but insisted on growing; it was begun in December 1884 and not finished until late February 1885. There is an ironic contrast between Jukes's racial complacency and professional efficiency, and the nightmarish situation in which he finds himself. Cornell interprets the story allegorically as

> a genuine Anglo-Indian nightmare . . . a vision of what it would be like to be one of the least of the ruled instead of one of the rulers. . . . The trap at the bottom of the sand-hills is a world where none of the customary rules of decent behaviour can be applied, where the Englishman must eat and sleep, not only in the manner of his fellow-victims, but in a way that differs little from that of many Indian paupers in the normal world outside.

Angus Wilson's interpretation is similar: he finds it 'one of the most powerful nightmares of the precariousness of a ruling group, in this case of a group haunted by memories of the Mutiny not yet twenty years old'. Wilson suggests that 'only the inartistic and improbable escape of Jukes at the end of the story prevents it from being among the first dozen of all Kipling's stories'. John Bayley, who regards it as 'one of the most memorable though least discussed of Kipling's *oeuvre*', states that it affords 'a real look into the abyss, reminiscent of both Poe and Kafka, but with none of the former's stagy melodrama or the latter's devoted neurosis'; he adds that it 'conveys sparely and without insistence the nightmare that Kipling found in India, as in all uncovenanted and unorganized human experience, and which his art fights off in any way it can'.

SWELLING OF JORDAN, THE. See 'The Story of the Gadsbys'.

'SWEPT AND GARNISHED'. *Century Magazine*, January 1915; *Nash's Magazine*, January 1915; *A Diversity of Creatures* (1917). Its position as the penultimate story in the latter volume, immediately preceding 'Mary Postgate', is significant. Written in October 1914, it concerns a German woman who, apparently in a state of delirium produced by influenza, sees in a vision the child-victims of her country's war-mongering. She has learned of the children's death in a letter from her son, who is serving in Belgium. Angus Wilson notes that the story appeared 'hotfoot upon the terrible stories of the atrocities in Belgium', and describes it as 'a masterly parable of cosiness brutally dispersed'. (The story ends with the obsessively house-proud *Hausfrau* trying to remove from her floor – and, by implication, from her consciousness and conscience – the drops of blood she believes to have been left by the children.) Carrington points out that it is an example of Kipling's 'growing interest in the mental processes of elderly women': compare in this respect 'Mary Postgate' and 'The Wish House'. Tompkins dismisses the suggestion that it can be interpreted as a story of the supernatural; and if indeed the woman's experience involves an hallucination, this strengthens the case for seeing the story as a companion-piece to 'Mary Postgate'. The title-phrase appears both in Matthew 12:44 and Luke 11:25.

TAKING OF LUNGTUNGPEN, THE. *Civil & Military Gazette*, 11 April 1887; *Plain Tales from the Hills* (1888). Mulvaney recalls how twenty-six men, after swimming a river and 'as nakid as Vanus', captured a native town and killed seventy-five Burmese without any losses to their own party. He argues that it was the innocence of the inexperienced troops that inspired them to such an improbable act of heroism. Gosse called the story 'a little masterpiece' and 'one of the best short stories not merely in English, but in any language'. It is said to have been based on an actual incident involving two British regiments, the Queen's and the Hampshire; Carrington notes that the incident was 'reported in the *Civil & Military* as an actual achievement of the 2nd Queen's Regiment, a few weeks before Kipling wrote it up as fiction'.

TENDER ACHILLES, THE. *London Magazine*, December 1929; *Limits and Renewals* (1932). A former army surgeon has a breakdown as a result of the strains imposed by his wartime experiences, but is tricked back into sanity by his colleagues at St Peggotty's medical school. The story is accompanied by a revealing poem, 'Hymn to Physical Pain'. The title seems likely to be a pun on the anatomical term 'tendo Achilles' (Achilles tendon). The magazine version adds at the end: 'they both seemed to know all about it, but it was full time for me to go home'. The character of Sir James Betton is said to be based on Sir John Bland-Sutton, a friend of Kipling and an eminent surgeon who operated on him.

TENTS OF KADAR, THE. See 'The Story of the Gadsbys'.

THEIR LAWFUL OCCASIONS. *Collier's Weekly*, 3 and 10 October, 1903; *Traffics & Discoveries* (1904). The source of the title is the *Book of Common Prayer* ('Forms of Prayer to be Used at Sea'). This two-part story is narrated by Pyecroft, 'late second-class petty officer of H.M.S. Archimandrite, an unforgettable man'. Angus Wilson describes him as 'the Mulvaney of the naval stories' but finds him 'an empty narrating device, compounded only of comic knowingness, cockney accent and naval jargon'. For other Pyecroft stories, see 'Steam Tactics', 'Mrs Bathurst', 'The Horse Marines' and 'The Bonds of Discipline'.

THEY. *Scribner's Magazine*, August 1904; *Traffics and Discoveries* (1904). This very personal story, hinting at Kipling's feelings about the death of his daughter Josephine, was begun in Cape Town in February 1904. Several years earlier, Lockwood Kipling had written in a letter: 'The house and garden are full of the lost child and poor Rud told his mother how he saw her [i.e., Josephine] when a door opened, when a space was vacant at table, coming out of every green dark corner of the garden.' A motorist driving in Sussex stumbles across a remote country-house inhabited by a blind woman and a number of children to whom she devotes her life. In a series of visits he gradually learns that the children are ghosts, and at last makes contact with his own dead child – but tells the woman that he will come no more, adding that 'For you it is right. . . . For me it would be wrong.' As Bodelsen points out, the reference to the fact that the

narrator comes from 'the other side of the county' is repeated no
fewer than six times, the repetition underlining the symbolism
('he is a visitor from the country of the living to the country of
the dead'). T. S. Eliot alludes to this story (without citing it) in
'Burnt Norton' (*Four Quartets*).

THREE AND —— AN EXTRA. *Civil & Military Gazette*, 17 November 1886; *Plain Tales from the Hills* (1886). A woman whose child
has died mourns inconsolably and her husband looks elsewhere
for amusement, finding it eventually in the company of Mrs
Hauksbee (introduced in this story as 'a little, brown, thin,
almost skinny, woman, with big, rolling, violet-blue eyes, and
the sweetest manners in the world'). The wife lays a plan to win
her husband back: she turns up at a dance which her husband is
attending with Mrs Hauksbee, having first made herself look as
attractive as possible. Her plan succeeds, and Mrs Hauksbee is
left high and dry. Other Mrs Hauksbee stories include 'The
Rescue of Pluffles', 'Consequences', 'Kidnapped', 'The Education of Otis Yeere', 'A Second-rate Woman', 'Venus Annodomini', as well as 'A Supplementary Chapter' (*Abaft the Funnel*)
and 'Mrs Hauksbee Sits Out' (*Illustrated London News*, Christmas Number, 1890; uncollected). Elsewhere ('Kidnapped') she
is described as 'the most wonderful woman in India', and in
'The Rescue of Pluffles' her age is given as about forty-three.
'Three and —— an Extra' introduces the phrase 'But that is
another story', which appears seven times more in *Plain Tales
from the Hills* and was widely quoted. On Mrs Burton as a
prototype for Mrs Hauksbee, see p. 36.

THREE MUSKETEERS, THE. *Civil & Military Gazette*, 11 March
1887; *Plain Tales from the Hills* (1888). This story marks the first
appearance of the 'soldiers three', Mulvaney, Learoyd and
Ortheris. (There are altogether eighteen stories about the trio:
four in *Plain Tales from the Hills*, seven in *Soldiers Three*, three in
Life's Handicap, three in *Many Inventions*, and one in *Actions and
Reactions*.) Mulvaney relates how a visiting nobleman is made
the victim of a practical joke (he believes himself to be set upon
by thieves and is 'rescued' by the trio, who receive his reward).

THROUGH THE FIRE. *Civil & Military Gazette*, 28 May 1888; *Life's
Handicap* (1891). An elderly charcoal-burner's young wife runs
away with a young lover, but the husband puts a curse upon her
and, believing in its efficacy, she begins to fade. At last she
returns to her home, but her lover insists on accompanying her.

They find there a stack of wood ready for the next day's charcoal-burning, climb on to the ready-made funeral pyre, and the lover shoots first the woman and then himself. The final touch of the story is the husband's lament that four rupees' worth of wood has been wasted. The policeman called in to investigate the case describes it as an Indian version of 'the story of Francesca da Rimini' (a story of tragic love from thirteenth-century Italy, referred to in Dante's *Inferno*). The tale is a neat miniature example of Kipling's attempts in fiction to show that the Indian and European minds work in quite different ways.

THROWN AWAY. No magazine publication; *Plain Tales from the Hills* (1888). A boy brought up by devoted but foolish parents has been carefully sheltered from the harsher side of life. When as a young man he goes to India he quickly succumbs to dissipation and commits suicide. His major and the narrator, realizing that the truth would kill his parents, arrange matters so that he appears to have died of cholera. Their discovery of his body and their subsequent actions are narrated with great vividness. Edmund Gosse praised the story as 'hopelessly tragic' and 'very remarkable'.

TIE, THE. No magazine publication; *Limits and Renewals* (1932). This story, which Carrington describes as 'an ill-natured anecdote, written long since and dredged up from the bottom of his notebooks where it might better have been allowed to stay', was probably written as early as 1915 (Mrs Kipling's diary entry for 22 April of that year refers to Kipling starting a 'story about Army food'). It concerns a contractor who supplies appalling food to the army; when this profiteer falls into the hands of the men who have had to eat it, they manhandle him and force him to eat his own food. W. W. Robson dismisses the story as 'negligible and unpleasant'; as a very late example of the revenge-story involving physical humiliation, it can be compared with such very early instances as 'A Friend's Friend' and 'The Judgment of Dungara'. Tompkins has answered the criticism that the schoolboyish behaviour and conversation of those involved is unconvincing: Kipling's detail that the old boys' tie worn by the victim 'saved us and steadied us' indicates that it 'suggested to them the methods of the prefects' study and, availing themselves of these, they avoided more serious violence' – and that it is, in fact, an example of the 'limits' referred to in the volume-title. For better or worse, the story certainly transplants the world of *Stalky & Co.* into an adult wartime setting. There is of course no such thing as an 'Old E. H. W. School tie', the initials presumably standing for Eton, Harrow and Winchester.

To Be Filed for Reference.   No magazine publication; *Plain Tales from the Hills* (1888). McIntosh Jellaludin, an Englishman educated at Oxford and formerly a brilliant scholar, has 'gone native', marrying a native woman and becoming a convert to Islam as well as (somewhat inconsistently) taking to drink. Just before he dies of pneumonia, he gives the narrator the manuscript of a book he has written which he believes will guarantee his immortality. It includes 'an account of the life and sins and death of Mother Maturin', a curious allusion to Kipling's own unfinished novel (see p. 3). On the protagonist, Cornell comments:

> By every Anglo-Indian standard he has failed utterly. And yet he has captured Kipling's imagination: the conversations between McIntosh and the reporter suggest in a curious way that two conflicting impulses in Kipling himself are debating against one another; McIntosh embodies that part of Kipling's mind for which the restraints of Anglo-Indian life were intolerably burdensome. . . . McIntosh is enviable to the extent that he has seen to the bottom of Indian life, and can therefore laugh at Strickland as an ignorant man. He is enviable as the author of 'Mother Maturin', the novel Kipling had begun but was never to complete.

Tods' Amendment.   *Civil & Military Gazette*, 16 April 1887; *Plain Tales from the Hills* (1888). Tods, 'about six years old', is an English child living at Simla; he is 'precocious for his age, and his mixing with natives had taught him some of the more bitter truths of life'; 'Of course, he spoke Urdu', and when necessary he translates in his mind 'from the vernacular to English, as many Anglo-Indian children do' (much of this, of course, being true of the young Kipling). Tods is petted by high officials, but also frequents the bazaar and thus picks up native gossip as his elders could hardly do. When the talk at a dinner-party turns to a new Land Bill 'affecting a few hundred thousand people', Tods tells a legal official of the native attitude towards an important measure proposed by the new legislation. The official is impressed by what the child reports, and as a result an amendment is introduced. Gosse described the story as 'a political allegory' and suggested that Kipling wanted to emphasize the need of the government in India to understand the point of view of the natives, as the child does but the high-ranking officials in the story do not.

TOMB OF HIS ANCESTORS, THE. *Pearson's Magazine*, December 1897; *McClure's Magazine*, December 1897; *The Day's Work* (1898). John Chinn is a young man whose family have served in India for generations and whose early childhood has been spent there. After fifteen years' absence in England, he returns to India as an army officer and finds Bukta, an old native who has known him as a child and who now declares, 'I am your servant, as I was your father's before you.' The native population come to believe that the young man is a reincarnation of his grandfather, a belief fortified by a birthmark that appears in alternate generations of the Chinn family. The Bhil people revere the memory of John's grandfather and namesake, who had brought law and justice to them. They believe that his ghost rides a tiger that lives near his tomb 'among the Satpura hills'. John comes to be regarded as a 'demi-god twice born – tutelary deity of their land and people'. By exploiting these superstitions the young subaltern deals with a potentially serious situation: he persuades the native people to be vaccinated, and he kills the tiger that lives in the neighbourhood of his grandfather's tomb and has fuelled the people's belief in a ghost-rider. The hero is said to have been based on James Outram (see Philip Woodruff, *The Guardians* [1963]).

UNCOVENANTED MERCIES. No magazine publication; *Limits and Renewals* (1932). This allegory of the after-life may be compared with the earlier story 'On the Gate'. Tompkins stresses the contrast between the two: 'The Hell of "Uncovenanted Mercies" is not a tender jest, like the Heaven of "On the Gate". It is a realization of human suffering in terms of sick hope and repeated disappointment.'

UNITED IDOLATERS, THE. *Nash's Magazine*, June 1924; *Hearst's International Magazine*, June 1924; *Debits and Credits* (1926). Kipling seems to have begun the writing of this school story, later included in *The Complete Stalky & Co.* (1929), in 1923. An unpopular temporary master, Brownell, is scandalized by certain aspects of school discipline, his conventional notions being contrasted with the Head's unorthodox wisdom. The boys are infected with a craze for the 'Uncle Remus' stories of Joel Chandler Harris, and manufacture 'idols' of Brer Terrapin and the Tar-Baby, staging an elaborate mock-battle in which some damage is done. This has the intended effect of causing Brownell to resign. The boys' devious skill in manipulating the situation for their own ends is demonstrated: compare, in the same volume, 'The Propagation of Knowledge'.

UNPROFESSIONAL. *The Story-Teller*, October 1930; *Limits and Renewals* (1932). A complex story of cancer, medical research, astrological forces, and a battle with 'the cheated grave'. Four doctors investigate the connection between the heavenly bodies and the behaviour of cancer cells. Dobrée has drawn attention to Kipling's view that medical researchers should use less science and more imagination. The *Reader's Guide* points out the significance of the fact that the first operation is performed in the afternoon on the ebb-tide, the second in the morning on the flood tide. St Peggotty's Hospital is also referred to in 'The Tender Achilles'.

VALLEY OF THE SHADOW, THE.   See 'The Story of the Gadsbys'.

VENUS ANNODOMINI.   *Civil & Military Gazette*, 4 December 1886; *Plain Tales from the Hills* (1888). A callow young Englishman falls in love with a well-preserved woman old enough to be his mother. He is disillusioned when he learns that she has a daughter near his own age, and when his father turns up and reveals that in his youth *he* was infatuated with the same woman. The title probably contains a punning reference to Venus Anadyomene ('rising from the sea').

VILLAGE THAT VOTED THE EARTH WAS FLAT, THE.   No magazine publication; *A Diversity of Creatures* (1917). The narrator and three friends, motoring together, are charged with speeding through a village and are convicted and fined by a pompous J.P. In collaboration with a music-hall impresario who has also been victimized, he embarks on an elaborate scheme of revenge which results in ridicule being heaped on the village. Tompkins suggests that the story's starting-point was 'a conviction, at once zestful and misgiving, of the enormous power of the modern Press and the other publicizing industries and arts, especially the Music Hall, that were linked with it.' Kipling states that the story was written in 1913, but Carrington quotes from Mrs Kipling's diary of 7 May 1914 ('R. hard at work on *Village that Voted*') to show that his memory may have been unreliable. It was finished on 8 June 1914. *KJ* (XLVI, September 1979) reports a Flat-Earth Society founded in 1888 as still flourishing in California in 1979. This is one of the best of Kipling's farcical tales of punitive practical joking.

VORTEX, THE. *Scribner's Magazine*, August 1914; *A Diversity of Creatures* (1917). The normal life of an English village is suddenly thrown into disarray when several swarms of bees are released as a result of a minor collision between a car and a bicycle. There is the usual orgy of uncontrollable mirth ('that mirth which is more truly labour than any prayer'); and there is also a punitive element, since the pompous bore Lingnam is physically humiliated by being obliged first to take refuge in a pond, then to dress in wildly unsuitable clothes.

WALKING DELEGATE, A. *Century Magazine*, December 1894; *The Day's Work* (1898). Set in Vermont, this fantasy describes how a horse from Kansas tries in vain to stir up rebellion among the other horses by persuading them of their right to freedom and of the tyranny of their human masters. A reviewer in *Macmillan's Magazine* noted that the allegory expressed 'Kipling's profound antipathy to Socialism, and . . . profound belief in "the day's work" ', but dismissed the story as 'nonsense'. This is Kipling's only story with a Vermont setting; Angus Wilson notes that 'in the atmosphere of the Vermont countryside life was essentially horsey', and that much of Kipling's time outdoors there was spent with horses. Wilson finds the political satire, directed at American labour politics, 'superficial, though vehemently felt'.

WANDERING JEW, THE. *Civil & Military Gazette*, 4 April 1889; *Life's Handicap* (1891). This study of a rich man's monomania tells how John Hay, on learning that 'If you go once round the world in an easterly direction, you gain one day', obsessively circumnavigates the globe in order to prolong his life. At last a doctor persuades him that he would do better to be suspended from the ceiling of a room, letting the earth 'swing free beneath him' and thus gaining 'a day in a day . . . the equal of the undying sun'. Hay follows his advice and sits, 'an old and worn man . . . a stop-watch in his hand, racing against eternity'. The story's central idea is ingenious and even powerful, and it hardly deserves the *Athenaeum*'s coupling of it with 'The Lang Men o' Larut' as 'tawdry trifles'.

WATCHES OF THE NIGHT. *Civil & Military Gazette*, 25 March
1887; *Plain Tales from the Hills* (1888). A disagreeable and
narrowly religious woman, wife of a colonel, becomes convinced by circumstantial evidence that bears no relation to the
truth that her husband is being unfaithful to her. The delusion
is fostered by 'a frivolous lady', Mrs Larkyn, and the colonel
and his lady continue to live in misery. 'What begins as
potential farce becomes a savage portrait of puritanical distrust
in the process of destroying itself' (Cornell).

WAYSIDE COMEDY, A. *The Week's News*, 21 January 1888; *Under
the Deodars* (1888). Five English inhabitants of a lonely hill-
station play out a drama of marital infidelity, jealousy,
heartlessness and complacent ignorance, narrated with a
controlled cynicism and an irony that anticipate the mode of
Somerset Maugham. Though most of the characters end up
feeling contempt, if not hatred, for each other, they continue to
go through the motions of an amicable social life: 'But of course,
as the Major says, "in a little Station we must all be friendly".'
The presentation of sexual immorality and its emotional effects
is, for the date, very striking. E. B. Adams has discussed this
story in *English Literature in Transition*, III (1968).

WEE WILLIE WINKIE. *The Week's News*, 28 January 1888; *Wee
Willie Winkie* (1888). A six-year-old, son of the Colonel, goes to
the rescue of a young lady who has fallen among hostile natives,
and thus 'enters into his manhood'. Even Gosse felt that
Kipling had been 'led away by sentiment and a false ideal'; and
the modern reader is likely to find the tale embarrassing in its
attitudes and irritating in its presentation (of, for example,
childish speech-defects). Carrington suggests that this story
and 'His Majesty the King' belong to a genre once popular but
now totally out of fashion – the kind of fiction dealing with the
doings of 'angel-children whose innocent pranks reconcile
quarrelling lovers and unite broken families' – and reminds us
that they belong to the same decade as Mrs Frances Hodgson
Burnett's *Little Lord Fauntleroy* (1886). J. I. M. Stewart concurs
in finding both stories 'thickly sentimental', and comments:
'Kipling was to write with genius for children, not invariably
with genius about them'. For more successful attempts, see
'Tods' Amendment' and the autobiographical 'Baa Baa, Black
Sheep'; also 'The Story of Muhammad Din' as an example of
sentimentality avoided.

WILLIAM THE CONQUEROR. *The Gentlewoman*, December 1895 and January 1896 (and simultaneously in *The Ladies' Home Journal*); *The Day's Work* (1898). Contemporary reviewers waxed enthusiastic about this two-part story of Miss Martyn, a tomboyish girl nicknamed William the Conqueror, who insists on accompanying her brother when he is sent to deal with an emergency caused by a famine in South India. She falls in love with his colleague Scott, an energetic man of action, and they become engaged. The story was written in the spring of 1895. The heroine is said to have been based on Mrs Edmonia Hill (see 'A Kipling Who's Who'); more interestingly, she seems to exemplify a character-type prominent in the fiction of the mid-nineties, the independent, energetic young woman who seems determined to break loose from the Victorian stereotype of 'the angel in the house' (compare Sue Bridehead in Hardy's precisely contemporary novel *Jude the Obscure*). Angus Wilson suggests that the heroine is a tribute to 'the intrepid, easy-going, boyish, American girls [Kipling] so much admired' as well as to Carrie Kipling's qualities.

WIRELESS. *Scribner's Magazine*, August 1902; *Traffics and Discoveries* (1904). A consumptive chemist's assistant in an English seaside town falls into a trance-like state under the influence of drugs and composes fragments of poems by Keats (whom he has never read). His situation in many respects parallels that presented in Keats's 'The Eve of St Agnes', and he himself is 'a deliberately coarsened and inaccurate reproduction of Keats' (Tompkins). At the same time the chemist's nephew is operating a wireless set with which he is trying to pick up Morse messages. This is a story of extraordinary ingenuity (though, according to Gilbert, 'a little too clever to be wholly satisfying'), its powerful central idea not unworthy of the imagination of Jorge Luis Borges. Tompkins suggests that the story was 'generated by the excitement of finding in the new development of wireless telegraphy parallels to his conception of the mysterious nature of inspiration', but argues that the 'absorbed and rampant cleverness of the working-out over-stimulates the reader's detective sense and also deflects it from the centre of the story'. Amis shares this view: 'The reader's attention is directed more to the skilful counterpointing of its two themes – communication in space by telegraphy and in time by some means or other – than to the pathos of the consumptive chemist's-assistant whose mind becomes attuned to that of Keats.' Carrington notes that 'radio techniques had engaged [Kipling's] attention since his cruise with the Channel Fleet in 1898, when the Navy was experimenting with Marconi's new devices'. For an earlier story on the theme of reincarnation (related but not, of course, identical to the theme of this story), see 'The Finest Story in the World'. Compare, too, Kipling's remark in 1918 to Rider Haggard concerning artistic creativity: 'We are only telephone wires' (*Rudyard Kipling to Rider Haggard: The Record of a Friendship* [1965], ed. M. Cohen, p. 100). As a schoolboy Kipling had parodied Keats, and the following is written in a copy of *Longer English Poems* that formerly belonged to him and is now in the Library of Congress (see *KJ*, xxxix, September 1936):

> The first day back, ay bitter cold it was
> And I tho' rugged and wrappered was acold.
> Like boiléd spinach was the playground grass,
> Yellow our boots, y-clogged with goosey mould,
> Malarious vapours over *Goosey* rolled.
> Stale bread, bad butter, filled our hungry maw,
> Damp were the sheets, huddled in frousy fold,
> Loud voicéd laughter shook the form room floor
> And pale and pinched boys peered down the corridor.

It is, of course, loosely based on the opening stanza of 'The Eve of St Agnes' and is in the same metrical form. *Goosey* is Goosey Pool in the neighbourhood of the United Services College.

WISH HOUSE, THE. *Maclean's Magazine*, 15 October 1924; *Hearst's International Magazine*, November 1924; *Nash's and Pall Mall Magazine*, December 1924; *Debits and Credits* (1926). Two elderly women meet in a Sussex village for an afternoon's chat: 'the two had been friends since childhood; but, of late, destiny had separated their meetings by long intervals'. As they talk over their past lives, one tells of her faithful but unrequited love for a man, and relates how she has taken upon herself, by supernatural means, the physical pain and suffering with which he was at various times afflicted. She has learned of the Wish House, an empty house in a London street, from a child who has herself been told of it by a gipsy girl: a visit to the Wish House enables one to take upon oneself the sufferings of another. Towards the end of the story, we learn that one old woman is suffering from cancer, the other going blind. It ends with their parting, evidently for the last time. This tender but unsentimental story is one of the few Kipling wrote entirely about women, and is a good example of the more sympathetic presentation of women, especially older women, in his later work. As Carrington aptly observes, the setting is, for a story of the supernatural, markedly original: 'The "Wish House" is no picturesque haunted grange but a dingy villa in a suburban street, infested by a shabby, wheezing, down-at-heel, fumbling elemental, the dregs of ghosthood.' Tompkins praises the story as 'a marvel of structure', and for Angus Wilson it is 'probably Kipling's most successful single story', successfully avoiding 'all Kipling's many hazards'. J. I. M. Stewart also speaks of it in superlatives, declaring that it establishes Kipling's claim as 'a supreme master' of the short story. It was begun early in 1924; for Kipling's relevant illness at the end of 1922 see under 'A Madonna of the Trenches', a slightly earlier story in which cancer also plays a part (as it again does in 'Dayspring Mishandled' and 'The Children of the Zodiac'). In an interesting passage in *Light on C. S. Lewis* (1965), p. 63, Neville Coghill writes, with reference to the Christian doctrine of co-inherence:

> This was a power which Lewis found himself later to possess, and which, he told me, he had been allowed to use to ease the suffering of his wife, a cancer victim. . . . 'You mean,' I said, 'that the pain left her, and that you felt it for her in your body?' 'Yes,' he said, 'in my legs. It was crippling. But it relieved hers.' [I owe this quotation to the *Reader's Guide*.]

WITH ANY AMAZEMENT. See 'The Story of the Gadsbys'.
WITH THE MAIN GUARD. *The Week's News*, 4 August 1888; *Soldiers Three* (1888). Mulvaney recalls an episode in which Irish troops successfully fought a band of Pathans. An enthusiastic reviewer in *Blackwood's* compared the description of fighting to 'Homer or Sir Walter [Scott]'.
WITH THE NIGHT MAIL. *McClure's Magazine*, November 1905; *Actions and Reactions* (1909). This science-fiction story recounts an Atlantic crossing by airship in the year 2000 and provides various glimpses of the future (war has been abolished in 1967 and nationalism has disappeared). Carrington praises the

prophetic quality of this Wellsian vision: 'Although a few ships were fitted with wireless telegraphy, there was no radio-telephony, no hint or suggestion of public broadcasting; but Kipling's air-liner moved through a world-wide network of radio services, supplying weather-forecasts, and allotting safety-levels and landing priorities, thirty years before anyone else had dreamed of "flying control".' There is, as Carrington nicely observes, 'a debauch of technical writing' as well as a collection of documents – official reports, correspondence, advertisements – skilfully concocted to lend verisimilitude. Arnold Bennett, however, was unimpressed, describing the story as 'a glittering essay in the sham-technical' in his unfavourable review of *Actions and Reactions* in *New Age* (4 November 1909). 'As Easy as A.B.C.' is a sequel to this story.

WITHOUT BENEFIT OF CLERGY. *Macmillan's Magazine*, June 1890; *Harper's Weekly*, 7 and 14 June 1890; *The Courting of Dinah Shadd* (1890); *Mine Own People* (1891); *Life's Handicap* (1891). John Holden, an English official, falls in love with Ameera, a sixteen-year-old girl, 'a Mussulman's daughter bought two years before from her mother'. He has established the two women in a house that he visits regularly and comes to regard as home, though naturally his compatriots know nothing of this secret life and regard him as unattached. When the story opens, Ameera is expecting his child; he returns from a short absence on duty to find that a son has been born and, despite his fears, that Ameera is well. The child is adored by both of them, begins to walk and talk, but then dies of 'the seasonal autumn fever . . . as many things are taken away in India – suddenly and without warning'. Though their grief is profound, their love for each other is undiminished. Then a cholera epidemic breaks out: 'The English sent their wives away to the hills', and Holden is told 'You're a lucky chap. You haven't got a wife to send out of harm's way.' He tries to persuade Ameera to go, but she insists on remaining near him, falls ill, and dies in his arms. Her mother removes the furniture from the house which, battered by the rains, soon looks as if it 'had been untenanted for thirty years instead of three days'. The landlord announces that he will have it pulled down and that a road will be made across the site, 'so that no man may say where this house stood'. Gosse praised this story as 'by far the most tender page which Mr Kipling has written'. There is a long discussion of it by Gilbert, who makes a curious error in referring to the 'marriage' of the couple: the title, apart from other evidence, makes it clear that the union is irregular, and Holden's consciousness of this produces a feeling of guilt that helps to explain his sense of vulnerability – a crucial element in the story. Jeffrey Meyers (*KJ*, xxxvi, December 1969) notes that the 'destruction of love between English and Indian' is also to be found in several of Kipling's earlier stories, including 'Lisbeth' and 'Beyond the Pale', though these are 'more didactic and less successful'. Meyers regards 'Without Benefit of Clergy' as 'one of Kipling's best', though at the same time 'seriously flawed': the intrusion of the Member for Lower Tooting is 'aesthetically unsound', and the mother's cruelty and rapacity 'entirely gratuitous'; moreover, Kipling attempts to express strong emotion in 'banal and unconvincing physiological terms'. The Kipling Papers include a script for a silent film based on this story, but it seems never to have been made.

WOMAN IN HIS LIFE, THE. *McCall's Magazine*, September 1928; *London Magazine*, Christmas Number, 1928; *Limits and Renewals* (1932). A young man who has served as a sapper in the war builds up a successful post-war business but suffers a break-down through overwork. He recovers through the acquisition of a dog at the suggestion of his ex-batman (Kipling himself had kept Aberdeen terriers, the breed in the story). When the dog becomes trapped in a badger set he has to overcome his traumatic memories of the trenches in order to rescue her. Bodelsen cites this as an example of Kipling's use of significant repetition of words and phrases, which he sees as one species of 'pointers' supplied by Kipling to assist the reader in interpret-ing the story. Bodelsen notes that the curious phrase 'repetition work' is used 'three times in entirely different connections' early in the story, and suggests plausibly that it 'helps to prepare the way for the realization that Marden's victory of the repressed fears behind his trauma is achieved by re-enacting ('repeating') the experience under the Messines Ridge from which it originated'. For other examples of this device, see 'The Dog Hervey' and 'They'.

WORLD WITHOUT, THE. See 'The Story of the Gadsbys'.

WRESSLEY OF THE FOREIGN OFFICE. *Civil & Military Gazette*, 20 May 1887; *Plain Tales from the Hills* (1888). An official self-importantly devoted to his work falls in love with a shallow-minded girl. Idealistically believing that 'the best work of a man's career should be laid reverently at [the] feet' of the woman he loves (a notion derived from Ruskin's *Sesame and Lilies*), he writes a learned book on Indian history and presents it to her. He is shattered – 'smashed . . . by this one frivolous little girl' – when she totally fails to appreciate it, and he thereupon destroys the printed copies, becomes an embittered man, and never does anything so good again. According to Birkenhead, the girl, Tillie Venner (the name is perhaps intended to suggest 'veneer'), is based on Florence Garrard. This is one of several early stories in which a woman is seen as a threat to a man's work: see, for instance, 'The Story of the Gadsbys' for a more fully developed treatment of the same theme.

YOKED WITH AN UNBELIEVER. *Civil & Military Gazette*, 7 December 1886; *Plain Tales from the Hills* (1888). Phil Garron is a ne'er-do-well sent out to India to work on a tea plantation. He leaves behind Agnes, who loves him, but she is soon persuaded by her parents to marry a more eligible suitor. Phil has thought little of Agnes after quitting her; but news of the marriage prompts him to write, declaring his eternal loyalty. Soon he marries a native girl and settles down happily. When Agnes' husband dies after three years of marriage, she, an incurable romantic, goes to find Phil in order to offer him herself and her fortune, but she finds him married. Thus a man 'who really is not worth thinking of twice' is loved by two women.

.007. *Scribner's Magazine*, August 1897; *The Day's Work* (1898). This is the story of a new railway engine, its conversation with other engines, and its admission to the Amalgamated Brotherhood of Locomotives. Contemporary reviewers complained, not without reason, of being bewildered by Kipling's use of technical jargon; compare in this respect 'The Devil and the Deep Sea' and, as an example of animistic fantasy and Kipling's enthusiasm for machines, 'The Ship that Found Herself'.

The Novels

THE LIGHT THAT FAILED

When Kipling arrived in London towards the end of 1889, he had already begun to make a name as a writer of vivid and original tales, sketches and verses, but he had not yet taken up the challenge of the full-length novel. Dickens had been dead for nearly twenty years, and no obvious successor had arisen to fill his place. Thackeray, George Eliot, Trollope and Reade were all dead; neither Meredith nor Hardy had the prodigious popular appeal of a Dickens. But Kipling possessed in generous measure the Dickensian vitality, fertility and self-assurance; and his claim to the vacant throne was taken seriously by some (p. xii). It was now clearly up to him to show his paces in the larger, more demanding field of a full-length work of fiction. *The Light that Failed* represents his first attempt to meet this demand.

Like much of his work, the novel has a complex bibliographical history. It – or a version of it – seems to have been written in 1890, and before the end of the year it had been published in New York as No. 25 in Lovell's Westminster Series. In January 1891 it reappeared in *Lippincott's Monthly Magazine* (Philadelphia). This version contained twelve chapters, was considerably shorter than the one that later became widely available, and ended happily with the engagement of the hero and heroine. As Carrington notes, 'the author allowed Lippincott's a good run with the magazine version before releasing the book in normal form to the English trade'. When, in March 1891, Macmillan published the first English edition, it was a substantially longer book than the one that had filled fewer than a hundred pages of the American magazine: it now contained fifteen chapters, and an unhappy ending was substituted. (Professor Tompkins notes that

141

the latter half of Chapter 6 as well as Chapters 7 and 8 of the standard edition appeared for the first time.)

In the preface that was also added at this time, Kipling makes the puzzling statement that the new version was 'as it was originally conceived by the Writer'. Why his original conception should have been modified and then returned to is unclear: there is no evidence of the kind of pressure that had, for example, led Dickens to change the ending of *Great Expectations* or Hardy that of *The Return of the Native*. The later version is about one-third as long again as the version first published; and if in fact this longer version was the one originally written it may have been *too* long for the magazine – though 'originally conceived' does not mean the same as 'originally written', and in any case this explanation does not account for the changed ending. The text was subjected to further revisions for editions published in 1897 and 1899. A dramatic version was successfully produced in 1903, and the book has several times been filmed.

Like many first novels, *The Light that Failed* seems to have incorporated ideas derived from literary models as well as a large dose of autobiography. In *Something of Myself* Kipling claims (perhaps as a red herring) to have been influenced by the Abbé Prévost's *Manon Lescaut* (1731), the story of a young man corrupted by his love for an unworthy woman. As a schoolboy visiting the Paris Exhibition with his father, Kipling had seen a picture of the death of Manon which he 'never forgot'; a few years later he had read the novel; and his claim, or suggestion, was that *The Light that Failed* was 'a sort of inverted, metagrobolised phantasmagoria based on *Manon*'. Carrington, however, has very persuasively demonstrated the influence of an English model, Mrs Browning's once-popular verse-novel *Aurora Leigh* (1856), which also provided Kipling with a title. Several features, including the hero's blindness and the heroine's role as artist, are shared by Kipling's novel and Mrs Browning's long poem but not by the French work. Of the autobiographical elements, the most important is derived from the revival of Kipling's feelings for his lost love Florence Garrard (see 'A Kipling Who's Who'). He had run into her in London in February 1890, and at the beginning of May had visited her in Paris, where she was living an artist's life. Kipling gained nothing but heartache from this brief renewal of their relationship, and according to Carrington the novel 'came off his pen red-hot; he lived it as he wrote it'. J. I. M. Stewart has described the book as 'a fantasy of propitiatory self-punishment'.

This painful experience must lie behind the view of woman embodied in the book, a view amounting to misogyny and including a marked hostility to feminist aspirations. Carrington goes so far as to describe it as 'an anti-feminist tract'; in even stronger terms Angus Wilson deplores its 'blind, self-flattering misogyny'; and long ago Max Beerbohm drew attention to what he saw as Kipling's 'cheap cynicism about the female sex'. Maisie is a strikingly early example of what came to be called 'the new woman': she predates by several years, for example, both the heroine of Grant Allen's *succès de scandale The Woman Who Did* (1895) and Sue Bridehead in Hardy's *Jude the Obscure* (1895). The subject was intensely topical: Ibsen's *A Doll's House* had been produced in England in 1889, and at the beginning of 1890 Sir Walter Besant, who later in the year was to support Kipling's candidacy for membership of the Savile Club, had published an article 'The Doll's House – and After' in the *English Illustrated Magazine*. Maisie's feminism, therefore, reflects Kipling's awareness of current issues. But, as the phrases quoted from Carrington, Wilson and Beerbohm indicate, it was far from being endorsed by the narrator. The love of a woman is depicted as a distraction from the work that is the real business of life – work that a woman is incapable of valuing properly. As the narrator, anticipating the manner of Somerset Maugham, comments in Chapter 14:

A woman will forgive the man who has ruined her life's work so long as he gives her love: a man may forgive those who ruin the love of his life, but he will never forgive the destruction of his work.

In contrast to the predatory and destructive relationship offered by a woman, Kipling sets up a world of masculine chumminess and loyalty that at times seems little more than a version of the simple delights of public school life:

Dick fell upon eggs and bacon and gorged till he could gorge no more. Torpenhow handed him a filled pipe, and he smoked as men smoke who for three weeks have been deprived of good tobacco. (Chapter 3)

And again: 'Dick went whistling to his chambers with a strong yearning for some man-talk and tobacco after his first experience of an entire day spent in the society of a woman.' For 'chambers' read 'study', and we are not far from the world of *Stalky and Co.*, with its similar celebration of what are seen as the distinctively masculine pleasures. To be fair, however, the relationship of Dick and Torpenhow goes beyond this, based as it is not on mere congeniality but on shared experience of work: as Kipling puts it in Chapter 5, with somewhat more intensity than in the previous quotations, 'Torpenhow . . . looked at Dick with his eyes full of the austere love that springs up between men who have tugged at the same oar together and are yoked by custom and use and the intimacies of toil.' Kipling's commitment to the gospel of work and his prizing of 'the intimacies of toil' – to be enunciated in many short stories set in diverse circumstances – is already strong thus early in his career, and is indeed evident even earlier, in *Plain Tales from the Hills* and *The Story of the Gadsbys*.

The melodrama and sentimentality of *The Light that Failed* have not caused it to find favour with some modern critics, while its misogyny, as noted above, has aroused stronger disapproval. Angus Wilson judges it 'a novel that would be very distasteful if it were not absurd'. J. M. S. Tompkins, however, though conceding that some scenes display 'a lack of emotional reserve', accords the book a full and sympathetic discussion. It has also been defended more recently by Kingsley Amis, who finds it 'undervalued' and notes its 'curious knack of staying in print'. Among Kipling's contemporaries, Henry James anticipated many later verdicts in finding it 'the most youthfully infirm of his productions (in spite of great "life"), much wanting in composition and in narrative and explicative, or even implicative, art' (it should be added that James based this judgement, communicated to Stevenson in a letter of 12 January 1891, on a reading of the shorter *Lippincott's* version). Andrew Lang found it inferior to the short stories Kipling had already published: 'The central interest is not so powerful, the characters are not so sympathetic, as are the interest and the characters of his short pieces'; and J. M. Barrie, also writing in 1891, found it seriously defective ('his boy and girl . . . are a man and woman playing in vain at being children'; 'Maisie, the heroine, is utterly uninteresting, which is the one thing a heroine may not be'), but concluded that Kipling had 'produced a real novel, though not a great one'. Lionel Johnson deplored the happy ending as 'impossible, upon the stated premises', and found the substituted version 'finely and desperately logical'.

No one seems to have seen it as offering grounds for supposing that Kipling was capable of becoming a great novelist, though Barrie comes nearest ('Here is proof that there are latent capabilities in him which may develop, and show him by-and-by grown out of knowledge'). Perhaps the damaging factor was that Kipling stood in this novel too close to his experience to transform it into a work of fiction in which incident and dialogue, feeling and tone, came fully under control: the suffering was too recent, the attitudes and emotions insufficiently distanced, and to have 'lived it as he wrote it' was ultimately a source not of power but of weakness. To the student of Kipling it remains interesting as exhibiting, albeit in a markedly and sometimes painfully crude form, preoccupations that in his more mature work he was to be more successful in bringing under artistic control.

THE NAULAHKA

This novel, the joint work of Kipling and his friend Wolcott Balestier, is subtitled 'A Story of West and East'. It was serialized in the *Century Magazine* from November 1891 to July 1892, Balestier's sudden death occurring shortly after serialization began (5 December 1891). Volume publication in London and New York followed in 1892. The title refers to a necklace, and is more properly spelt *Naulakha*; Kipling later adopted the name (and the correct spelling) for his home in Vermont.

The Naulahka did not prove, any more than *The Light that Failed* had done a year or so earlier, that Kipling was capable of writing a great novel, or even a very good one. It is an exercise in a specialized genre, that of the novel of adventure. As some of Kipling's contemporaries recognized, however, it is by no means a failure. J. H. Millar, writing in *Blackwood's* in 1898, said that it was 'as thrilling as *Treasure Island*' and that 'the description of life at a Rajput King's Court . . . is worth countless blue-books and innumerable tracts'. (Stevenson's novel earlier in the decade, together with the work of such contemporaries as Rider Haggard, had popularized the adventure tale with an exotic setting.) More recently, Kingsley Amis has found it 'by no means a bad book', and Angus Wilson has gone further and deemed it 'excellent reading'.

The exact nature of the collaboration is unclear. Birkenhead's statement that 'Balestier was writing the American scenes, Kipling the Indian' is misleading; if this were the case, it would have been a very unequal partnership, since – in spite of the subtitle – only the first four chapters are set in America. Balestier, who certainly wrote these, must also have had a large hand in the Indian chapters, though he no doubt relied a good deal on Kipling's notes for local detail, which is abundant and precise. Work on the book seems to have been begun in the summer of 1890: on 12 July Balestier wrote to William Dean Howells that he had 'been seeing even more of Kipling with whom I am writing a story in collaboration. The scene is to be partly Western American (W. B.) and partly Indian (R. K.)'. This does indeed sound as though the original notion involved a simple division of labour, with the American element envisaged as considerably more prominent than it eventually became. As it turned out, after the hero leaves Colorado at the end of the fourth chapter, there are frequent reminders of his distant home but the rest of the scene is laid in India and his return is not depicted. On 18 February 1891 Balestier wrote to Howells: 'Kipling and I have been wading deep into our story lately, and have written rather more than two thirds of it. It begins in the West, where I have a free hand for several chapters. Then we lock arms and march upon India.' In August Kipling set off to sail round the world, and never saw Balestier again; it may be that the book was nearly finished by that time, though the final instalment seems to have been still unwritten when Balestier died in December.

As Carrington points out, the characterization strongly recalls that of *The Light that Failed*: Nicholas Tarvin is 'Dick Heldar with an American accent', and Kate Sheriff 'a more submissive, more alluring Maisie' (though Kate's bump of submissiveness is surely, until the very end, very small). Both Tarvin and Kate are, in their quite different ways, idealists: he wants to put the small Colorado town of Topaz on the map by bringing the railway to it (and there is genuine disinterestedness – the urge to create a flourishing community in the new West – mingled with his political and financial ambitions); she has been moved by learning of the plight of Indian women, and trains as a nurse in order to bring to them the blessings of enlightened Western medical knowledge. (Carrington surely errs in stating that Tarvin wants to get his hands on the celebrated jewel 'as an act of bravado with which to impress a woman in his native town': his overriding preoccupation is with the future greatness of the town, itself appropriately named after a jewel.) Tarvin, who wants to marry Kate, is impatient with her yearnings and exasperated that she will not accept the conventional role of home-maker and decorative appendage to his own brilliant career; the novel is thus, in one of its aspects and to a limited extent, a treatment of what the decade came to call 'the woman question'. (For further comments on this point, see p. 143.) Kate is one of those strong-willed, short-haired heroines who chafes at the limitations of women's role – a type that was to become familiar in English fiction. In Chapter 18 she tells Tarvin:

> Marriage means that – to be absorbed into another's life: to live your own, not as your own but another's. It is a good life. It's a woman's life. I can like it; I can believe in it. But I can't see myself in it. A woman gives the whole of herself in marriage – in all happy marriages. I haven't the whole of myself to give.

As this quotation makes clear, Kate's feminism is of a distinctly limited kind: she argues not for her sex, on whose behalf she indeed endorses the traditional restrictions, but for herself as a special case. (There are moments when she recalls the Dorothea of *Middlemarch*.)

The effect of the plot-manipulation is to show that Kate's longing to work wonders single-handed in India is an impossible dream: defeated by thousands of years of tradition and superstition, she retreats at the end of the novel into acquiescence and marriage, and acknowledges the error of her former convictions: 'she realized nothing more than a woman's complete contentment with the fact that there was a man in the world to do things for her.' The novel thus turns out to be anti-feminist in its main thrust. In a passage at the end of Chapter 20, an Indian queen tells Kate that she cannot help other women because she knows nothing of what they feel; in other words, she needs to become a wife and mother before she can begin to be useful or respected as a nurse. At the end of the book it is hinted, rather unfairly, that she will feel 'remorse' for her earlier errors.

But if Kate has to abandon her ideals as unworkable in the real world, Tarvin too has to make adjustments. He is a rather ironically observed hero. His energy and resourcefulness (if Kate aspires to be a New Woman, Tarvin is the New Man of the newly opened West) make him not only a pioneer *par excellence* but a natural leader, and he is clearly destined to become governor of his state. But he is in many respects naive, and he learns a good deal in the course of the story; in winning Kate he is obliged to abandon some of his fiercely held ideas and values. Soon after his arrival in India, his jaunty self-confidence receives a nasty jolt when it comes home to him that, while he can succeed in impressing the Colorado voters, he simply does not understand Indians: 'He began to feel as if he should have to go back and learn his ABC's over again.' The Naulahka is a necklace of legendary beauty and value, and he promises to obtain it for the empty-headed wife of a railway president; in return she will use her influence on her husband to bring the coveted railway to Topaz. His adventures, therefore, are a version of the traditional quest; but his Holy Grail is an object required to satisfy a woman's vanity, and to make Tarvin the hero of his community and thus advance his political career. He obtains the necklace, but returns it, and is certainly a better and a wiser man at the end of the story.

The real strength of the book, however, lies not in its characterization, which is distinctly thin, nor in the working out of its themes, which seems somewhat confused, but in its presentation of the two backgrounds: on a small scale, the American frontier town with its emerging social identity, and much more richly and fully the Indian scene. The plot-contrivances are sometimes far-fetched (it is a remarkable major coincidence that the necklace should be available in precisely that part of the sub-continent to which Kate has undertaken to go), but they are at least the occasion for some authentic and vividly detailed evocations of the sights, sounds and smells of India that must have come from Kipling's notebook if not in every instance actually from his pen. Tarvin, like Kipling, has a 'ceaseless and fruitful curiosity about all new things', and it is largely through his eyes that we see the exotic world. In Chapter 12 he sets out on a 'strange ride' that, as Carrington has shown, is based on one of Kipling's own journalistic exploits when he rode thirty miles across country by night in order to send off his copy in advance of his rivals. Similarly based on Kipling's own experience is Tarvin's exploration of the ruined city of Gunnaur. In these scenes the use of telling detail is often masterly: the smell of 'the acrid juice of bruised camel-thorn beneath his horse's hoofs'; the 'rustle of quills' and the 'evil stench' as a porcupine crosses his path; the moonlit fields 'silver-white with the opium poppy, or dark with sugar-cane'. Later, when Tarvin visits a Hindu temple, he hears 'a soft rustle and scratching of nesting bats'. It is in these passages, not in the often stagey dialogue – strongly reminiscent at times, like some of the hero's hair's-breadth escapes, of the *Boys' Own Paper* ('Your life isn't worth an hour's purchase here') – that are to be found the freshest portions of this novel by two young men.

Finally, and surely from Kipling's hand, one may quote a passage from Chapter 14 that catches with economical poignancy the expatriate experience from the woman's point of view – as it might have been that of Kipling's own mother. When Tarvin meets an agent's wife, 'belonging to one of those families which from the earliest days of the East India Company have administered the fortunes of India', he finds that she is totally devoid of interest in the legendary necklace:

> No; she knew nothing of the Naulahka. Her thoughts were bounded by the thought of going home in the spring. Home for her meant a little house near Surbiton, close to the Crystal Palace, where her three-year-old boy was waiting for her; and the interests of the other English men and women seemed equally remote from Rajputana. . . . It was only inferentially that Tarvin could gather that they had spent the greater part of their working lives within the limits of the country. They talked as gipsies might talk by the roadside a little before the horses are put into the caravan. The ways were hot, they implied, and very dusty; and they hoped one day to be able to rest. The wedding was only one more weary incident on the line of march, and they devoutly wished it over. One of them even envied Tarvin for coming to the State with his fresh eye and his lively belief in the possibility of getting something out of the land beside a harvest of regrets.

CAPTAINS COURAGEOUS

The title of this short novel is taken from an old ballad, 'Mary Ambree', which is to be found in Percy's *Reliques of Ancient English*

Poetry and other collections; the opening line of the ballad is
'When captaines couragious, whom death cold not daunte'. The
novel is subtitled 'A Story of the Grand Banks', and the original
title was 'Harvey Cheyne – Banker'. The American edition was
dedicated to Dr Conland (see 'A Kipling Who's Who'); Kipling
also presented him with the manuscript, which is now in the
Pierpont Morgan Library, New York.

The novel was written in 1896. Mrs Kipling's diary for 11
February of that year notes: 'Captains C. taking shape'; and on 19
May she records: 'Rud leaves for Gloucester with Conland'
(Gloucester, Massachusetts, was still at that time an important
centre of the fishing industry). It was serialized in *McClure's
Magazine* from November 1896 to March 1897, and in *Pearson's
Magazine* from December 1896 to April 1897; and was published
in volume form in London and New York in 1897. There is a
modern edition by J. Ferguson (New York, 1959). Carrington
notes that the story is 'closely modelled' upon Pierre Loti's *Pêcheurs
d'Islande* (1886).

J. I. M. Stewart has pointed out that *Captains Courageous* is
Kipling's 'only book in which the characters and setting are
wholly American' and is 'the most substantial direct product of
the Vermont period'. The central character is the indulged and
pasty-faced son of a millionaire father and a doting mother (this
unattractive boy is said to be based on a spoilt American child
encountered by Kipling on a voyage from Calcutta to San
Francisco in 1889). He is washed overboard from an Atlantic liner
en route for Europe, and picked up by a fishing-boat, where he
works, of necessity, as one of the crew and is transformed thereby
into a healthy, decent youth before being restored to his family.
The slight story thus traces his initiation into manhood and his
conversion to the gospel of work. The book has also been seen as
offering a diagnosis of the moral life of America; the traditional
values of hard work, energy and enterprise are represented in
different ways by the cod fishermen and the railroad millionaire,
and the corrupting self-indulgence that Kipling saw emerging in
American society is represented by the boy's mother and by
Harvey himself at the beginning of the story.

Carrington's observation that it is 'an enlarged short story' is
just. Paradoxically, indeed, the story is incomparably simpler and
clearer in outline, less ambitious and less subtle, than a story such
as 'Mrs Bathurst'. Kipling was fond of the book; its writing was a

labour of love at a time when politics and family troubles were causing him great anxiety. The book provides evidence of his extraordinary capacity for absorbing detailed knowledge of specialized activities and for presenting them with enormous relish and loving detail: see, for example, the vigorous description of gutting cod in Chapter 2, with its admiration for 'the miraculous dexterity of it all'. (A dissenting view is that of Angus Wilson, who finds the technicalities in this case too much of a good thing.) Significantly, again, in Chapter 9, after Harvey has been rather perfunctorily reunited with his parents (though he is an only child, and has been supposed dead), there follow several pages of fascinated discussion of the logistics of a private railway carriage crossing the continent.

As in Kipling's other tales of work, the cod-fishermen constitute a 'caste' (the word is used at the beginning of Chapter 5, where the sores on the boy's arm caused by the wet jersey and oilskins cutting into his flesh are seen as 'the mark of the caste that claimed him'); they enjoy the exclusivity of a male club or a religious sect, and it comes as no surprise to find at the end of the same chapter that one of the sailors is a freemason. As in Conrad's tales, the world of the ship is its own self-sufficient society and an appropriate scene for the boy's education in the truest sense of the word – the experiences that qualify him for admission to the world of men.

KIM

Kim took considerably longer to grow than most of Kipling's books: according to J. I. M. Stewart, 'there was nothing which gave him more trouble'. Its origins belong to the period of residence in Vermont, and it is 'said to have been first conceived during a visit of Lockwood Kipling's to Naulakha' (Hilton Brown). It perhaps grew out of the early abandoned Anglo-Indian novel *Mother Maturin* (see p. 157), and Kim has also something in common with the Mowgli of the *Jungle Books*. But its deeper origins belong to Kipling's childhood and his earliest experiences of the sights, sounds and smells of India. It has been suggested, on the basis of internal evidence, that the dating of the action precedes by a generation or so the date of composition, and that Kim was born in 1865 and joined the Lama in 1878; if so, it may be significant that Kipling, who gave his own initial to his boy-hero, was himself born in 1865. The book is, among other things, an exploration of the writer's earliest memories, and Hilton Brown has called it '*the* nostalgic throwback of his career'.

The book was serialized in *McClure's Magazine* (December 1900 to October 1901) and almost simultaneously in *Cassell's Magazine* (January–November 1901), and appeared in book form in England and America in 1901. The New York edition includes ten illustrations by John Lockwood Kipling. For Kipling's own comments on the book, see *Something of Myself*, Chapter 5.

By general consent *Kim* is the best of Kipling's longer works of prose fiction and by any standards a masterpiece. There is less agreement on what kind of book it is and on what is its central theme. Kipling himself characterized it as 'nakedly picaresque and plotless', but even a careless reading suggests that it contains something more than a mere string of colourful incidents. J. I. M. Stewart considered that it ought to be seen primarily as 'a book for young people'. Edmund Wilson claimed that the book deals with 'the gradual dawning of [Kim's] consciousness that he is really a Sahib'. Rupert Croft-Cooke took the line that it is really two stories in one, and that one of them is greatly inferior to the other:

> But the Great Game follows them. It is made eventful, even exciting . . . but the secret service story is no better than John Buchan might have written and never ceases to be a tiresome distraction from the 'nakedly' – and magnificently – picaresque.

Charles Carrington probed somewhat deeper in stressing that Kim has to face a decision how to live:

> he must choose between contemplation and action. . . . Though it is not expressly stated, the reader is left with the assurance that Kim, like Mowgli and like the Brushwood Boy, will find reality in action, not in contemplation.

Edward Shanks stated the theme somewhat differently: 'it must be said that *Kim* is *about* the infinite and joyous variety of India for him who has the eyes to see it and the heart to rejoice in it.' This view is endorsed by Arnold Kettle: 'There is in fact a strong case for describing *Kim* as being essentially about India the subcontinent rather than about Kim the boy.'

A brief outline of the main action will indicate some of the book's main features. Kimball O'Hara, the son of an Irish Colour-Sergeant and a nursemaid in a Colonel's family (the mother's race and nationality are unspecified, but there are grounds for supposing she might have been a Eurasian), is an orphan who runs wild in the streets of Lahore. When we first see him he is seated astride an antique bronze gun in front of the Museum (Kipling's father was, of course, curator of the latter). He meets a Tibetan lama who has embarked on a quest for a river that will wash away sins, and the two set off on a pilgrimage to the Buddhist holy places of India. Since the priest is a kind of saintly innocent and the boy is precocious and knowing, the quasi-paternal and quasi-filial roles are to some extent reversed. The situation is traditionally picaresque in so far as the hero and a companion set forth on a journey and encounter numerous persons and adventures along the way.

They travel widely by railway and along the Grand Trunk Road, but when Kim encounters the Mavericks, his father's regiment, he falls into the clutches of the chaplains, who cause him to be sent to school (with the Lama's agreement and at his expense) in order to be turned into a sahib. During the school holidays, however, Kim escapes and returns to his old ways; he is taken up by British agents and trained for secret service work ('the Great Game'). In the latter part of the book he travels to the Himalayas with the Lama, who eventually finds the river he is seeking. His goal is therefore achieved, but Kim's position at the end of the story remains a little ambiguous.

As this summary shows, *Kim* presents a man's world and most of the major characters are male. Women appear fleetingly in minor roles, but at one point Kim reflects: 'How can a man follow the Way or the Great Game when he is so-always pestered by women?' (The narrator informs us that Kim 'thought in the vernacular' on this occasion, and we are bound to recall the young Rudyard Kipling thinking and talking in the vernacular in his early years.)

'The Way' and 'the Great Game' are the two antithetical sets of values – the life of contemplation versus the life of action, asceticism versus materialism – that confront Kim. In a sense both reach their climax towards the end of the novel, for not only

does the Lama find his river but Kim succeeds in obtaining vital
documents and delivering them to the authorities. When it comes
to the choice, however, Kim does not opt exclusively for either. As
Arnold Kettle says:

> Kim is a man in the world of men, neither more nor less. It is a
> real world, not an illusion (as the Lama's philosophy would
> have it), a world of Doing in which action is neither an
> irrelevance nor an end in itself but a necessary element in the
> relationship between men and nature, man and man. This is
> what Kim has come through to. . . . Kim has escaped from the
> false antithesis, the choice between action on the one hand and
> truth on the other, between an amoral materialism and an
> unworldly idealism. The new materialism to which he
> advances, and of which the emblem is his sense of identity with
> the earth and its processes, no longer excludes the human
> values encompassed in his relationships with the Lama.
> ('What is Kim?', in *The Morality of Art*, ed. D. W. Jefferson
> [1969] pp. 219–20.)

In other words, Kim opts for a synthesis or golden mean, avoiding
both fanaticism and a crass rejection of the spiritual life. His
'sense of identity with the earth and its processes' is a natural
outcome of the sustained picture of India's teeming landscapes
and townscapes that the novel has presented.

There is a large descriptive element in *Kim* but Kipling's scenes
are only occasionally presented as set-pieces; more often the
touches, while intensely vivid, are highly economical, as a few
quotations will suggest:

> [during a railway journey] Golden, rose, saffron, and pink, the
> morning mists smoked away across the flat green levels. All the
> rich Punjab lay out in the splendour of the keen sun. The lama
> flinched a little as the telegraph-posts swung by. . . .
>   They all unloosed their bundles and made their morning
> meal. Then the banker, the cultivator, and the soldier prepared
> their pipes and wrapped the compartment in choking, acrid
> smoke, spitting and coughing and enjoying themselves. The
> Sikh and the cultivator's wife chewed *pan*; the lama took snuff
> and told his beads, while Kim, cross-legged, smiled over the
> comfort of a full stomach.   (Ch. 2)

The lama squatted under the shade of a mango, whose shadow played checkerwise over his face; the soldier sat stiffly on the pony; and Kim, making sure that there were no snakes, lay down in the crotch of the twisted roots.

There was a drowsy buzz of small life in hot sunshine, a cooing of doves, and a sleepy drone of well-wheels across the fields. . . . (Ch. 3)

And truly the Grand Trunk Road is a wonderful spectacle. It runs straight, bearing without crowding India's traffic for fifteen hundred miles – such a river of life as nowhere else exists in the world. They looked at the green-arched, shade-flecked length of it, the white breadth speckled with slow-pacing folk; and the two-roomed police-station opposite. (Ch. 3)

For an example of more sustained description, see the account of the Great Trunk Road and its travellers in Chapter 4, beginning: 'They met a troop of long-haired, strong-scented Sansis with baskets of lizards and other unclean food on their backs, their lean dogs sniffing at their heel.'

After all, it is India that binds together the two main strands of the novel, for its restless, endlessly varied life is both the scene of adventure and 'the very Wheel itself, eating, drinking, trading, marrying, and quarrelling – all warmly alive' (Ch. 12) from which the holy man seeks escape. The India of *Kim* is not that of the early short stories – primarily, that is, the India of the sahibs and tourists – but the land of the Indian peoples themselves in all their diversity. As J. I. M. Stewart has said, 'At least to a Western reader, it is the Indian characters in the story who appear most real and, in a deep sense, most beloved.' When Kim is asked in Chapter 8 'And who are thy people, Friend of all the World?', he replies, 'This great and beautiful land.' Kipling, who was never to see India again, enshrined in the book his own love for the land to which his earliest memories belonged.

'Why did the author of the brilliant short stories never develop into an important novelist?' asked Edmund Wilson in 1941. The answer surely has to be the obvious one: that the gifts demanded of a writer of 'brilliant short stories' will not necessarily sustain the same writer through a full-length work of fiction. In his early stories, Kipling is indeed brilliant in contriving situations that present a crisis in one or more human lives: a crisis that may be comic, serious or tragic. But the characters who enact the drama are usually conceived and presented in the sketchiest terms: it is significant that most of Kipling's descriptive writing evokes places rather than people. Rarely do his characters develop, and this not because the form of the short story cannot accommodate development but because the matter holds little interest for him. Much of his work shows the strengths and the limitations of a journalist of genius: he is superb at catching the quality of a moment or an episode, but virtually a non-starter when it comes to tracing the slow evolution of a personality or a relationship. And it is after all the latter – to endow a character (in Henry James's phrase) with 'the high attributes of a Subject', and to describe (in George Eliot's phrase) 'the stealthy convergence of human lots' – that was seen in Kipling's time as the business of the novelist. The absorbing concern of the modern novel is with inwardness, and its techniques have been largely devoted to the task of conveying a sense of the inner life. But Kipling, fascinated by externals of every kind and every degree of significance, had little time for inwardness. That indifference did not vitiate his work as a writer of short stories (though he is significantly different even in this genre from, say, James Joyce or Katherine Mansfield); but it prevented him from becoming a novelist in the main realistic tradition of English fiction. In fact, with the exception of the strongly autobiographical *The Light that Failed*, he never even attempted to write a novel of this kind.

Some of Kipling's later stories are more ambitious and even constitute fragmentary novels (like 'Mrs Bathurst') or incredibly compressed novels-in-miniature (like 'The Gardener'). In such characters as Helen Turrell and Mary Postgate he succeeded in giving a sense not just of a passage of experience but of the quality of a whole life. But compression was an essential condition of high quality.

Miscellaneous Prose

Kipling was an enormously prolific writer, and the list of his minor writings is a very long one. Bibliographically speaking, the matter is complicated by his habit of reprinting and collecting (often with extensive revisions) work that had already appeared elsewhere, and by hundreds of 'pirated' editions of his work that led him to bring out authorized editions in very small numbers not intended for sale but simply in order to secure the copyright.

The following is only a brief selection of the more interesting titles. For further information, see the standard bibliography by J. McG. Stewart. *The New Cambridge Bibliography of English Literature*, vol. III, pp. 1024–6, has useful lists of 'Stories, Poems, and Speeches published separately' and 'Contributions to Books not reprinted elsewhere' (the Kipling entry is by R. L. Green). Appendix I of Louis L. Cornell's *Kipling in India* is a chronology of Kipling's writings until his departure from India in 1889 and includes many uncollected items. Appendix III of the same work discusses 'Kipling's Uncollected Newspaper Writings'.

MOTHER MATURIN

Kipling worked on this unfinished and unpublished novel during 1885 – that is, while he was living in Lahore and working for the *Civil & Military Gazette*. On 7 March he wrote in his diary that 'The idea of "Mother Maturin" dawned on me today'; and by the end of July he had written 237 foolscap pages (subsequently lost or destroyed). In a letter to his aunt Edith Macdonald he described it as 'an Anglo-Indian episode', and added:

It's not one bit nice or proper but it carries a grim sort of a moral with it and tries to deal with the unutterable horrors of lower class Eurasian and native life as they exist outside reports. . . . Trixie [his sister] says it's awfully horrid; Mother says it's nasty but powerful and I know it to be in large measure true. It is an unfailing delight to me.

According to Carrington, part of the material was salvaged for *Kim*. 'The Book of Mother Maturin' is mentioned in the story 'The Gate of a Hundred Sorrows'.

A FLEET IN BEING

Published in 1898 and subtitled 'Notes of Two Trips with the Channel Squadron', it reprints six articles published in the *Morning Post*, 5–11 November 1898.

FROM SEA TO SEA

Published in two volumes in New York (June 1899) and London (March 1900); the full title is *From Sea to Sea and other Sketches. Letters of Travel*. The volume contains a series of letters written during Kipling's journey from India to England in 1889 and for the most part originally published in *The Pioneer* and *The Pioneer Mail* (Allahabad) between 17 April 1889 and 2 April 1890. The letters were considerably abridged for reprinting, and several in the original series were omitted. Kipling's account of his visit to Mark Twain (No. 37 in the collection) was not one of the original series but was first published in the *New York Herald* (17 August 1890).

ABAFT THE FUNNEL

This title was originally given to a series of eight stories that appeared in the *Civil & Military Gazette* in 1889. In 1909 the title was used by an American publisher (Dodge & Co.) for an unauthorized collection containing four of the stories together with twenty-six others originally printed in various Indian newspapers and the poem 'In Partibus'. Kipling's American publisher, Doubleday, responded to this pirated edition by immediately issuing, at the irresistible price of nineteen cents, an almost identical edition of the same collection. The volume was not issued in England, but its contents were later included in the 'Sussex Edition'.

A SCHOOL HISTORY OF ENGLAND

Kipling was the co-author (with C. R. L. Fletcher) of this textbook, published in 1911. The final section, on the blessings of modern inventions, seems to show Kipling's hand.

WARTIME WRITINGS

The New Army in Training (1915) contains six articles reprinted with revisions from the *Daily Telegraph*.

France at War (1915) contains six articles reprinted from the *Daily Telegraph*. The American edition bears the title *France at War on the Frontier of Civilization*.

The Fringes of the Fleet (1915) contains six articles reprinted from the *Daily Telegraph*.

Tales of 'the Trade' (New York, 1916) contains three articles reprinted from *The Times*.

Destroyers at Jutland is the title of four pamphlets published in New York in 1916, containing articles that had already appeared in the *Daily Telegraph* and the *New York Times*.

The last three collections listed above were brought together in the volume *Sea Warfare* (1916); there were many revisions, and the poem 'The Neutral' was added.

The War in the Mountains is a series of five pamphlets published in New York in 1917 and reprinting five articles from the *Daily Telegraph*. They were immediately translated into Italian (Milan, 1917).

The Eyes of Asia (New York, 1918) reprints four articles from newspapers.

An aftermath of the war was *The Irish Guards in the Great War* (1923), a two-volume contribution to the history of the regiment in which John Kipling had served.

LETTERS OF TRAVEL

This volume, published in 1920, collects essays published in various British, American and Canadian periodicals.

LAND AND SEA TALES

Published in 1923; the English edition has the subtitle 'For Scouts and Guides', the American edition 'For Boys and Girls'. The volume brings together eleven stories, all previously published in various magazines, as well as a number of poems.

A BOOK OF WORDS

A volume containing thirty-one speeches, published in 1928.

THY SERVANT A DOG

A volume bearing this title appeared in 1930 and contained three stories, of which two had appeared earlier in *Cassell's Magazine*. An enlarged edition (1938) contains five stories.

SOUVENIRS OF FRANCE

Published in 1933, the volume reprints travel sketches that had already appeared in newspapers.

SOMETHING OF MYSELF

Kipling's uncompleted autobiographical sketch, serialized in various newspapers and published in volume form in 1937. Kipling wrote it in the closing years of his life, and the title hints at its discretion: as Carrington notes, 'it contains no mention of Flo Garrard or of Mrs Hill, of Wolcott or Beatty Balestier, no allusion to the deaths of Josephine and John Kipling. There are few dates and those not always accurate.' It remains, however, of great interest to the student of Kipling.

The Verse

Kipling was a prolific poet over an unusually long period. The most complete editions of his verse include seven or eight hundred items, and he published verse over a longer period than Hardy and over nearly as long a period as Yeats. When his first slim volume, *Schoolboy Lyrics*, appeared, Tennyson and Browning were still writing and Hardy and Yeats were unheard of as poets; and although his output dwindled in his later years, his last poems belong to the thirties – the age, that is, of Eliot and Auden (in the year in which Kipling dies, Auden's *Look, Stranger!*, Eliot's *Collected Poems 1909–35*, and Dylan Thomas's *Twenty-Five Poems* all appeared). His verse, then, cannot be regarded merely as a minor appendage of his major achievement in prose, but demands serious consideration both in its own right and in its relationship to the prose – the more so since, in his later years, Kipling came to integrate stories and poems much more closely, with the result that the meaning of a story cannot always be properly determined without taking into account the poem or poems that accompany it.

The most important of Kipling's collections of verse are the following (the dates given are of first publication, regardless of place; in many cases later editions were expanded to include additional poems):

Schoolboy Lyrics (1881) (private printing of fifty copies)
Echoes (1884) (32 of the poems are by Kipling, the rest by his
  sister)
Departmental Ditties and Other Verses (1886)
Barrack-Room Ballads and Other Verses (1892)
The Seven Seas (1896)
The Five Nations (1903)

161

Songs from Books (1912)
The Years Between (1919)

The most important collected editions are:

Collected Verse (New York, 1907; London, 1912)
Inclusive Edition (1919; originally in three volumes but in one
    volume from 1921; expanded editions appeared in 1927 and
    1933)
Definitive Edition (1940)
Sussex Edition, mainly in vols xxxii–xxxv (1938–9)
Burwash Edition (1941)

T. S. Eliot's famous and influential selection, *A Choice of
Kipling's Verse*, was first published in 1941; its preface was revised
and reprinted as 'In Praise of Kipling' and included in *On Poetry
and Poets* (1957). Charles Carrington has edited *The Complete
Barrack-Room Ballads of Rudyard Kipling* (1973).

Eliot's essay addresses the question: What kind of a poet is
Kipling? and the question is clearly a central one in relation to
both his achievements and his limitations. It will be noted that the
title of Eliot's selection refers not to 'poetry' but to 'verse', and this
looks at first glance like an admission of second-rateness (poets
write poetry, versifiers write verse, the latter term embracing such
effusions as those which are to be found on greetings cards and in
the 'In Memoriam' columns of local newspapers). But Eliot
quickly disabuses us of this assumption. Writing in the modernist
age, he recognizes that a defence of Kipling needs to be of a rather
unusual kind: 'We expect to have to defend a poet against the
charge of obscurity: we have to defend Kipling against the charge
of excessive lucidity.'

The eighteenth century, and even the nineteenth, would have
found it very odd that a writer should be charged with 'excessive
lucidity'; but Kipling's qualities were not those exemplified by the
most widely admired poets, or desiderated by the most influential
Anglo-American critics, of the thirties and forties – for paradox,
ambiguity, startling imagery, linguistic experiment, literary
allusiveness, subtlety and obliqueness, one may for the most part
search his verse in vain. No wonder Eliot felt obliged to treat him
as a special case:

It should be clear that when I contrast 'verse' with 'poetry' I am not, *in this context*, implying a value judgment. I do not mean, here, by verse, the work of a man who would write poetry if he could: I mean by it something which does what 'poetry' could not do.

In reviewing *The Years Between* more than twenty years earlier (the review is reprinted in *Kipling: The Critical Heritage*), Eliot had described Kipling as 'very nearly a great writer'. But Kipling's popularity was already waning in the post-war world, and we need to go back a full generation to 1890 in order to sense the impact of his early verse upon readers and critics.

Departmental Ditties had received a favourable but unenthusiastic review from Andrew Lang in *Longman's Magazine*, the first review of Kipling in a British periodical. Lang found the volume 'quaint and amusing', classified its contents as *vers de société*, and judged one poem ('Giffen's Debt') 'worthy of Bret Harte'. (The *Bombay Gazette* had earlier, and appropriately, invoked the names of W. M. Praed and Frederick Locker-Lampson, both respected practitioners of light verse.) A longer review by Sir William Hunter (*Academy*, 1 September 1888) observed that 'Although . . . Mr Kipling's stage is a narrow one, his players are very much alive.'

It was *Barrack-Room Ballads*, however, which aroused real enthusiasm – partly, no doubt, because its author had by the time of its publication already risen to fame on account of his short stories. Even before the volume appeared in 1892, individual poems had been printed in Henley's *Scots Observer* (later *National Observer*), beginning resoundingly with 'Danny Deever' on 22 February 1890, and had attracted widespread attention. Sir Arthur Quiller-Couch wrote that the collection contained verse 'for which "splendid" is the only term – so radiantly it glitters with incrustations of barbaric words' (*English Illustrated Magazine*, September 1893), and the comment suggests that English readers of the time were fascinated by Kipling's exoticism of style as well as subject-matter. Forty-three years later, the *Times Literary Supplement* in its obituary article on Kipling (25 January 1936) was to find little of value in the early verse (of *Departmental Ditties* the anonymous writer opines magisterially that 'these popular ballads, parodies, society verses, satires, clever and witty as they are, do not warrant the bestowal of the title of poet'), but to praise the later lyrics such as 'Cities and Thrones and Powers' (now canonized by inclusion in the *New Oxford Book of English Verse*) – the Georgian and English Kipling, that is, rather than the Victorian and Anglo-Indian Kipling. Eliot's selection four years later was to be more tolerant and eclectic, and to do justice to the best of the ballads, dramatic monologues and public poems as well as the lyrics.

Kipling's earliest surviving verses belong to his early teens, and the *Schoolboy Lyrics* contain poems of 1879–82. Very little of this material was included in the later collections, and one is hardly surprised at the mature Kipling's rejection of his juvenilia. (The final item of *Schoolboy Lyrics*, however, does appear in the Definitive Edition: this is 'Ave Imperatrix!', prompted by the attempt in March 1882 to assassinate Queen Victoria, and a curious anticipation by a boy of sixteen of the later public style.) The volume contains much skilful versifying, some clever parody, a comic rendering of the Devonshire dialect, and, in rather different vein, some disillusioned reflections on life with titles like 'Conventionality'. In short, these are the verses, serious and gay, that one would expect of a clever and precocious boy who had read a good deal of English poetry and was adept at hitting off, for serious or comic purposes, the styles of famous poets. 'The Jam-Pot (in the manner of Robert Browning)' indicates his early awareness of a poet who was to become a significant influence; and the note of indignant scorn in 'Reading the Will' recalls *Maud* and reminds us that around 1880 Tennyson was still a force to be reckoned with.

'Reading the Will' offers, indeed, hints of the kind of use of vivid detail that was soon to become a hallmark of Kipling's style:

> And scarcely the bell had ceased to toll
> Ere they crowded together over the cake,
>   Ferret-eyed women and keen-faced men, . . .
>   See that woman, her yellow teeth
> Pressing the lip's thin line of red;
>   Mark the struggle that lies beneath
> The outer surface of weepers and veils. . . .

But for the most part there is no personal voice, only clever ventriloquism, in *Schoolboy Lyrics*, and it would be unreasonable to expect to find anything else in the work of so young an author.

Echoes is a more specialized collection, consisting of parodies mainly of nineteenth-century poets from Wordsworth and Tennyson to Swinburne and Wilfred Blunt; and while engaged in poking fun at the idiosyncrasies of respected poets, Kipling can be seen to be in the process of finding his own manner. 'The Sudder Bazaar' contains touches that reappear in the subsequent stories, and the germs of many of the *Plain Tales from the Hills* can perhaps be detected in the rather startling set of 'Nursery Rhymes for Little Anglo-Indians':

> Sing a Song of Sixpence,
>   Purchased by our lives –
> Decent English gentlemen
>   Roasting with their wives
>
> In the plains of India,
>   Where like flies they die.
> Isn't that a wholesome risk
>   To get our living by?

And again:

> I had a little husband
>   Who gave me all his pay.
> I left him for Mussoorie,
>   A hundred miles away.
>
> I dragged my little husband's name
>   Through heaps of social mire,
> And joined him in October,
>   As good as you'd desire.

Even a parody of Christina Rossetti has an unexpected sharpness:

> Daffodils in English fields
>   And breezes in the clover;
> But here's a sun would strike you dead
>   Seven times over!

Some of the parodies in *Echoes* had played with the notion of English poets writing on Indian themes ('A.Vision of India' in the manner of Tennyson is another example). In *Departmental Ditties* the Indian point of view predominates; and although the poems originally appeared in Indian publications it is hard not to believe that Kipling had one eye fixed on an audience at home, for a part of his purpose seems to be to bring to the bosoms of his readers the truth about Anglo-Indian life in all its harshness. His characters in these anecdotal verses are for the most part Anglo-Indians, civilian and military, and official visitors; and some of the poems stress unsparingly the adverse conditions, climatic and otherwise, under which Englishmen lived and worked in India – conditions generally unappreciated by those at home who talked of the Empire in easy generalizations. Kipling is intent upon truth-telling; and his aim, while partly to amuse, is also, importantly, to instruct and even to rebuke.

His manner is that of what the nineteenth century liked to call *vers de société*: sophisticated, often witty light verse in the tradition of Hood, Calverley, Praed, Locker-Lampson and Gilbert (notably exemplified in our own time by John Betjeman). Like some of these poets, he favours long lines of fourteen or more syllables that carry the reader forward at a brisk pace, as in 'A Code of Morals':

Now Jones had left his new-wed bride to keep his house in order,
And hied away to the Hurrum Hills above the Afghan border,
To sit on a rock with a heliograph; but ere he left he taught
His wife the working of the Code that sets the miles at naught.

(The verse-form is that of Gilbert's well-known 'Etiquette'.) The language often has a vigorous audacity, as in the reflections of a man who had been driven into a 'main drain sewage-outfall' by a stampeding elephant:

'You may hold with surface-drainage, and the sun-for-
        garbage cure,
Till you've been a periwinkle shrinking coyly up a sewer.
I believe in well-flushed culverts. . . .
                        This is why the death-rate's small;
And, if you don't believe me, get *shikarred* yourself.
        That's all.'   ('Municipal')

Earlier Kipling had parodied Browning, but now he gleefully
exploits the colloquial, parenthetical, button-holing manner of
the *Dramatic Monologues*, as in 'Pagett, M.P.', one of the best of the
collection. The speaker is an old India hand, the subject a visiting
politician who, a self-appointed expert on India, is forced to
confront the realities of life in the sub-continent:

July was a trifle unhealthy – Pagett was ill with fear;
Called it the 'Cholera Morbus', hinted that life was dear.
He babbled of 'Eastern exile', and mentioned his home with tears;
But I hadn't seen *my* children for close upon seven years.

The jaunty dactyls and trochees suggest a gusto reminiscent, or
anticipatory, of Kipling's revenge-stories and punitive farces, and
one almost expects Pagett, M.P., to be debagged; but in the last
line of the stanza quoted, and in the final stanza of the poem, the
tone suddenly deepens, as it sometimes does at the end of a
Kipling story. The satire is not far from savage indignation, the
laughter not far from tears.

The article devoted to Kipling in *The Times* on 25 March 1890
(unsigned, but by T. H. Ward) notes that 'He is even now a very
young man, in spite of his seven or eight small volumes; in fact, we
believe he is not yet twenty-five' (the belief was quite correct).
Later in the article Ward comments that 'the volume called
Departmental Ditties, clever and bright as it is, is in no respect on the
same level as certain verses which have appeared with and
without his name during the present year in British periodicals'.
The 'certain verses' included the 'Barrack-Room Ballads', later
incorporated in the volume of that name; and Ward was right in
thinking that they represented a notable advance on anything
Kipling had done earlier in the medium of verse. The published
volume contains a large number of Kipling's most memorable
poems, and many of them are not least remarkable for a curious
and powerful ambiguity of tone. Such items as 'Shillin' a Day' and
'Gunga Din' were favourite recitation-pieces for so long that it is
easy to suppose that they are no more than colourful and vigorous,
if somewhat crude and brash, light verse, and that they owed their
huge popularity to a combination of exotic subject-matter, catchy
rhythms and comic Cockney dialect.

Actually Kipling's effects are often considerably more subtle.
In 'The Widow at Windsor', for example, the loyal tribute to the

Queen is undercut in two ways: first by the colloquial familiarity with which Victoria is referred to ('the Widow at Windsor / With a hairy [famous, splendid] gold crown on her head'; 'Missis Victorier's sons'), and then by the parenthetical refrain that echoes the tribute with significant variations that shift the centre of interest from the Queen to her soldiers:

> That takes us to various wars.
> 　(Poor beggars! – barbarious wars!) . . .

> When the Widow at Windsor says 'Stop!'
> 　(Poor beggars: – we're sent to say 'Stop!') . . .

> To the bloomin' old rag over'ead.
> 　(Poor beggars! – it's 'ot over'ead!) . . .

The effect is to turn a patriotic poem into one that has as its real theme not monarch or Empire but the sufferings of the ill-paid, unsung common soldier.

That this is Kipling's primary and fairly consistent concern is shown by the poem 'To T. A. [Tommy Atkins]' that stands as an epigraph to the collection:

> I have tried for to explain
> Both your pleasure and your pain,
> And, Thomas, here's my best respects to you.

Already in his implied attitude to imperialism Kipling is anticipating such poems as 'Recessional': rather than idealizing or celebrating the fact that Victoria ruled a large proportion of the earth's surface, he compels us to confront the human cost in specific, dramatic and disturbing detail. 'The Widow at Windsor' may in the matter of tone be compared with Housman's '1887' (the opening poem of *A Shropshire Lad*) later in the same decade, and contrasted with the unqualified patriotism of Newbolt's poetry in the same period.

Even though 'The Widow at Windsor' and many of the other poems in the collection are monologues, there is no attempt to present the speaker as a unique individual: rather he is a representative and communal voice, and in this respect Kipling is closer to the traditional ballad and street-song than to the mainstream of poetic tradition in the late Victorian period. The point is of some historical significance. The most original poets of the time, such as Thomas Hardy and Gerard Manley Hopkins (the latter had died in 1889), had broken with the long tradition of fluid, musical verse that runs from Spenser to Tennyson and had turned to the freer, more varied and even more awkward rhythms of speech and song as a basis for their verse-forms. Kipling, whose verses are closer to the Scots ballads of the later middle ages and the songs he heard at Gatti's music hall than they are to the contents of the *Golden Treasury*, lacked the major innovative genius of a Hardy or a Hopkins but had nevertheless set himself firmly in the same direction.

His debt to the traditional tragic ballad can be seen quite specifically in 'Danny Deever', where the haunting repetitions, the question-and-answer form, and the indirectness of the narrative all recall such anonymous poems as 'Edward, Edward' and 'Lord Randal':

'What makes the rear-rank breathe so 'ard?' said Files-on-
   Parade.
'It's bitter cold, it's bitter cold,' the Colour-Sergeant said.
'What makes that front-rank man fall down?' said Files-on-
   Parade.
'A touch o' sun, a touch o' sun,' the Colour-Sergeant said.

which may be compared with:

'What became of your bloodhounds, Lord Randal, my son?
What became of your bloodhounds, my handsome young
   man?' –
'O they swell'd and they died; mother, make my bed soon,
For I'm weary wi' hunting, and fain wald lie down.'

'Mandalay', on the other hand, is closer to the music-hall ditty and, especially in its languorous, slow-moving refrain, almost creates its own melody. (It was, of course, long popular in a musical setting; one is glad to find its poetic currency affirmed by inclusion in the *New Oxford Book of English Verse*.)

India and its army is still prominent in *The Seven Seas*, which contains a further substantial group of soldier-ballads that includes such uncompromisingly unVictorian items as 'The

Sergeant's Wedding' and 'Mary, Pity Women!' The volume also
contains 'McAndrew's Hymn', perhaps the best of all Kipling's
attempts at the longer dramatic monologue. Its speaker-
protagonist is a kind of Holy Willie of the engine-room:

Lord, Thou hast made this world below the shadow of a dream,
An', taught by time, I tak' it so – exceptin' always Steam.
From coupler-flange to spindle-guide I see Thy Hand, O God –
Predestination in the stride o' yon connectin'-rod.

The dialect is now Scots rather than Cockney, and Kipling again
employs his favourite fourteen-syllable line to good effect, as the
monologuist holds forth with rolling, irresistible eloquence, his
complacent sententiousness stressed by the rhyming couplets.
Like some of the narrators of Kipling's stories, he is simultaneously engaged in saying his piece and in unconscious
self-revelation.

By the time *The Five Nations* appeared seven years later (1903),
Kipling was in his late thirties and had settled at Bateman's.
Although there are still signs of the earlier manner in a poem such
as 'Boots', a new voice is now clearly audible – or, rather, two
voices. One is the reflective, personal voice exemplified by
'Sussex'; the other the public, 'official' voice of 'The White Man's
Burden', 'The Islanders' and 'Recessional' (the last of these is
placed prominently at the end of the volume). In the latter type of
poem – and Kipling was to write many of this type, and to reach
an extraordinarily wide audience through them – he speaks not as
a journalist exposing a particular scandal or bringing specific
grievances to the attention of an ignorant public, but as a
representative of the nation or even the race in its wiser, more
sober moods. We can see, or hear, the strongly marked difference
between these voices if we put side by side brief extracts from three
poems in this collection:

        The bachelor 'e fights for one
            As joyful as can be;
        But the married man don't call it fun,
            Because 'e fights for three –
        For 'Im and 'Er an' It
            (An' Two an' One makes Three)

'E wants to finish 'is little bit,
   An' 'e wants to go 'ome to 'is tea!
                ('The Married Man')

Clean of officious fence or hedge
   Half-wild and wholly tame,
The wise turf cloaks the white cliff edge
   As when the Roman came.
What sign of those that fought and died
   At shift of sword and sword?
The barrow and the camp abide,
   The sunlight and the sward.
                     ('Sussex')

For heathen heart that puts her trust
   In reeking tube and iron shard,
All valiant dust that builds on dust,
   And guarding, calls not Thee to guard,
For frantic boast and foolish word –
   Thy Mercy on Thy People, Lord!
                   ('Recessional')

The tone of these three passages is very different. The strong rhythms of the first (thumping like a bass-drum in lines five and six, and jaunty as a music-hall chorus in the last two lines) are utterly unlike the subdued precision of the second extract, and the measured, sternly declamatory manner of the third is different again. On the level of diction, the first is colloquial, the second more literary (consider the unpredictable epithets in 'officious fence' and 'wise turf'), the third biblical and liturgical (the poem ends, indeed, with an 'Amen').

In his later years Kipling's verse-writing, rather than running alongside his prose-writing with occasional points of contact, was often closely integrated with it. In the later volumes of stories, each tale is normally accompanied (preceded and/or followed) by one or more poems. As a result, T. S. Eliot has called him 'an integral prose-and-verse writer', commenting that 'the later unit is a poem and a story together – or a story and two poems – combining to make a form which no-one has used in the same way and in which no-one is ever likely to excel him'. 'Mary Postgate', for example, needs to be read and pondered in conjunction with the poem that follows it ('The Beginnings'), and 'The Tender Achilles' in conjunction with 'Hymn to Physical Pain', while the historical stories in *Puck of Pook's Hill* gain an extra dimension from the delicate, evocative verses that are a feature of the volume (for example, 'Puck's Song' and 'The Way through the Woods').

Kipling's output of verse in his later years continued to be substantial; the Great War, for instance, prompted many poems, including the cogently and poignantly brief 'Epitaphs of the War'. But English poetry was developing more rapidly during these years than the work of an elderly and often grievously unhappy man was likely to do, and the later Kipling was left behind by the generation that saw the appearance of *The Waste Land*, the early poems of Pound, and (a little later) the early work of the Auden generation. Kipling was after all a Victorian, already on the verge of middle age when the Queen died; and for all his prodigious talent he lacked the poetic genius of a Yeats, whose style was able to undergo a series of metamorphoses. Modernism in turn gave rise to new critical ideologies that found their particular tools ill-suited to the dissection of Kipling and many of his contemporaries; so that even before he died he seemed to many of the new generation a curiously old-fashioned figure, a quaint survivor from a vanished world or (to some) the embodiment of unenlightened and unpalatable attitudes, aesthetic as well as ideological.

And yet he continued to find readers, and the Definitive Edition of his verse, published in 1940, was reprinted ten times before the decade was out (and that in the face of wartime difficulties over book-production). Kipling is one of those writers of verse (and much the same is true of his prose) who is virtually ignored by the academic establishment of teachers and critics but who none the less enjoys a continuing popular fame and a recognized status as a living classic (nearly everyone who reads at all has read some Kipling). It is not difficult to see why this should be so. The most influential academic fashions of the last two or three generations have tended to equate poetic excellence with difficulty; conversely, the writer who offers little grist to the slow-grinding mills of 'explicative' criticism is likely to be ignored (for every one who teaches or writes on, say, Edward Thomas a hundred teach or write on T. S. Eliot – which does not necessarily mean that Eliot is a hundred times better as a poet than Thomas).

Kipling, as Eliot himself pointed out long ago, is not a poet who requires or indeed suffers laborious or ingenious exegesis. His meaning is usually readily accessible; his effects are direct and unmistakable in their impact on the reader; his music is more often that of the brass band than that of the string quartet. (The odd thing is, of course, that his *prose* is often subtle, ambiguous, allusive and obscure to the point of opacity – a curious appropriation by the popular form of the short story of characteristics more readily associated with modern poetry.) Most of the time his verse operates within a relatively narrow emotional and stylistic range (though some contrasts of tone have been noted); and for this reason he could never be considered a major poet. Keats deplored poetry that has 'a palpable design upon us', and many have disliked Kipling's poetry for this reason. I have suggested earlier that the best of Kipling's verse can be considerably more subtle than is often supposed. It may be, however, that even his more direct and didactic verse may come back into fashion, rather as did the poetry of Pope, after a period of neglect or disparagement. Kipling could easily have become a very different kind of poet from the one he turned out to be: Louis L. Cornell has shown in *Kipling in India* that the manuscript book of poems written after he fell in love with Florence Garrard and titled (ominously) *Sundry Phansies* 'faintly hints at the kind of poet Kipling might have become – an "aesthete" of the nineties, . . . a thin and minor version of the early Yeats'. (The manuscript is now in the Berg Collection at the New York Public Library.) In the event, of course, though a contemporary of the aesthetes and the decadents, he was no more of their party than Hardy was. Kipling turned instead to rhetoric, the use of a language 'simple, sensuous, passionate' to stir strong (though not necessarily profound) emotions in a large number of people. And if rhetoric may be regarded not simply as a term of abuse but as having a legitimate role among the diverse repertoire of poetic styles – and if it does not, then a great deal of the work of such poets as Byron and Whitman must be surrendered – the best of Kipling's verse deserves to remain current. Rhetoric is not, of course, to the taste of every individual or every generation; and it is Kipling's misfortune, and ours, that – for reasons that are partly and perhaps largely extra-literary – rhetoric in our time tends to arouse distrust. When Henry James read *The Seven Seas* he was both fascinated and repelled; in a letter of 5 November 1896, he writes:

I am laid low by the absolutely uncanny talent – the prodigious special faculty of it. It's all *violent*, without a dream of nuance or a hint of 'distinction'; all prose trumpets and castanets and such – with never a touch of the fiddle-string or a note of the nightingale.

But for all the incompatibility of sensibilities, James was honest enough to conclude, as anyone must: 'But it's magnificent and masterly in its way, and full of the most insidious art.'

A Select Guide to Kipling's Verse

'ABSENT-MINDED BEGGAR, THE'.   Written in October 1899, the month in which the South African War broke out; published in the *Daily Mail* on 31 October. On its extraordinary success as a fund-raiser to aid the families left behind by soldiers who had gone to South Africa, see p. 21. It is unashamedly propagandist, toughly unsentimental, ironic and reproachful towards patriotic words unbacked by deeds. Kipling commented that 'Sir Arthur Sullivan wedded the words to a tune guaranteed to pull teeth out of barrel-organs', and J. McG. Stewart notes that 'Handkerchiefs, pillow cases, plates, tobacco jars, ash trays, cigarette packages, etc., were produced bearing all or part of the poem, and a part of the sale price in each case went into the fund.' A facsimile of the manuscript can be found in Sotheby & Co.'s catalogue for 23 March 1936.

'APPEAL, THE'.   This request that a writer's personal privacy be respected, posthumously as well as during his lifetime, was not published until 1939 and is printed at the end of collections of his verse.

'BALLAD OF EAST AND WEST, THE'.   Written in 1889; published in *Macmillan's Magazine*, December 1890; collected in *Barrack-Room Ballads* (1892). It became immediately popular on its appearance. The opening line – one of Kipling's most familiar – has often been quoted out of context and, as a result, has been widely misunderstood. According to Kingsley Amis, this single line, which is considerably qualified by the three that follow it, has been responsible for 'most of the ignorant castigation of Kipling as a racialist'. Carrington notes that the poem recounts 'a romantic version of a tale that was in print long before Kipling's day'.

'BEGINNINGS, THE'.   First published in *A Diversity of Creatures* (1917), where it accompanies the powerful and disturbing story 'Mary Postgate', and included subsequently in the Inclusive Edition (1919). Amis describes it as 'literally a hymn of hate'. It needs to be read in conjunction with the story to which it stands as a postscript.

'BOOTS'.   Published in *The Five Nations* (1903). One of a group of soldier-poems written in or about 1901, it became a popular recitation-piece.

'CRAFTSMAN, THE'.   Published in *The Years Between* (1919). Purporting to give an account of the origins of some of Shakespeare's greatest characters in commonplace incidents, it deals with the subject of artistic creation. For a story dealing with Shakespeare, see 'Proofs of Holy Writ', written in 1932, published in the *Strand Magazine* in April 1934, and included in vol. xxx of the Sussex Edition.

'DANNY DEEVER'.   Published in the *Scots Observer*, 22 February 1890 (the first of the series of 'Barrack-Room Ballads' to appear in that paper). An outstanding example of Kipling's use of the ballad form: W. B. Yeats said that it exhibited 'the matter but not the form of old street ballads'. Amis has described it as 'the most harrowing poem in our language'. T. S. Eliot commented that it is 'a poem which is technically (as well as in content) remarkable':

> The regular recurrence of the same end-words, which gain immensely by imperfect rhyme (*parade* and *said*), gives the feeling of marching feet and the movement of men in disciplined formation – in a unity of movement which enhances the horror of the occasion and the sickness which seizes the men as individuals; and the slightly quickened pace of the final lines marks the change in movement and in music.

For David Masson's reaction to this poem, see p. xii.

'EPITAPHS OF THE WAR'.   Published in *The Years Between* (1919). T. S. Eliot notes that 'Good epigrams in English are very few' but that this is a form of verse in which Kipling excelled; Eliot cites this group of poems in support of his claim.

'EVARRA AND HIS GODS'.   Published in the *Scots Observer*, 4 October 1890; collected in *Barrack-Room Ballads* (1892). Kipling imagines man, 'the craftsman of gods, shaping his divinity in accordance with his circumstances' (Tompkins).

'FABULISTS, THE'. Published in *A Diversity of Creatures* (1917). Another poem about Kipling's conception of art.

'FEMALE OF THE SPECIES, THE'. Published in the *Morning Post*, 20 October 1911. Kipling's satiric comment on the Suffragette Movement; the title has, of course, become proverbial, and the refrain 'For the female of the species is more deadly than the male' is one of Kipling's most familiar lines. On 23 October 1911 a retort, 'The Species of the Female', by Sidney Low was published in the *Standard* (see Amy Cruse, *After the Victorians* [1938] p. 135).

'FUZZY-WUZZY'. Published in the *Scots Observer*, 15 March 1890; collected in *Barrack-Room Ballads* (1892). The subtitle is 'Soudan Expeditionary Force. Early Campaigns'. The poem expresses admiration for the fighting qualities of the enemy (though it does so with a touch of patronage that is not much to present-day tastes).

'GUNGA DIN'. Published in the *Scots Observer*, 7 June 1890; collected in *Barrack-Room Ballads* (1892). Though (like 'Fuzzy-Wuzzy') too paternalistic for most modern tastes, this was an enormously popular recitation-piece familiar to millions. Orwell coupled it with 'Danny Deever' as an example of Kipling 'at his worst, and also his most vital'; 'Gunga Din' has not, however, enjoyed the same respect as has been accorded to 'Danny Deever' by recent critics.

'HYMN OF BREAKING STRAIN'. This very late poem (1935) forms an interesting comment on Kipling's preoccupation in some of his later stories with strain, breakdown, and recovery, physical and psychological (compare the title of his last collection, *Limits and Renewals*). The poem was published in both the *Daily Telegraph* and (appropriately) *The Engineer* on 15 March 1935.

'HYMN TO PHYSICAL PAIN'. In *Limits and Renewals* (1932) this poem precedes the story 'The Tender Achilles', one of Kipling's tales of healing. Written in a stanza-form that recalls *Hymns Ancient and Modern*, and employing a diction that perhaps consciously echoes 'O God, our help in ages past', this powerful and disturbing poem can serve as a gloss on the preoccupation with disease and suffering in Kipling's later fiction. For his feelings concerning cancer, see p. 104.

'IF——'. Published in the *American Magazine* in October 1910, and in 'many subsequent editions . . . in the form of broadsides, leaflets, and pamphlets' (J. McG. Stewart), this poem was included in *Rewards and Fairies* (1910) and is probably not only Kipling's best-known poem but one of the most widely familiar in the language. According to Kipling it was based on the character of Dr Jameson, who had visited Kipling at Bateman's in October 1909. Sir Maurice Bowra pointed out that both theme and metre recall Browning's 'Epilogue' to *Asolando*, which traditionally concludes all editions of Browning's verse.

'IN SPRINGTIME'. Published in the *Pioneer* (Allahabad), 20 March 1885 and reprinted in the *United Services College Chronicle*, 29 October 1888; collected in *Departmental Ditties* (1886). This very early poem is an Anglo-Indian version of Browning's well-known 'Home Thoughts from Abroad': the bell-like song of an Indian bird is 'the knell of exile', and the poem is interesting as an expression of Kipling's feeling for English landscape, later to find fuller expression in some of his short stories. Reviewing *Departmental Ditties* in *Longman's Magazine* in October 1886 – apparently the first Kipling review published in Britain – Andrew Lang singled out 'In Springtime' for special commendation and printed it in full.

'ISLANDERS, THE'.   Dated 1902 and published in *The Times* on 4 January 1902; collected in *The Five Nations* (1903). Described by Angus Wilson as a 'scornful attack on [England's] determined blindness to its dangers': Kipling inveighs against the complacency of the ruling classes in the face of the German menace and other perils. As Wilson nicely observes, he 'takes each sacred cow of the clubs and senior common rooms and slaughters it messily before its worshippers' eyes'. It contains the famous contemptuous phrases on 'flannelled fools at the wicket' and 'muddied oafs at the goals', of which Orwell notes that the line 'sticks like an arrow to this day'. Kipling's point was that games were regarded as more important than military preparedness. According to Carrington, 'no earlier pronouncement of Rudyard's had touched so many victims on the raw'.

'LAND, THE'.   Published in *A Diversity of Creatures* (1917) as a pendant to the story 'Friendly Brook'; collected in *Songs for Youth* (1924). The poem expresses Kipling's sense of the continuity of the English tradition as personified by the recurring figure of the independent yeoman – a theme earlier

developed in such stories as those contained in *Puck of Pook's Hill*.
'LA NUIT BLANCHE'. Published in the *Civil & Military Gazette* (Lahore), 7 June 1886, under the title 'Natural Phenomena'; collected in *Departmental Ditties* (1886). Tompkins contrasts the 'horrific facetiousness' of this poem with the 'pure horror' of the short story 'The End of the Passage'.
'LAST DEPARTMENT, THE'. Published in the *Civil & Military Gazette* (Lahore), 13 April 1886; collected in *Departmental Ditties* (1886). One of Kipling's earliest critics, Sir William Hunter (*Academy*, 1 September 1888), concluded his review of *Departmental Ditties* by remarking:

> His serious poems seem to me the ones most full of promise. Taken as a whole, his book gives hope of a new literary star of no mean magnitude rising in the east. An almost virgin field of literary labour there awaits some man of genius. The hand which wrote 'The Last Department' in this little volume is surely reserved for higher work than breaking those poor pretty Simla butterflies on the wheel.

The poem is written in the stanza-form popularized by Edward FitzGerald's *Rubáiyát of Omar Khayyám*, and expresses something of the fatalism of Omar–FitzGerald, though Kipling's own grim humour is also strongly in evidence:

> Transferred to the Eternal Settlement,
> Each in his strait, wood-scantled office pent,
>   No longer Brown reverses Smith's appeals,
> Or Jones records his Minute of Dissent.
>
> And One, long since a pillar of the Court,
> As mud between the beams thereof is wrought;
>   And One who wrote on phosphates for the crops
> Is subject-matter of his own Report.

Compare 'The Rupaiyat of Omar Kal'vin'.
'LOOT'. Published in the *Scots Observer*, 29 March 1890; collected in *Barrack-Room Ballads* (1892). The speaker is an experienced soldier instructing a novice; Kipling's own attitude – sympathetic or sardonic – remains ambiguous. T. S. Eliot suggests

that we need not suppose him to be 'commending the rapacity and greed of such irregularities, or condoning rapine', but the question is not an easy one to settle, though it would clearly be a mistake to equate the poet too readily with the speaker of this dramatic monologue. (For an example of such an error, consider the comment made by Edward Shanks, quoted by Eliot: 'this is wholly detestable, and it makes the commentator on Kipling turn red when he endeavours to explain it'. Commentators on Browning's 'My Last Duchess' have not been notable for turning red, and the case is arguably a parallel one.)

'MCANDREW'S HYMN'. Dated 1893; published in *Scribner's Magazine*, December 1894 (Kipling was paid $500, at that time a record price for a poem in the United States, according to Carrington); collected in *The Seven Seas* (1896). A dramatic monologue showing the influence of Browning: the speaker is a 'dour Scots engineer' who has spent his life at sea. Ostensibly a prayer to God, it is actually a hymn in praise of machines and the men who create and tend them, McAndrew regarding the making of a new machine as a God-like act of creation. Angus Wilson describes this and 'The Mary Gloster' as 'hymns to the life force'. A puzzling allusion in *Something of Myself* to 'my worst slip' has been plausibly explained (*KJ*, XII, December 1945) as a reference to the phrase 'knots an hour' in this poem, later amended to 'miles an hour'.

'MANDALAY'. Published in the *Scots Observer*, 22 June 1890; collected in *Barrack-Room Ballads* (1892). A haunting, still effective poem of nostalgia, expressing Kipling's sensuous response to life in the East. The phrase 'somewhere east of Suez' originates here. Its metre is said to have been based on a popular waltz tune; significantly, Mrs Kipling's diary more than once refers to her husband 'singing a new poem'.

'MARY GLOSTER, THE'. Dated 1894; first published in *The Seven Seas* (1896). A Browningesque dramatic monologue: compare 'McAndrew's Hymn', with which T. S. Eliot bracketed it. The speaker is a wealthy ship-owner on his deathbed: Eliot comments that 'The rapacious old ship owner . . . is not easily dismissed, and the presence of the silent son gives a dramatic quality absent from McAndrew's soliloquy.' Henry James, who had just read *The Seven Seas* (sent to him by Kipling), wrote in a letter dated 5 November 1896: 'There's a vilely idiotic reference

to his "coarseness" in this a.m.'s *Chronicle*. The coarseness of
"The Mary Gloster" is absolutely one of the most triumphant
"values" of that triumphant thing.'

'MARY, PITY WOMEN!' Included in *The Seven Seas* (1896). A
dramatic monologue in ballad form; the speaker is a woman
who has been abandoned by her lover, a soldier who is to 'sail
tomorrow'. The idea is said to have been based on a story told to
Kipling by a barmaid during his early years in London. Angus
Wilson has praised the realism of the poem's 'mixture of crude
sexual passion and pathetic desire for respectability'. For a
prose parallel, see the story 'The Record of Badalia Herodsfoot'.

'NATIVE-BORN, THE'. Dated 1894; published in *The Times*, 14
October 1895; collected in *The Seven Seas* (1896). The first of the
'public poems' that appeared in *The Times* over a period of many
years and that included such famous pieces as 'Recessional'
and 'The White Man's Burden'. They were, according to
Kipling, 'given to *The Times* because for this kind of work I did
not take payment'; according to Carrington, they led to his
being regarded as 'the people's laureate' even though he never
occupied the official position of Poet Laureate.

'OUR LADY OF THE SNOWS'. Dated 1897; published in *The Times*,
27 April 1897; collected in *The Five Nations* (1903). Subtitled
'Canadian Preferential Tariff, 1897', it commemorates
Canada's granting of preferential tariffs for British imports –
not, one might be forgiven for supposing, a very promising
poetic subject, but these vigorous lines won a place in Eliot's
selection. Other parts of the Empire are called on to follow
Canada's lead.

'PUCK'S SONG'. First published in *Puck of Pook's Hill* and
expanded for inclusion in the collected editions. Like some of
the later stories, it traces the connections between English
landscape and English history.

'RECESSIONAL'. Published in *The Times*, 17 July 1897; collected
in *The Five Nations* (1903). Subtitled '1897', the date of
Victoria's Diamond Jubilee: celebrations of the Queen's acces-
sion on 20 June 1837 extended through the latter part of June
1897 and into July (on 22 June, for instance, over 2500 beacon
fires burned from Cornwall to Caithness). Predictably, an
excess of patriotic fervour was provoked; one of the ironies of
literary history is that Kipling's poem, actually a warning

against the arrogance to which a world power is inevitably prone, should have come to be regarded by many as jingoistic and imperialistic. The phrase that has given most trouble is 'lesser breeds without the Law', on which Hilton Brown has commented pertinently:

> The sense of the phrase . . . is to be seen in the last three words and not in the first two. There is room for all within the Law, which sees no breed which has accepted it as greater or lesser than another. And the whole poem is an admonition to the English as to a people which must humbly keep the law as a special trust.

As usual, Kipling's emphasis is not so much on the advantages of possessing an Empire as on the responsibilities this entails: he does not *celebrate* the imperial idea – and to this extent he was, of course, distinctly out of line with the public mood of 1897 – being rather intent on reminding the mother country of its burden of duty. Angus Wilson points out that this poem and 'The White Man's Burden' (see below) had the effect of turning 'a popular, very well-known writer into a controversial figure of world fame'.

According to the manuscript, a photographic reproduction of which is included in Lord Birkenhead's biography, the original title was 'After'.

Something of Myself contains Kipling's account of the composition of the poem. According to his daughter Elsie, 'Much of his best known verse was written to a tune, the "Recessional" to "Melita", the tune usually sung to "Eternal Father, strong to save".' T. S. Eliot declared: 'I call Kipling a great hymn writer on the strength of "Recessional".' A 'recessional' is, in the strict sense of the word, a hymn sung while clergy and choir withdraw from the chancel at the end of a service: in the poem the idea of withdrawal is pervasive and far-reaching (see, for example, stanza 2 – 'The Captains and the Kings depart' – and stanza 3 – 'Far-called, our navies melt away'). The poem has been translated into many languages, including Latin (see *Journal of Education*, February 1898) and Greek (see *The Times*, 13 November 1920).

'RHYME OF THE THREE CAPTAINS, THE'. Dated 1890; published in the *Athenaeum*, 6 December 1890; collected in *Barrack-Room*

Ballads (1892). On 4 October 1890 the *Athenaeum*, an influential London literary weekly, published in its 'Literary Gossip' column an item by Kipling claiming that Harper & Brothers, the American publishers, were guilty of literary piracy in publishing the unauthorized collection *The Courting of Dinah Shadd and Other Stories*, which had appeared in the previous month. A controversy ensued, in the course of which (on 22 November) the *Athenaeum* published a letter over the signature of three authors – Walter Besant, William Black and Thomas Hardy – stating that in their experience the New York firm had treated foreign authors fairly. Kipling's satirical ballad was a reaction to this letter, and the title and the opening lines refer to the three signatories. Carrington (pp. 206–12) gives a full account of the episode. For further information concerning Kipling's relations with Hardy, see under the latter in 'A Kipling Who's Who'.

'RHYME OF THE THREE SEALERS, THE'. Published in the *Pall Mall Budget*, 14 December 1893 (the first thirteen lines had appeared in *The Times* and elsewhere on 2 November 1892); collected in *The Seven Seas* (1896). A manuscript of this poem on four quarto sheets is in the British Library (Ashley 4880); see Plate 8a for a reproduction of the first sheet. Although described as an 'original holograph manuscript' it appears to be a fair copy with a few minor revisions.

'SETTLER, THE'. Published in *The Times*, 27 February 1903; collected in *The Five Nations* (1903). Written soon after the end of the Boer War, it consists of 'verses put into the mouth of an Englishman, turning the furrows of the land he has fought over, and now serves' (Tompkins).

'SONG OF THE GALLEY-SLAVES, THE. Published in *Many Inventions* (1893), where it accompanies 'The Finest Story in the World'. T. S. Eliot describes it as 'a very good poem, in rather free verse'.

'SUSSEX'. Dated 1902 and apparently written in South Africa early in that year (the move to Bateman's, Kipling's Sussex home for the remainder of his life, followed later in the year); included in *The Five Nations* (1903). It was prompted by the same intense and rather proprietorial attachment to England that finds expression in such stories as 'An Habitation Enforced', 'Friendly Brook' and 'My Son's Wife'.

'TOMLINSON'. Dated 1891; published in the *National Observer*, 23

January 1892; collected in *Barrack-Room Ballads* (1892). A rich man who has died is welcome in neither heaven nor hell. Angus Wilson suggests that the poem expresses Kipling's 'hatred of urban civilized nullity'.

'Tommy'.   Published in the *Scots Observer*, 1 March 1890; collected in *Barrack-Room Ballads* (1892). An eloquent, unsentimental protest against the nation's ingratitude to those who risk their lives on its behalf. It contains the memorable phrase 'makin' mock o' uniforms that guard you while you sleep', of which George Orwell remarked that 'it would be difficult to hit off the one-eyed pacificism of the English in fewer words'.

'Vampire, The'.   Published in April 1897 in a catalogue of The New Gallery, London, to accompany the description of a picture of the same title by Philip Burne-Jones, Kipling's cousin (see 'A Kipling Who's Who'). It also appeared in the *Daily Mail* on 17 April 1897 and was often reprinted without Kipling's permission (he had given it to Burne-Jones and it was never copyrighted), but he did not include it in an authorized collection of his verse until 1919.

'White Man's Burden, The'.   Published in *The Times*, 4 February 1899; collected in *The Five Nations* (1903). The poem seems to have been begun in June 1897, the month of Victoria's Diamond Jubilee celebrations, but completed only about eighteen months later: see also 'Recessional' above. The poem was addressed to the people of the United States, who were involved with Spain in a war over Cuba. 'His message to America was the positive side of his Imperial creed, as "Recessional" was the negative side of the coin' (Angus Wilson).

'Widow at Windsor, The'.   Published in the *Scots Observer*, 26 April 1890; collected in *Barrack-Room Ballads* (1892). There seems to be no foundation for the legend that Victoria took offence at this poem and refused to appoint Kipling to the Laureateship vacated in 1892 by the death of Tennyson.

Kipling and Freemasonry

Kipling became a freemason in 1886, while still below the minimum age of twenty-one (it seems that the Lodge of Hope and Perseverance in Lahore was in sore need of a secretary, and he immediately filled that position). For the various stages of his admission, see p. 3. According to his account in *Something of Myself*, he was 'entered by a member of the Brahmin Somaj, passed by a Mohammedan, and raised by an Englishman. Our tyler was an Indian Jew.' Carrington comments that 'In caste-ridden India, freemasonry was the only ground on which adherents of different religions could meet "on the level" '; elsewhere Carrington concedes that the attraction of the 'masculine self-sufficiency' offered by freemasonry must also have been strong. Angus Wilson notes that 'Freemasonry had been a solvent of the fiercely disciplined and caste-bound life of the British Army in India from the late eighteenth century', and by this time there were no fewer than five lodges in Lahore alone.

Kipling resigned from the lodge in August 1887 on moving to Allahabad, and joined the lodge there. Later in his life he is said to have joined the Authors' Lodge in London (founded in 1910), and he appears also to have been a founder-member of two lodges connected with the War Graves Commission.

B. M. Bazley suggests that allusions to freemasonry are 'scattered about in nearly every book that bears Kipling's name'. There are a couple of passing references in *Plain Tales from the Hills*, a fuller reference in 'With the Main Guard' (*Soldiers Three*), and a marked prominence in 'The Man Who Would Be King' (*Wee Willie Winkie*). In *Kim* there are, according to Bazley, 'about a dozen' references, and the topic again becomes important in several of the later stories, including 'Fairy-Kist', 'The Tender Achilles', 'A Madonna of the Trenches', 'A Friend of the Family',

'The Janeites' and 'In the Interests of the Brethren'. Bazley notes that in *Puck of Pook's Hill* 'Kipling seems to be tracing an analogy between Mithraism and Masonry'. See also the poems 'The Mother-Lodge' and 'Banquet Night'. A reference in *Something of Myself* to a story concerning Masonic lions has been identified by R. L. Green, who suggests that the source may be 'King Lion', probably by James Greenwood, serialized in the *Boys' Own Magazine* in 1864; the story is interesting as a possible source of the *Jungle Books* (see Green's useful article, 'Kipling's Early Reading', *KJ*, XXIII, July 1956). Bazley has published three articles on Kipling's freemasonry: for a comprehensive list of allusions in his writings, see *KJ*, XVII (April 1950); see also *KJ*, XVI (December 1949) and XXVIII (December 1961). Two other articles on this topic in *KJ* are by H. S. Williamson (XXXI, September 1934) and Albert Frost (IX, October 1942).

Points of View

The brief selection of extracts that follows is in no sense offered as an anthology of the best that has been thought and said about Kipling; rather, it comprises a small bouquet of comments chosen for their diversity and their provocative quality. Further information concerning sources will be found in the Select Bibliography.

'Ruddy thirsts for a man's life and a man's work' (Lockwood Kipling to a friend in 1881).

'I must do the work I have to do' (Kipling, on learning in 1915 that his only son was missing in action).

'There is no anaesthesia so complete as a man's absorption in his own job' (Kipling speaking to the Royal College of Surgeons in 1923).

'When your Daemon is in charge, do not try to think consciously. Drift, wait, and obey' (Kipling, *Something of Myself*).

'The evidence of his senses bewilders and staggers him' (William Barry, writing in the *Quarterly Review* in July 1892).

'In the middle nineties this spectacled and moustached little figure with its heavy chin and its general effect of vehement gesticulation, its wild shouts of boyish enthusiasm for effective force, its lyric delight in the sounds and colours, in the very odours of Empire, its wonderful discovery of machinery and cotton waste and the under-officer and the engineer, and "shop" as a poetic dialect, became almost a national symbol. He got hold of us wonderfully, he filled us with tinkling and haunting quotations, . . . he coloured the very idiom of our conversations' (H. G. Wells, *The New Machiavelli* [1911]).

'In his earliest time I thought he perhaps contained the seeds of an English Balzac; but I have given that up in proportion as he has come down steadily from the simple in subject to the more simple – from the Anglo-Indians to the natives, from the natives to the Tommies, from the Tommies to the quadrupeds, from the quadrupeds to the fish, and from the fish to the engines and screws' (Henry James, letter to Grace Norton of 25 December 1897).

'Kipling was someone who had spent six years in a concentration camp as a child; he never got over it. As a very young man he spent seven years in an India that confirmed his belief in concentration camps; he never got over this either . . . he was obsessed by – wrote about, dreamed about, and stayed awake so as not to dream about – many concentration camps, of the soul as well as of the body; many tortures, hauntings, hallucinations, deliria, diseases, nightmares, practical jokes, revenges, monsters, insanities, neuroses, abysses, forlorn hopes, last chances, extremities of every kind; these and their sweet opposites' (Randall Jarrell, 'On Preparing to Read Kipling').

'At times he seems to regard the world as an aggregation of secret and semi-secret societies, a pattern of circles, intersecting indeed, but closed – English Public Schools, religions, engine-rooms, messes, nationalities, clubs, services, and professions. . . . But Kipling was at times – and it grew on him – too eager to prove himself initiate of many mysteries; and it is a little annoying to be winked at by an augur when one isn't an augur oneself' (W. L. Renwick, 'Re-reading Kipling').

'What he loves better than anything in the world is the intimacy within a closed circle. . . . To belong, to be inside, to be in the know, to be snugly together against the outsiders – this is what really matters' (C. S. Lewis, 'Kipling's World').

'There was no glimpse anywhere of sober and self-respecting human beings – only a wild carnival of drunken, bragging, boasting Hooligans in red coats and seamen's jackets, shrieking to the sound of the banjo and applauding the English flag' (Robert Buchanan, 'The Voice of "The Hooligan" ').

'Instead of *becoming* a man of action like Rimbaud . . . he fell into the ignominious role of the artist who prostrates his art before the achievements of soldiers and merchants, and who is always declaring the supremacy of the "doer" over the man of ideas' (Edmund Wilson, 'The Kipling that Nobody Read').

'There is no line of my verse or prose which has not been mouthed till the tongue has made all smooth, and memory, after many recitals, has mechanically skipped the grosser superfluities' (Kipling, *Something of Myself*).

'On the whole, Kipling despised women; but in one or two tales he is glad to use them to vent feelings that he would be ashamed to attribute to a man, and above all to describe as being possible to himself' (Boris Ford, 'A Case for Kipling?').

'He is less interested in people than in social realities, and that is why his morality appears to be distorted. The centre of Kipling's world is society itself, and he related man to society in a way different from that of any other late Victorian writer. His understanding of society resembles that of a sociologist. . . . The impression which his work as a whole gives is that of a man who sees human beings moving in a definable network of social relationships which impose upon them a code of behaviour appropriate to their environment. . . . Kipling does not show us what the effect is of the social process on the individual, nor does he see that the writer creates a world peopled with characters who necessarily act and feel as isolated individuals as well as political animals . . . he is unaware of the problem set by the concept of roles. . . . He brilliantly sets out the conflict between different cultures, but he evades for the most part the conflict within the individual himself' (Noel Annan, 'Kipling's Place in the History of Ideas').

'Kipling was one of liberalism's major intellectual misfortunes' (Lionel Trilling, 'Kipling').

'It will only be possible to give him his rightful place when the political heats of his day have become coldly historical' (Bonamy Dobrée, 1929).

[The congregation at Kipling's funeral in Westminster Abbey] 'consisted of men of action, the men with whom he had spent his life, rather than men of letters' (Charles Carrington).

[Kipling has been] 'more grotesquely misunderstood, misrepresented, and in consequence denigrated, than any other known writer' (Bonamy Dobrée, 1967).

Collected Editions

There have been numerous collected editions of Kipling's work, of which the most important are the following:

The Outward Bound Edition (11 volumes published in 1897; others, to a total of 36, appeared at intervals to 1937).

The Edition De Luxe (limited edition of 38 volumes, 1897–1937).

The Swastika Edition (15 volumes, 1899; published in the USA).

The Uniform Edition (28 volumes, 1899–1938).

The Pocket Edition (37 volumes, 1907–38; published in London, but an American version was also published).

The Bombay Edition (31 volumes, 1913–38).

The Seven Seas Edition (27 volumes, 1913–26; published in the USA).

The Sussex Edition (35 volumes, 1937–9). This posthumous edition incorporates Kipling's final revisions made during his last years and is therefore of special textual interest; it includes two volumes of prose and a good deal of verse hitherto uncollected.

The Burwash Edition (28 volumes, 1941; published in New York) follows the text of the Sussex Edition but disposes its contents differently.

Filmography

Several of Kipling's works have been filmed, and some of these versions have achieved a wide popularity. There were no fewer than three silent versions of *The Light that Failed*: an Italian film of 1914, a Pathé film of 1916, and an American film in 1923 (this last directed by George Melford). A successful sound version was made by Paramount in 1939: directed by William A. Wellman, it starred Ronald Colman, Ida Lupino and Walter Huston. A television version of the same novel was made in 1961.

Captains Courageous was filmed by M.G.M. in 1937, with Spencer Tracy, Lionel Barrymore, Freddie Bartholomew, Mickey Rooney and Melvyn Douglas (director: Victor Fleming), and a television version was made in 1977.

Wee Willie Winkie is the title of a Twentieth Century-Fox film (1937) directed by John Ford and starring Shirley Temple and Victor McLaglen.

M.G.M. made *Soldiers Three* in 1951, with Stewart Granger, David Niven, Walter Pidgeon and Robert Newton (director: Tay Garnett).

The same company made *Kim* in 1950, with Errol Flynn (director: Victor Saville), and the novel was also filmed for television in 1960.

The *Jungle Books* have also provided popular material for film-makers. United Artists' 1942 version, entitled *Rudyard Kipling's Jungle Book*, was directed by Zoltan Korda and featured Sabu; the same actor had earlier appeared in the successful *Elephant Boy*, based on the story 'Toomai of the Elephants' (United Artists, 1936; directed by Robert Flaherty and Zoltan Korda). A Walt Disney version of *The Jungle Book* was made in 1967, and a television version (under the title *Mowgli's Brothers*) 1976.

The Man Who Would Be King (US, 1975) is a successful version of Kipling's short story. Directed by John Huston, it stars Sean Connery, Michael Caine and Christopher Plummer (the last as Kipling).

All the television versions mentioned were made in the USA. Australian television made a version of *Elephant Boy* in 1973, and BBC Television has recently (1982) shown a serial version of *Stalky & Co.*

A curiosity is the silent film *A Fool There Was* (1915), a six-reeler rather improbably based on Kipling's poem 'The Vampire'. This was directed by William Fox and starred Theda Bara; according to Philip French, the latter 'became the cinema's first and archetypal "vamp" and introduced that word, as noun and verb, into the language'. French describes the film as 'risible' but 'enormously successful' ('Kipling and the Movies', in *Rudyard Kipling: The Man, his Work and his World*, ed. John Gross [1972]).

Another film derived, at least in part, from a Kipling poem was *Gunga Din* (1939), directed by George Stevens and starring Douglas Fairbanks, Jr. This uses the characters of *Soldiers Three*, with Cary Grant and Victor McLaglen playing the other two soldiers; for some reason the protagonists were rechristened MacChesney, Cutter and Ballentine. For a later version of *Soldiers Three*, see above. A 1961 remake of *Gunga Din* was entitled *Sergeants Three*.

Lindsay Anderson's *If* (1968) borrows the title of Kipling's famous poem and has a very tenuous relationship to *Stalky & Co.*, but cannot properly be considered a Kipling adaptation.

As Philip French points out, Kipling did not involve himself with the cinema to the same extent as his contemporaries Wells and Shaw. His adaptation of the story 'Without Benefit of Clergy' in about 1920 was never filmed, and the same fate befell his adaptations of *Soldiers Three* and *Thy Servant a Dog* towards the end of his life. 'Mrs Bathurst' makes important use of allusions to the new medium of the cinema.

Select Bibliography

Bibliographies

The most useful work is J. McG. Stewart's *Rudyard Kipling: A Bibliographical Catalogue*, ed. A. W. Yeats (Halifax, Nova Scotia, 1959). Also useful are two earlier works: E. W. Martindell's *A Bibliography of the Works of Rudyard Kipling, 1881–1921* (1922; new edition with additions, 1923), and Flora V. Livingston's *Bibliography of the Works of Rudyard Kipling* (New York, 1927; reprinted 1968), with its *Supplement* (Cambridge, Mass., 1938; reprinted 1968), the latter incorporating revisions and corrections. An extensive annotated bibliography of writings about Kipling appeared in *English Literature in Transition*, III (1960), with a supplement in 1965. Recent Kipling criticism and scholarship is regularly listed in *The Year's Work in English Studies* and other annual bibliographies, including the journal *Victorian Studies*. There is a short but useful bibliography of primary and secondary works in *The New Cambridge Bibliography of English Literature*, III (1969).

Reference Books

F. L. Knowles's *A Kipling Primer* (1900) is still useful, though it naturally deals only with the early work. W. Arthur Young's *A Dictionary of the Characters and Scenes in the Stories and Poems of Rudyard Kipling, 1886–1911* (1912; reprinted New York, 1969) has been revised by J. H. McGivering as *A Kipling Dictionary* (1967). *The Reader's Guide to Rudyard Kipling's Work*, ed. R. E. Harbord (8 vols, 1961–72) is scarce – it appeared in a privately printed edition limited to 100 sets – and is inconveniently arranged, but contains a mass of detailed information, notably very full annotations to Kipling's writings.

Biographies

Charles Carrington's *Rudyard Kipling: His Life and Work* (1955; third edition, incorporating revisions, 1978) is the authorized biography; although somewhat pedestrian in style it contains a mass of reliable information. Lord Birkenhead's *Rudyard Kipling* (1978) suffered a curious fate: the first draft was written with the encouragement of Kipling's daughter, who gave the author access to family papers, and was completed in 1948; on being submitted to Mrs Bambridge for approval, however, it was rejected outright and, revised in the 1960s, was published only after Lord Birkenhead's (and Mrs Bambridge's) death. While naturally repeating much that is in Carrington, it is a useful and readable account and adds some fresh information. Angus Wilson's *The Strange Ride of Rudyard Kipling* (1977) is an invigorating critical biography, strong alike in its interpretation of Kipling's work and its assessment of the significance of his experience, with some occasional errors of detail but full of original insights. Kingsley Amis's *Rudyard Kipling and his World* and Martin Fido's *Rudyard Kipling* are briefer accounts of Kipling's life and work, accompanied by numerous interesting illustrations.

There are also many books and articles on specific aspects of Kipling's life. George C. Beresford's *Schooldays with Kipling* (1936) and Lionel C. Dunsterville's *Stalky's Reminiscences* (1928) are accounts by contemporaries of the United Services College years. Kipling's family troubles in Vermont are the subject of a monograph by Frederic F. Van de Water (New York, 1937) and an article by Lord Birkenhead (*Essays by Divers Hands*, xxx, 1961); there is also a monograph *Rudyard Kipling in New England* (Brattleboro, 1936) by Howard C. Rice. Dorothy Ponton, who was Kipling's secretary, published *Rudyard Kipling at Home and at Work* (Poole, n.d. [1953]). For various reminiscences by Kipling's friend Edmonia Hill, his sister Alice Fleming, and his former editor E. Kay Robinson, see under the appropriate entries in 'A Kipling Who's Who' earlier in this volume. Harold Orel's *Rudyard Kipling: Interviews and Recollections* (2 vols, 1983) is a substantial and useful selection of reminiscences, with helpful annotation.

Criticism: Books

This section naturally overlaps to some extent with the previous one, since some of the biographies (notably Angus Wilson's) contain critical discussion of Kipling's work, and some of the works of criticism include biographical material.

One of the earliest book-length studies was Richard Le Gallienne's *Rudyard Kipling: A Criticism* (1900), which included a bibliography by John Lane. The book opens by announcing that 'The smart young Anglo-Indian story-teller is now a prophet', and concludes: 'As a writer Mr Kipling is a delight; as an influence he is a danger.' Other studies to appear in Kipling's lifetime, or shortly afterwards, include André Chevrillon's *Rudyard Kipling* (Paris, 1936), Cyril Falls's *Rudyard Kipling: A Critical Study* (1915), and Edward Shanks's *Rudyard Kipling* (1940). Bonamy Dobrée's pioneering essay in *The Criterion*, VI (1927), reprinted and expanded in his *The Lamp and the Lute* (1929), was followed by two books: *Rudyard Kipling* (1951) and *Kipling: Realist and Fabulist* (1967); and during the same period there were studies by Hilton Brown (*Rudyard Kipling*, 1945) and Rupert Croft-Cooke (*Rudyard Kipling*, 1948), as well as three books of more than average interest: Joyce M. S. Tompkins's *The Art of Rudyard Kipling* (1959), C. A. Bodelsen's *Aspects of Kipling's Art* (Manchester, 1964), and J. I. M. Stewart's *Rudyard Kipling* (1967) (Stewart's chapter on Kipling in *Eight Modern Writers* (Oxford, 1963), forming vol. 12 of the *Oxford History of English Literature*, is also valuable). Tompkins's book, consistently perceptive and illuminating, remains after more than twenty years the best full-length account of Kipling's art. T. R. Henn's *Kipling* (1967) is a sound brief study. Two of Kipling's most recent critics are Robert F. Moss, whose *Rudyard Kipling and the Fiction of Adolescence* (1982) discusses the school stories, and Mary Lascelles, whose *The Story-Teller Retrieves the Past* (Oxford, 1980) includes many references to his historical fiction. Elliot L. Gilbert has published a somewhat selective study of Kipling's short stories under the title *The Good Kipling* (1972). Louis L. Cornell's *Kipling in India* (1966) is an excellent discussion of Kipling's apprenticeship as a writer and his early journalism. S. S. Husain's *Kipling and India* (Dacca, 1964) and K. B. Rao's *Kipling's India* (Norman, Oklahoma, 1967) also cover the early years, as does an earlier study, Arnley Munson's *Kipling's India* (1916). Shamsul Islam's

Kipling's 'Law' (1975) is subtitled 'A Study of his Philosophy of Life'. John A. McClure's *Kipling and Conrad* (Harvard, 1981) is a comparative study. Roger Lancelyn Green's *Kipling and the Children* (1965) can be recommended as a study of the children's books, and Green has also edited the very useful volume *Kipling: The Critical Heritage* (1971), which brings together reviews and criticism of Kipling's writings from the period 1886 to 1936. On Kipling's early reception, see also Holbrook Jackson's *The Eighteen-Nineties* (1913; revised edition 1922). Philip Mason's *Kipling: The Glass, the Shadow and the Fire* (1975) is a general study, and there is a good collection of essays, *Rudyard Kipling: The Man, his Work and his World*, ed. John Gross (1972). (For two other important symposia, edited by E. L. Gilbert and A. Rutherford, see below.)Kipling's poetry has received little extended discussion, though two earlier works deserve mention: Ralph Durand's *Handbook to the Poetry of Rudyard Kipling* (1914) and A. M. Weygandt's *Kipling's Reading and its Influence on his Poetry* (Philadelphia, 1939). For M. Van Wyk Smith's recent book, see p. 21. John Gross's collection, mentioned above, includes an essay on the verse by Robert Conquest.

Criticism: Articles and Essays

'In Gilbert' after an item below indicates that it is to be found reprinted in *Kipling and the Critics*, ed. Elliot L. Gilbert (1966); 'In Rutherford' that it is included in *Kipling's Mind and Art*, ed. Andrew Rutherford (Edinburgh, 1964).

A dozen items of outstanding interest are:

Noel Annan, 'Kipling's Place in the History of Ideas', *Victorian Studies*, III (1960) (in Rutherford).
W. H. Auden, 'A Poet of the Encirclement', *New Republic*, CIX (25 October 1943).
John Bayley, discussion of Kipling in *The Uses of Division* (1976).
T. S. Eliot, Introduction to *A Choice of Kipling's Verse* (1941), later expanded and reprinted in *On Poetry and Poets* (1957).
Henry James, Introduction to Kipling's *Mine Own People* (New York, 1891) (in Gilbert).
C. S. Lewis, 'Kipling's World' (given as a lecture in 1948; included in *They Asked for a Paper*, 1963) (in Gilbert).

Randall Jarrell, 'On Preparing to Read Kipling', in *A Sad Heart at the Supermarket* (New York, 1962) (in Gilbert).

George Orwell, 'Rudyard Kipling', first published in 1942, revised and reprinted in *Critical Essays* (1946) (in Gilbert and Rutherford).

W. L. Renwick, 'Re-reading Kipling', *Durham University Journal*, XXXII (1940) (in Rutherford).

Andrew Rutherford, 'The Subaltern as Hero: Kipling and Frontier War', in *The Literature of War* (1978).

Lionel Trilling, 'Kipling', first published in 1943, reprinted in *The Liberal Imagination* (New York, 1949) (in Gilbert and Rutherford).

Edmund Wilson, 'The Kipling that Nobody Read', first published in 1941, reprinted in *The Wound and the Bow* (New York, 1941) (in Rutherford).

Boris Ford's 'A Case for Kipling?' (*Scrutiny*, XI, 1942–3; reprinted in Gilbert) presents the case *against* Kipling in strong terms. Several critics have explored Kipling's relationship to and influence upon other writers. H. M. McLuhan has an essay on 'Kipling and Forster' (*Sewanee Review*, LII, 1944); J. C. McCauley has discussed his influence on Shaw (*Shaw Review*, XVII, 1974); and Robert Platzner his influence on H. G. Wells (*Victorian Newsletter*, XXXVI, 1969). Michael Morley has examined his influence on Brecht (*Modern Language Notes*, LXXXVIII, 1973), and there is a monograph on the same subject (subtitled 'A Marxist's Imperialist Mentor') by J. K. Lyon (The Hague, 1975). J. C. Trewin has an essay on 'Kipling and the Theatre' in *Essays and Studies*, n.s. XX (1967).

Among other, mainly recent, essays are the following:

Robert Buchanan, 'The Voice of the Hooligan', *Contemporary Review*, LXXVI (December 1899) (in Gilbert).

Dennis Duffy, 'Kipling and the Dialect of the Tribe', *Dalhousie Review*, XLVII (1967).

Michael Edwardes, 'Kipling and the Imperial Imagination', *Twentieth Century* (June 1953).

S. T. Fisher, 'Kipling's Hysterical Laughter', *Notes and Queries*, n.s. XXV (1978).

Christopher Harvie, ' "The Sons of Martha": Technology, Transport, and Rudyard Kipling', *Victorian Studies*, XX (1977).

Peter Hinchcliffe, 'Coming to Terms with Kipling', *University of Toronto Quarterly*, XLV (1975).

Janet Montefiore, 'Day and Night in Kipling', *Essays in Criticism*, XXVII (1977).

Harold Orel, 'Rudyard Kipling and the Establishment: a Humanistic Dilemma', *South Atlantic Quarterly*, LXXXI (1982).

Norman Page, 'Kipling's World of Men', *Ariel*, X (1979).

D. M. E. Roskies, 'Telling the Truth in Kipling and Freud', *Etudes Anglaises*, XXXI (1982).

Index